PRINCIPLES OF AESTHETICS

PRINCIPLES OF AESTHETICS

DEWITT H PARKER

2011
Kaveri Books
New Delhi - 110 002

First Indian Edition 2011

ISBN: 978-81-7479-108-5

Published by
Kaveri Books
4832/24, Ansari Road
New Delhi-110002 (India)
Tel: 011-23288140, 23245799
Fax: 011 2328 8140
E-mail : kaveribooks@vsnl.com
Website: www.kaveribooks.com

Typeset in Baskerville BE Font at
Delta Book World, New Delhi - 110 002.

Printed at
Chawla Offset Printers, Delhi - 110 052

PRINTED IN INDIA

Preface

This book has grown out of lectures to students at the University of Michigan and embodies my effort to express to them the nature and meaning of art. In writing it, I have sought to maintain scientific accuracy, yet at the same time to preserve freedom of style and something of the inspiration of the subject. While intended primarily for students, the book will appeal generally, I hope, to people who are interested in the intelligent appreciation of art.

My obligations are extensive,–most directly to those whose influence is too indirect or pervasive to make citation profitable, or too obvious to make it necessary. For the broader philosophy of art, my debt is heaviest, I believe, to the artists and philosophers during the period from Herder to Hegel, who gave to the study its greatest development, and, among contemporaries, to Croce and Lipps. In addition, I have drawn freely upon the more special investigations of recent times, but with the caution desirable in view of the very tentative character of some of the results.

The appended bibliography is, of course, not intended to be in any sense adequate, but is offered merely as a guide to further reading; a complete bibliography would itself demand almost a volume.

Dewitt H Parker

Professor of Philosophy
in the University of Michigan

Contents

Chapter I

Introduction
Purpose and Method

Although some feeling for beauty is perhaps universal among men, the same cannot be said of the understanding of beauty. The average man, who may exercise considerable taste in personal adornment, in the decoration of the home, or in the choice of poetry and painting, is at a loss when called upon to tell what art is or to explain why he calls one thing "beautiful" and another "ugly." Even the artist and the connoisseur, skilled to produce or accurate in judgment, are often wanting in clear and consistent ideas about their own works or appreciations. Here, as elsewhere, we meet the contrast between feeling and doing, on the one hand, and knowing, on the other. Just as practical men are frequently unable to describe or justify their most successful methods or undertakings, just as many people who astonish us with their fineness and freedom in the art of living are strangely wanting in clear thoughts about themselves and the life which they lead so admirably, so in the world of beauty, the men who do and appreciate are not always the ones who understand.

Very often, moreover, the artist and the art lover justify their inability to understand beauty on the ground that beauty is too subtle a thing for thought. How, they say, can one hope to distill into clear and stable ideas such a vaporous and fleeting matter as Aesthetic feeling? Such men are not only unable to think about beauty, but skeptical as to the possibility of doing so,–contented mystics, deeply feeling, but dumb.

However, there have always been artists and connoisseurs who have striven to reflect upon their appreciations and acts, unhappy until they have understood and justified what they were doing; and one meets with numerous art-loving people whose intellectual curiosity is rather quickened than put to sleep by just that element of elusiveness in beauty upon which the mystics dwell. Long acquaintance with any class of objects leads naturally to the formation of some definition or general idea of them, and the repeated performance of the same type of act impels to the search for a principle that can be communicated to other people in justification of what one is doing and in defense of the value which one attaches to it. Thoughtful people cannot long avoid trying to formulate the relation of their interest in beauty, which absorbs so much energy and devotion, to other human interests, to fix its place in the scheme of life. It would be surprising, therefore, if there had been no Shelleys or Sidneys to define the relation between poetry and science, or Tolstoys to speculate on the nature of all art; and we should wonder if we did not everywhere hear intelligent people discussing the relation of utility and goodness to beauty, or asking what makes a poem or a picture great.

Now the science of aesthetics is an attempt to do in a systematic way what thoughtful art lovers have thus always been doing haphazardly. It is an effort to obtain a clear general idea of beautiful objects, our judgments upon them, and the motives underlying the acts which create them,–to raise the aesthetic life, otherwise a matter of instinct and feeling, to the level of intelligence, of understanding. To understand art means to find an idea or definition which applies to it and to no other activity, and at the same time to determine its relation to other elements of human nature; and our understanding will be complete if our idea includes all the distinguishing characteristics of art, not simply enumerated, but exhibited in their achieved relations.

How shall we proceed in seeking such an idea of art? We must follow a twofold method: first, the ordinary scientific method of observation, analysis, and experiment; and second, another and very different method, which people of the present day often profess to avoid, but which is equally necessary, as I shall try to show, and actually employed by those who reject it. In following the first method we treat beautiful things as objects given to us for study, much as plants and animals are given to the biologist. Just as the biologist watches the behavior of his specimens, analyzes them into their various parts and functions, and controls his studies through carefully devised experiments, arriving at last at a clear notion of what a plant or an animal is–at a definition of life; so the student of aesthetics observes works of art and other well-recognized beautiful things, analyzes their elements and the forms of connection of these, arranges experiments to facilitate and guard his observations from error and, as a result, reaches the general idea for which he is looking,–the idea of beauty.

A vast material presents itself for study of this kind: the artistic attempts of children and primitive men; the well-developed art of civilized nations, past and present, as creative process and as completed work; and finally, the everyday aesthetic appreciations of nature and human life, both by ourselves and by the people whom we seek out for study. Each kind of material has its special value. The first has the advantage of the perspicuity which comes from simplicity, similar for our purposes to the value of the rudimentary forms of life for the biologist. But this advantage of early art may be overestimated; for the nature of beauty is better revealed in its maturer manifestations, even as the purposes of an individual are more fully, if not more clearly, embodied in maturity than in youth or childhood.

Yet a purely objective method will not suffice to give us an adequate idea of beauty. For beautiful things are created by men, not passively discovered, and are made, like other things which men make, in order to realize a purpose. Just as a saw is a good saw only when it fulfills the purpose of cutting wood, so works of art are beautiful only because they embody a certain purpose. The beautiful things which we study by the objective method are selected by us from among countless other objects and called beautiful because they have a value for us, without a feeling for which we should not know them to be beautiful at all. They are not, like sun and moon, independent of mind and will and capable of being understood in complete isolation from man. No world of beauty exists apart from a purpose that finds realization there. We are, to be sure, not always aware of the existence of this purpose when we enjoy a picture or a poem or a bit of landscape; yet it is present none the less. The child is equally unaware of the purpose of the food which pleases him, yet the purpose is the ground of his pleasure; and we can understand his hunger only through a knowledge of it.

The dependence of beauty upon a relation to purpose is clear from the fact that in our feelings and judgments about art we not only change and disagree, but correct ourselves and each other. The history of taste, both in the individual and the race, is not a mere process, but a progress, an evolution. "We were wrong in calling that poem beautiful," we say; "you are mistaken in thinking that picture a good one"; "the eighteenth century held a false view of the nature of poetry"; "the English Pre-Raphaelites confused the functions of poetry and painting"; "to-day we understand what the truly pictorial is better than Giotto did"; and so on. Now nothing can be of worth to us, one thing cannot be better than another, nor can we be mistaken as to its value except with reference to some purpose which it fulfills or does not fulfill. There is no growth or evolution apart from a purpose in terms of which we can read the direction of change as forward rather than backward.

This purpose cannot be understood by the observation and analysis, no matter how careful, of beautiful *things*; for it exists in the mind primarily and only through mind becomes embodied in things; and it cannot be understood by a mere inductive study of aesthetic experiences–the mind plus the object–just as they come; because, as we have just stated, they are changeful and subject to correction, therefore uncertain and often misleading. The aesthetic impulse may falter and go astray like any other impulse; a description of it in this condition would lead to a very false conception. No, we must employ a different method of investigation–the Socratic method of self-scrutiny, the conscious attempt to become clear and consistent about our own purposes, the probing and straightening of our aesthetic consciences. Instead of accepting our immediate feelings and judgments, we should become critical towards them and ask ourselves, What do we really seek in art and in life which, when found, we call beautiful? Of course, in order to answer this question we cannot rely on an examination of our own preferences in isolation from those of our fellow-men. Here, as everywhere, our purposes are an outgrowth of the inherited past and are developed in imitation of, or in rivalry with, those of other men. The problem is one of interpreting the meaning of art in the system of culture of which our own minds are a part. Nevertheless, the personal problem remains. Aesthetic value is emphatically personal; it must be felt as one's own. If I accept the standards of my race and age, I do so because I find them to be an expression of my own aesthetic will. In the end, my own will to beauty must be cleared up; its darkly functioning goals must be brought to light.

Now, unless we have thought much about the matter or are gifted with unusual native taste, we shall find that our aesthetic intentions are confused, contradictory, and entangled with other purposes. To become aware of this is the first step towards enlightenment. We must try to distinguish what we want of art from what we want of other things, such as science or morality; for something unique we must desire from anything of permanent value in our life. In the next place we should come to see that we cannot want incompatible things; that, for example, we cannot want art to hold the mirror up to life and, at the same time, to represent life as conforming to our private prejudices; or want a picture to have expressive and harmonious colors and look exactly like a real landscape; or long for a poetry that would be music or a sculpture that would be pictorial. Finally, we must make sure that our interpretation of the aesthetic purpose is representative of the actual fullness and manysidedness of it; we should observe, for example, that sensuous pleasure is not all that we seek from art; that truth of some kind we seek besides; and yet that in some sort of union we want both.

This clearing up can be accomplished only in closest touch with the actual experience of beauty; it must be performed upon our working preferences and judgments. It must be an interpretation of the actual history of art. There is no a priori method of establishing aesthetic standards. Just as no one can discover his life purpose apart from the process of living, or the purpose of another except through sympathy; so no one can know the meaning of art except through creating and enjoying and entering into the aesthetic life of other artists and art lovers.

This so-called normative–perhaps better, critical–moment in aesthetics introduces an inevitable personal element into every discussion of the subject. Even as every artist seeks to convince his public that what he offers is beautiful, so every philosopher of art undertakes to persuade of the validity of his own preferences. I would not make any secret of this with regard to the following pages of this book. Yet this intrusion of personality need not be harmful, but may, on the contrary, be valuable. It cannot be harmful if the writer proceeds undogmatically, making constant appeals to the judgment of his readers and claiming no authority for his statements except in so far as they find favor there. Influence rather than authority is what he should seek. In presenting his views, as he must, he should strive to stimulate the reader to make a clear and consistent formulation of his own preferences rather than to impose upon him standards ready made. And the good of the personal element comes from the power which one strong preference or conviction has of calling forth another, and compelling it to the discovery and defense of its grounds.

In so far as aesthetics is studied by the objective method it is a branch of psychology. Aesthetic facts are mental facts. A work of art, no matter how material it may at first seem to be, exists only as perceived and enjoyed. The marble statue is beautiful only when it enters into and becomes alive in the experience of the beholder. Keys and strings and vibrations of the air are but stimuli for the auditory experience which is the real nocturne or etude. Ether vibrations and the retina upon which they impinge are nothing more than instruments for the production of the colors which, together with the interpretation of them in terms of ideas and feelings, constitute the real picture which we appreciate and judge. The physical stimuli and the physiological reactions evoked by them are important for our purpose only so far as they help us to understand the inner experiences with which they are correlated. A large part of our work, therefore, will consist in the psychological analysis of the experience of art and the motives underlying its production. We shall have to distinguish the elements of mind that enter into it, show their interrelations, and differentiate the total experience from other types of experience. Since, moreover, art is a social phenomenon, we shall have to draw upon our knowledge of social psychology to illumine our analysis of the individual's experience. Art is a historical, even a technical, development; hence the personal enjoyment of beauty itself is conditioned by factors that spring from the traditions of groups of artists and art lovers. No one can understand his pleasure in beauty apart from the pleasure of others.

In so far, on the other hand, as aesthetics is an attempt to define the purpose of art and so to formulate the standards presupposed in judgments of taste, it is closely related to criticism. The relation is essentially that between theory and the application of theory. It is the office of the critic to deepen and diffuse the appreciation of particular works of art. For this purpose he must possess standards; but he need not be, and in fact often is not, aware of them. A fine taste may serve his ends. Not infrequently, however, the critic endeavors to make clear to himself and his readers the principles he is employing. Now, on its normative side, aesthetics is ideally the complete rationale of criticism, the systematic achievement, for its own sake, of what the thoughtful critic attempts with less exactness and for the direct purpose of appreciation. It is beyond the province of aesthetics to criticize any particular work of art, except by way of illustration. The importance of illustration for the sake of explaining and proving general principles is, however, fundamental; for, as we have seen, a valuable aesthetic theory is impossible unless developed out of the primary aesthetic life of enjoyment and estimation, a life of contact with individual beautiful things. No amount of psychological skill in analysis or philosophical aptitude for definition can compensate for want of a real love of beauty,– of the possession of something of the artistic temperament. People who do not love art, yet study it from the outside, may contribute to our knowledge of it through isolated bits of analysis, but their interpretations of its more fundamental nature are always superficial. Hence, just as the wise critic will not neglect aesthetics, so the philosopher of art should be something of a critic. Yet the division of labor is clear enough. The critic devotes himself to the appreciation of some special contemporary or historical field of art–Shakespearean drama, Renaissance sculpture, Italian painting, for example; while the philosopher of art looks for general principles, and gives attention to individual works of art and historical movements only for the purpose of discovering and illustrating them. And, since the philosopher of art seeks a universal idea of art rather than an understanding of this or that particular work of art, an intimate acquaintance with a few examples, through which this idea can be revealed to the loving eye, is of more importance than a wide but superficial aesthetic culture.

In our discussion thus far, we have been assuming the possibility of aesthetic theory. But what shall we say in answer to the mystic who tells us that beauty is indefinable? First of all, I think, we should remind him that his own thesis can be proved or refuted only through an attempt at a scientific investigation of beauty. Every attempt to master our experience through thought is an adventure; but the futility of adventures can be shown only by courageously entering into them. And, although the failure of previous efforts may lessen the probabilities of success in a new enterprise, it cannot prove that success is absolutely impossible. Through greater persistence and better methods the new may succeed where the old have failed. Moreover, although we are ready to grant that the pathway to our goal is full of pitfalls, marked by the wreckage of old theories, yet we claim that the skeptic or the mystic can know of their existence only by traveling over the pathway himself; for in the world of the inner life nothing can be known by hearsay. If, then, he would really know that the road to theoretical insight into beauty is impassable, let him travel with us and see; or, if not with us, alone by himself or with some one wiser than we as guide; let him compare fairly and sympathetically the results of theoretical analysis and construction with the data of his firsthand experience and observe whether the one is or is not adequate to the other.

Again, the cleft between thought and feeling, even subtle and fleeting aesthetic feeling, is not so great as the mystics suppose. For, after all, there is a recognizable identity and permanence even in these feelings; we should never call them by a common name or greet them as the same despite their shiftings from moment to moment if this were not true. Although whatever is unique in each individual experience of beauty, its distinctive flavor or nuance, cannot be adequately rendered in thought, but can only be felt; yet whatever each new experience has in common with the old, whatever is universal in all aesthetic experiences, can be formulated. The relations of beauty, too, its place in the whole of life, can be discovered by thought alone; for only by thought can we hold on to the various things whose relations we are seeking to establish; without thought our experience falls asunder into separate bits and never attains to unity. Finally, the mystics forget that the life of thought and the life of feeling have a common root; they are both parts of the one life of the mind and so cannot be foreign to each other.

The motive impelling to any kind of undertaking is usually complex, and that which leads to the development of aesthetic theory is no exception to the general rule. A disinterested love of understanding has certainly played a part. Every region of experience invites to the play of intelligence upon it; the lover of knowledge, as Plato says, loves the whole of his object. Yet even intelligence, insatiable and impartial as it is, has its predilections. The desire to understand a particular type of thing has its roots in an initial love of it. As the born botanist is the man who finds joy in contact with tree and moss and mushroom, so the student of aesthetics is commonly a lover of beauty. And, although the interest which he takes in aesthetic theory is largely just the pleasure in possessing clear ideas, one may question whether he would pursue it with such ardor except for the continual lover's touch with picture and statue and poem which it demands. For the intelligent lover of beauty, aesthetic theory requires no justification; it is as necessary and pleasurable for him to understand art as it is compulsive for him to seek out beautiful things to enjoy. To love without understanding is, to the thoughtful lover, an infidelity to his object. That the interest in aesthetic theory is partly rooted in feeling is shown from the fact that, when developed by artists, it takes the form of a defense of the type of art which they are producing. The aesthetic theory of the German Romanticists is an illustration of this; Hebbel and Wagner are other striking examples. These men could not rest until they had put into communicable and persuasive form the aesthetic values which they felt in creation. And we, too, who are not artists but only lovers of beauty, find in theory a satisfaction for a similar need with reference to our preferences.[1]

1. Compare Santayana: The Sense of Beauty, p. 11.

More important to the average man is the help which aesthetic theory may render to appreciation itself. If to the basal interest in beauty be added an interest in understanding beauty, the former is quickened and fortified and the total measure of enjoyment increased. Even the love of beauty, strong as it commonly is, may well find support through connection with an equally powerful and enduring affection. The aesthetic interest is no exception to the general truth that each part of the mind gains in stability and intensity if connected with the others; isolated, it runs the risk of gradual decay in satiety or through the crowding out of other competing interests, which if joined with it, would have kept it alive instead. Moreover, the understanding of art may increase the appreciation of particular works of art. For the analysis and constant attention to the subtler details demanded by theory may bring to notice aspects of a work of art which do not exist for an unthinking appreciation. As a rule, the appreciations of the average man are very inadequate to the total possibilities offered, extending only to the more obvious features. Often enough besides, through a mere lack of understanding of the purpose of art in general and of the more special aims of the particular arts, people expect to find what cannot be given, and hence are prejudiced against what they might otherwise enjoy. The following pages will afford, I hope, abundant illustrations of this truth.

Finally, aesthetic theory may have a favorable influence upon the creation of art. Not that the student of aesthetics can prescribe to the artist what he shall or shall not do; for the latter can obey, for better or worse, only the inner imperative of his native genius. Yet, inevitably, the man of genius receives direction and cultivation from the aesthetic sentiment of the time into which he is born and grown; even when he reacts against it, he nevertheless feels its influence; a sound conception of the nature and purpose of art may save him from many mistakes. The French classical tradition in sculpture and painting, which is not merely academic, having become a part of public taste, prevented the production of the frightful crudities which passed for art in Germany and England during the present and past centuries. By helping to create a freer and more intelligent atmosphere for the artist to be born and educated in, and finer demands upon him when once he has begun to produce and is seeking recognition, the student of aesthetics may indirectly do not a little for him. And surely in our own country, where an educated public taste does not exist and the fiercest prejudices are rampant, there is abundant opportunity for service.

Chapter II

The Definition of Art

Since it is our purpose to develop an adequate idea of art, it might seem as if a definition were rather our goal than our starting point; yet we must identify the field of our investigations and mark it off from other regions; and this we can do only by means of a preliminary definition, which the rest of our study may then enrich and complete.

We shall find it fruitful to begin with the definition revived by Croce[1]: art is expression; and expression we may describe, for our own ends, as the putting forth of purpose, feeling, or thought into a sensuous medium, where they can be experienced again by the one who expresses himself and communicated to others. Thus, in this sense, a lyric poem is an expression–a bit of a poet's intimate experience put into words; epic and dramatic poetry are expressions–visions of a larger life made manifest in the same medium. Pictures and statues are also expressions; for they are embodiments in color and space-forms of the artists' ideas of visible nature and man. Works of architecture and the other industrial arts are embodiments of purpose and the well-being that comes from purpose fulfilled.

This definition, good so far as it goes, is, however, too inclusive; for plainly, although every work of art is an expression, not every expression is a work of art. Automatic

---

1. Benedetto Croce: *Estetica*, translated into English by Douglas Ainslie, under title *Aesthetic*, chap. i

expressions, instinctive overflowings of emotion into motor channels, like the cry of pain or the shout of joy, are not aesthetic. Practical expressions also, all such as are only means or instruments for the realization of ulterior purposes–the command of the officer, the conversation of the market place, a saw–are not aesthetic. Works of art–the *Ninth Symphony*, the *Ode to the West Wind*–are not of this character.

No matter what further purposes artistic expressions may serve, they are produced and valued for themselves; we linger in them; we neither merely execute them mechanically, as we do automatic expressions, nor hasten through them, our minds fixed upon some future end to be gained by them, as is the case with practical expressions. Both for the artist and the appreciator, they are ends in themselves. Compare, for example, a love poem with a declaration of love.[2] The poem is esteemed for the rhythmic emotional experience it gives the writer or reader; the declaration, even when enjoyed by the suitor, has its prime value in its consequences, and the quicker it is over and done with and its end attained the better. The one, since it has its purpose within itself, is returned to and repeated; the other, being chiefly a means to an end, would be senseless if repeated, once the end that called it forth is accomplished. The value of the love poem, although written to persuade a lady, cannot be measured in terms of its mere success; for if beautiful, it remains of worth after the lady has yielded, nay, even if it fails to win her. Any sort of practical purpose may be one motive in the creation of a work of art, but its significance is broader than the success or failure of that motive. The Russian novel is still significant, even now, alter the revolution. As beautiful, it is of perennial worth and stands out by itself. But practical expressions are only transient links in the endless chain of means, disappearing as the wheel of effort revolves. Art is indeed expression, but free or autonomous expression.

---

2. Contrast Croce's use of the same illustration: Esthetic, p. 22, English translation.

The freedom of aesthetic expression is, however, only an intensification of a quality that may belong to any expression. For, in its native character, expression is never merely practical; it brings its own reward in the pleasure of the activity itself. Ordinarily, when a man makes something embodying his need or fancy, or says something that expresses his meaning, he enjoys himself in his doing. There is naturally a generous superfluity in all human behavior. The economizing of it to what is necessary for self-preservation and dominion over the environment is secondary, not primary, imposed under the duress of competition and nature. Only when activities are difficult or their fruits hard to get are they disciplined for the sake of their results alone; then only does their performance become an imperative, and nature and society impose upon them the seriousness and constraint of necessity and law. But whenever nature and the social organization supply the needs of man ungrudgingly or grant him a respite from the urgency of business, the spontaneity of his activities returns. The doings of children, of the rich, and of all men on a holiday illustrate this. Compare, for example, the speech of trade, where one says the brief and needful thing only, with the talk of excursionists, where verbal expression, having no end beyond itself, develops at length and at leisure; where brevity is no virtue and abundant play takes the place of a narrow seriousness.

But we have not yet so limited the field of expression that it becomes equivalent to the aesthetic; for not even all of free expression is art. The most important divergent type is science. Science also is expression,–an embodiment in words, diagrams, mathematical symbols, chemical formula, or other such media, of thoughts meant to portray the objects of human experience. Scientific expressions have, of course, a practical function; concepts are "plans of action" or servants of plans, the most perfect and delicate that man possesses. Yet scientific knowledge is an end in itself as well as a utility; for the mere construction and possession of concepts and laws is itself a source of joy; the man of science delights in making appropriate formulations of nature's habits quite unconcerned about their possible uses.

In science, therefore, there is much free expression; but beauty not yet. No abstract expression such as Euclid's *Elements*, Newton's *Principia*, or Peano's *Formulaire*, no matter how rigorous and complete, is a work of art. We admire the mathematician's formula for its simplicity and adequacy; we take delight in its clarity and scope, in the ease with which it enables the mind to master a thousand more special truths, but we do not find it beautiful. Equally removed from the sphere of the beautiful are representations or descriptions of mere things, whether inaccurate or haphazard, as we make them in daily life, or accurate and careful as they are elaborated in the empirical sciences. No matter how exact and complete, the botanist's or zoologist's descriptions of plant and animal life are not works of art. They may be satisfactory as knowledge, but they are not beautiful. There is an important difference between a poet's description of a flower and a botanist's, or between an artistic sketch and a photograph, conferring beauty upon the former, and withholding it from the latter.

The central difference is this. The former are descriptions not of things only, but of the artist's reactions to things, his mood or emotion in their presence. They are expressions of total, concrete experiences, which include the self of the observer as well as the things he observes. Scientific descriptions, on the other hand, render objects only; the feelings of the observer toward them are carefully excluded. Science is intentionally objective,–from the point of view of the artistic temperament, dry and cold. Even the realistic novel and play, while seeking to present a faithful picture of human life and to eliminate all private comment and emotion, cannot dispense with the elementary dramatic feelings of sympathy, suspense, and wonder. sthetic expression is always integral, embodying a total state of mind, the core of which is some feeling; scientific expression is fragmentary or abstract, limiting itself to thought. Art, no less than science, may contain truthful images of things and abstract ideas, but never these alone; it always includes their life, their feeling tones, or values. Because philosophy admits this element of personality, it is nearer to art than science is. Yet some men of science, like James and Huxley, have made literature out of science because they could not help putting into their writings something of their passionate interest in the things they discovered and described.

The, necessity in art for the expression of value is, I think, the principal difference between art and science, rather than, as Croce[3] supposes, the limitation of art to the expression of the individual and of Science to the expression of the concept. For, on the one hand, science may express the individual; and, on the other hand, art may express the concept. The geographer, for example, describes and makes maps of particular regions of the earth's surface; the astronomer studies the individual sun and moon. Poets like Dante, Lucretius, Shakespeare, and Goethe express the most universal concepts of ethics or metaphysics. But what makes men poets rather than men of science is precisely that they never limit themselves to the mere clear statement of the concept, but always express its human significance as well. A theory of human destiny is expressed in Prospero's lines–

We are such stuff
As dreams are made of, and our littlelife
Is rounded with a sleep;

but with overtones of feeling at the core. Or consider the passion with which Lucretius argues for a naturalistic conception of the universe. And the reason why poets clothe their philosophical expressions in concrete images is not because of any shame of the concept, but just in order the more easily and vividly to attach and communicate their emotion. Their general preference for the concrete has the

3. *Estetica*, quarta edizione, p.27; English translation. p.36.

same motive; for there are only a few abstractions capable of arousing and fixing emotion.

Even as an element of spontaneity is native to all expression, so originally all expression is personal. This is easily observable in the child. His first uses of words as well as of things are touched with emotion. Every descriptive name conveys to him his emotional reaction to the object; disinterested knowledge does not exist for him; every tool, a knife or a fork, means to him not only something to be used, but the whole background of feelings which its use involves. Our first perceptions of things contain as much of feeling and attitude as of color and shape and sound and odor. Pure science and mere industry are abstractions from the original integrity of perception and expression; mutilations of their wholeness forced upon the mind through the stress of living. To be able to see things without feeling them, or to describe them without being moved by their image, is a disciplined and derivative accomplishment. Only as the result of training and of haste do the forms and colors of objects, once the stimuli to a wondering and lingering attention, become mere cues to their recognition and employment, or mere incitements to a cold and disinterested analysis and description. Knowledge may therefore enter into beauty when, keeping its liberality, it participates in an emotional experience; and every other type of expression may become aesthetic if, retaining its native spontaneity, it can acquire anew its old power to move the heart. To be an artist means to be, like the child, free and sensitive in envisaging the world.

Under these conditions, nature as well as art may be beautiful. In themselves, things are never beautiful. This is not apparent to common sense because it fails to think and analyze. But beauty may belong to our *perceptions* of things. For perception is itself a kind of expression, a process of mind through which meanings are embodied in sensations. Given are only sensations, but out of the mind come ideas through which they are interpreted as objects. When, for example, I perceive my friend, it may seem as if the man himself were a given object which I passively receive; but, as a matter of fact, all that is given are certain visual sensations; that these are my friend, is pure interpretation–I construct the object in embodying this thought in the color and shape I see. The elaboration of sensation in perception is usually so rapid that, apart from reflection, I do not realize the mental activity involved. But if it turns out that it was some other man that I saw, then I realize at once that my perception was a work of mind, an expression of my own thought. Of course, not all perceptions are beautiful. Only as felt to be mysterious or tender or majestic is a landscape beautiful; and women only as possessed of the charm we feel in their presence. That is, perceptions are beautiful only when they embody feelings. The sea, clouds and hills, men and women, as perceived, awaken reactions which, instead of being attributed to the mind from which they proceed, are experienced as belonging to the things evoking them, which therefore come to embody them. And this process of emotional and objectifying perception has clearly no other end than just perception itself. We do not gaze upon a landscape or a pretty child for any other purpose than to get the perceptual, emotional values that result. The aesthetic perception of nature is, as Kant called it, disinterested; that is, autonomous and free. The beauty of nature, therefore, is an illustration of our definition.

On the same terms, life as remembered or observed or lived, may have the quality of beauty. In reverie we turn our attention back over events in our own lives that have had for us a rare emotional significance; these events then come to embody the wonder, the interest, the charm that excited us to recollect them. Here the activity of remembering is not a mere habit set going by some train of accidental association; or merely practical, arising for the sake of solving some present problem by applying the lesson of the past to it; or finally, not unpleasantly insistent, like the images aroused by worry and sorrow, but spontaneous and self-rewarding, hence beautiful. There are also events in the lives of other people, and people themselves, whose lives read like a story, which, by absorbing our pity or joy or awe, claim from us a like fascinated regard. And there are actions we ourselves perform, magnificent or humble, like sweeping a room, which, if we put ourselves into them and enjoy them, have an equal charm. And they too have the quality of beauty.

Despite the community between beautiful nature and art, the differences are striking. Suppose, in order fix our ideas, we compare one of Monet's pictures of a lily pond with the aesthetic appreciation of the real pond. The pond is undoubtedly beautiful every time it is seen; with its round outline, its sunlit, flower-covered surface, its background of foliage, it is perhaps the source and expression of an unfailing gladness and repose. Now the painting has very much the same value, but with these essential differences. First, the painting is something deliberately constructed and composed, the artist himself controlling and composing the colors and shapes, and hence their values also; while the natural beauty is an immediate reaction to given stimuli, each observer giving meaning to his sensations without intention or effort. Like the beauty of woman, it is almost a matter of instinct. In natural beauty, there is, to be sure, an element of conscious intention, in so far as we may purposely select our point of view and hold the object in our attention; hence this contrast with art, although real and important, is not absolute. Moreover, beauty in perception and memory is the basis of art; the artist, while he composes, nevertheless partly transcribes significant memories and observations. Yet, although relative, the difference remains; art always consists of works of art, natural beauty of more immediate experiences. And from this difference follows another–the greater purity and perfection of art. The control which the artist exerts over his material enables him to make it expressive all through; every element conspires toward the artistic end; there are no irrelevant or recalcitrant parts, such as exist in every perception of nature. Last, the beauty of the painting, because created in the beholder through a fixed and permaneat mechanism constructed by the artist, is communicable and abiding, whereas the immediate beauty of nature is incommunicable and transient. Since the sthetic perception of nature has its starting point in variable aspects that never recur, no other man could see or feel the lily pond as Monet saw and felt it. And, although in memory we may possess a silent gallery of beautiful images, into which we may enter privately as long as we live, in the end the flux has its way and at death shatters this treasure house irrevocably. Hence, only if the beauty of the lily pond is transferred to a canvas, can it be preserved and shared.

The work of art is the tool of the aesthetic life. Just as organic efficiency is tied to the nerve and muscle of the workman and cannot be transferred to another, but the tool, on the other hand, is exchangeable and transmissible (I cannot lend or bequeath my arm, but I can my boat); and just as efficiency is vastly increased by the use of tools (I can go further with my boat than I can swim); so, through works of art, aesthetic capacity and experience are enhanced and become common possessions, a part of the spiritual capital of the race. Moreover, even as each invention becomes the starting point for new ones that are better instruments for practical ends; so each work of art becomes the basis for new experiments through which the aesthetic expression of life attains to higher levels. Monet's own art, despite its great originality, was dependent upon all the impressionists, and they, even when they broke away from, were indebted to, the traditions of French painting established by centuries. Through art, the aesthetic life, which otherwise would be a private affair, receives a social sanction and assistance.

That permanence and communication of expression are essential to a complete conception of art can be discerned by looking within the artistic impulse itself. However much the artist may affect indifference to the public, he creates expecting to be understood. Mere self- expression does not satisfy him; he needs in addition appreciation. Deprived of sympathy, the artistic impulse withers and dies or supports itself through the hope of eventually finding it. The heroism of the poet consists in working on in loneliness; but his crown of glory is won only when all men are singing his songs. And every genuine artist, as opposed to the mere improviser or dilettante, wishes his work to endure. Having put his substance into it, he desires its preservation as he does his own. His immortality through it is his boast.

Exegi monumentum aere perennius
Regalique situ pyramidum altius
* * * * *
Non omnis moriar.

Art is not mere inspiration, the transient expression of private moods, but a work of communication, meant to endure.

There are certain distinguishing characteristics of aesthetic expression all of which are in harmony with the description we have given of it. In the first place, in art the sensuous medium of the expression receives an attention and possesses a significance not to be found in other types of expression. Although every one hears, no one attends to the sound of the voice in ordinary conversation; one looks through it, as through a glass, to the thought or emotion behind. In our routine perceptions of nature, we are not interested in colors and shapes on their own account, but only in order that we may recognize the objects possessing them; in a scientific woodcut also, they are indifferent to us, except in so far as they impart correct information about the objects portrayed. Outside of art, sensation is a mere transparent means to the end of communication and recognition. Compare the poem, the piece of music, the artistic drawing or painting. There the words or tones must be not only heard but listened to; the colors and lines not only seen but held in the eye; of themselves, apart from anything they may further mean, they have the power to awaken feeling and pleasure. And this is no accident. For the aesthetic expression is meant to possess worth in itself and is deliberately fashioned to hold us to itself, and this purpose will be more certainly and effectively accomplished if the medium of the expression has the power to move and please. We enter the aesthetic expression through the sensuous medium; hence the artist tries to charm us at the start and on the outside; having found favor there, he wins us the more easily to the content lying within.

If the medium, moreover, instead of being a transparent embodiment of the artist's feelings, can express them in some direct fashion as well, the power of the whole expression will gain. This is exactly what the sound of the words of a poem or the colors and lines of a painting or statue can do. As mere sound and as mere color and line, they convey something of the feeling tone of the subject which, as symbols, they are used to represent. For example, the soft flowing lines of Correggio, quite apart from the objects they represent, express the voluptuous happiness of his "Venus and Mars"; the slow rhythm of the repeated word sounds and the quality of the vowels in the opening lines of *Tithonus* are expressive in themselves, apart from their meaning, of the weariness in the thoughts of the hero, and so serve to re-express and enforce the mood of those thoughts. When we come to study the particular arts, we shall find this phenomenon of re-expression through the medium everywhere.

A second characteristic distinguishing aesthetic expressions from other expressions is their superior unity. In the latter, the unity lies in the purpose to be attained or in the content of the thought expressed; it is teleological or logical. The unity of a chair is its purpose, which demands just such parts and in just such a mechanical arrangement; the unity of a business conversation is governed by the bargain to be closed, requiring such words and such only, and in the appropriate logical and grammatical order. The unity of an argument is the thesis to be proved; the unity of a diagram is the principle to be illustrated or the information to be imparted. Compare the unity of a sonnet or a painting. In a sonnet, there is a unity of thought and sentiment creating a fitting grammatical unity in language, but in addition a highly elaborate pattern in the words themselves that is neither grammatical nor logical. In a painting, besides the dramatic unity of the action portrayed, as in a battle scene; or of the spatial and mechanical togetherness of things, as in a landscape; there is a harmony of the colors, a composition of the lines and masses themselves, not to be found in nature. And, although the general shape and arrangement of the parts of a useful object is dominated by its purpose, if it is also beautiful–a Louis Seize chair, for example–there is, besides, a design that cannot be explained by use. In artistic expressions, therefore, there exists a unity in the material, superposed upon the unity required by the purpose or thought expressed. And this property follows from the preceding. For, since the medium is valuable in itself, the mind, which craves unity everywhere, craves it there also, and lingers longer and more happily on finding it; and, since the medium can be expressive, the unity of the fundamental mood of the thought expressed will overflow into and pervade it. Hence there occurs an autonomous development of unity in the material, raising the total unity of the expression to a higher power.

Chapter III

The Intrinsic Value of Art

Our definition of art can be complete only if it enables us to understand the value of art. The reader may well ask what possible value expression can have when it becomes an end in itself. "I can understand," he may say, "the value of expression for the sake of communication and influence, but what value can it have of itself?" At this point, moreover, we are concerned with the intrinsic value immediately realized in the experience of art, not with further values that may result from it. Art, no less than practical expression, may have effects on other experiences, which have to be considered in measuring its total worth; but these we shall leave for investigation in our last chapters, after we have reached our fullest comprehension of art; we are interested now, in order to test and complete our definition, in the resident value only. As a help toward reaching a satisfactory view, let us examine critically some of the chief theories in the field. First, the theory, often called "hedonistic," that the value of art consists in the satisfactions of sense which the media of aesthetic expression afford–the delight in color and sound and rhythmical movement of line and form. The theory finds support in the industrial arts, where beauty often seems to be only a luxurious charm supervening upon utility; but also in painting and sculpture when appreciated in their decorative capacity as "things of beauty." There is a partial truth in this theory; for, as we have seen, the sensuous media of all the arts tend to be developed in the direction of pleasure; and no man who lacks feeling for purely sensuous values can enter into the fullness of the aesthetic experience. But the theory fails in not recognizing the expressive function of sensation in art. As Goethe said, art was long formative, that is, expressive, before it was beautiful, in the narrow sense of charming. In order to be beautiful, it is not enough for a work of art to offer us delightful colors and lines and sounds; it must also have a meaning–it must speak to us, tell us something.

The second theory which I shall examine is the moralistic or Platonic. According to this, art is an image of the good, and has value in so far as through expression it enables us to experience edifying emotions or to contemplate noble objects. The high beauty of the "Sistine Madonna," for example, would be explained as identical with the worth of the religious feelings which it causes in the mind of the beholder. The advantage of art over life is supposed to consist in its power to create in the imagination better and more inspiring objects than life can offer, and to free and control the contemplation of them. This is the narrower interpretation of the theory. When the notion of the good is liberalized so as to include innocent happiness as well as the strictly ethical and religious values, beauty is conceded to belong to pictures of fair women and children, and to lyrics and romances, provided there is nothing in them to shock the moral sense. Aesthetic value is the reflection–the imaginative equivalent–of moral or practical value.

The prime difficulty of this theory is its inadequacy as an interpretation of the whole of actual art; for, in order to find support among existing examples, it is compelled to make an arbitrary selection of such as can be made to fit it. Actual art is quite as much an image of evil as of good; there is nothing devilish which it has not represented. And this part of art is often of the highest aesthetic merit. Velasquez's pictures of dwarfs and degenerate princes are as artistic as Raphael's Madonnas; Goethe's Mephistopheles is one of his supreme artistic achievements; Shakespeare is as successful artistically in his delineation of Lady Macbeth as of Desdemona. Now for us who claim that the purpose of art must be divined from the actual practice of artists, from the inside, and should not be an arbitrary construction, from the outside, the existence of such examples is sufficient to refute the theory in question. If the artist finds a value in the representation of evil, value exists there and can be discovered.

If, indeed, the sole effect of artistic expression were to bring to the mind objects and emotions in the same fashion that ordinary life does, then the value of art, the image of life, would be a function of the value of the life imaged. And just as one seeks contact with the good in real life and avoids the evil, so one would seek in art imaginative contact with the good alone. But expression, and above all artistic expression, does something more than present objects to the imagination and arouse emotions. Art is not life over again, a mere shadow of life; if it were, what would be its unique value? who would not prefer the substance to the shadow? The expression of life is not life itself; hence, even if the evil in life be always evil, the expression of it may still be a good.

Another theory, often called the "intellectualistic" theory, claims that the purpose of art is truth. "Beauty is truth; truth, beauty." The immediate pleasure which we feel in the beautiful is the same as the instant delight in the apprehension of truth. There is no difference in purpose or value between science and art, but only a difference in method–science presents truth in the form of the abstract judgment; art, in the form of the concrete image or example.

The difficulty with this theory is the uncertainty as to what is meant by truth; hence the many shapes it assumes. But before going deeply into this question, let us consider some of the simple facts which seem to tell for and against the theory. There can be no doubt that many examples of the representative arts–painting, sculpture, novel, and drama–are praised for their truth. We demand truth of coloring or line in painting, of form in sculpture, of character and social relation in the drama or novel. On the other hand, we admit aesthetic value to fanciful painting and literature, and to expressions of beliefs which no one accepts at the present time. We appreciate the beauty of Dante's descriptions of the Inferno and of the conversations between him and its inhabitants without believing them to be reports of fact. No one values the *Blue Bird* the less because it is not an account of an actual occurrence. Even with regard to the realistic novel and drama, no one thinks of holding them to the standards of historical or scientific accuracy. And, although we may demand of a landscape painting plausibility of color and line, we certainly do not require that it be a representation of any identifiable scene.

If by truth, therefore, be meant a description or image of matters of fact, then surely it is not the purpose of art to give us this truth. The artist, to be sure, may give this, as when the landscapist paints some locality dear to his client or the portraitist paints the client himself; but he does not need to do this, and the aesthetic value of his work is independent of it; for the picture possesses its beauty even when we know nothing of its model. In the language of current philosophy, truth in the sense of the correspondence of a portrayal to an object external to the portrayal, is not "artistic truth."

The partisans of the intellectualistic theory would, of course, deny that they ever meant truth with this meaning. "We mean by truth," they would say, "an embodiment in sensuous or imaginative form of some universal principle of nature and life. The image may be entirely fictitious or fanciful, but so long as the principle is illustrated, essential truth, and that is beauty, is attained." But if this were so, every work of art would be the statement of a universal truth, as indeed philosophical adherents of this theory have always maintained– witness Hegel. Yet what is the universal truth asserted in one of Monet's pictures of a lily pond? There is, of course, an observance of the general laws of color and space, but does the beauty of the picture consist in that? Does it not attach to the representation of the concrete, individual pond? I do not mean that there may not be beauty in the expression of universals; in fact, I have explicitly maintained that there may, under certain conditions; I am simply insisting that beauty may belong to expressions of the individual also, and that you cannot reduce these to mere illustrations of universal ideas. Because of its completeness and internal harmony, the philosopher may find the simplest melody a revelation of the Absolute; but even if it were, its beauty would still pertain to it primarily as a revelation of the individual experience which it embodies. Again, by reason of the freedom from the particular conditions out of which it arises acquired by a work of art, its individual meaning easily becomes typical, so that it often serves as a universal under which individuals similar to those represented are subsumed–as when we speak of "a Faust" or "a Hamlet"; nevertheless, the adequate expression of the individual is at once the basis of its beauty and of its extended, universalized significance. It is when works of art are profoundly individual that we generalize their meaning. In art the individual never sinks to the position of a mere specimen or example of a universal law. The intellectualistic theory is partly true of symbolic art, but not wholly, for even there, the individuality of the symbol counts. And yet, as we shall see, there is another meaning of artistic truth, which is legitimate.

Aesthetic value, therefore, is not alone sensuous value or ethical or scientific or philosophical value. A work of art may contain one or all of these values; but they do not constitute its unique value as art. The foregoing attempts to define the value of art fail because they renounce the idea of unique value, substituting goodness, sensuous pleasure, or truth-values found outside of art. But the intrinsic value of art must be unique, for it is the value of a unique activity–the free expression of experience in a form delightful and permanent, mediating communication. And this value we should be able to discover by seeking the difference which supervenes upon experience through expression of this kind.

Apart from expression, experience may be vivid and satisfactory as we feel and think and dream and act; yet it is always in flux, coming and going, shifting and unaware. But through expression it is arrested by being attached to a permanent form, and there can be retained and surveyed. Experience, which is otherwise fluent and chaotic, or when orderly too busy with its ends to know itself, receives through expression the fixed, clear outlines of a thing, and can be contemplated like a thing. Every one has verified the clarifying effect of expression upon ideas, how they thus acquire definiteness and coherence, so that even the mind that thinks them can hold them in review. But this effect upon feeling is no less sure. The unexpressed values of experience are vague strivings embedded in chaotic sensations and images; these expression sorts and organizes by attaching them to definite ordered symbols. Even what is most intimate and fugitive becomes a stable object. When put into patterned words, the subtlest and deepest passions of a poet, which before were felt in a dim and tangled fashion, are brought out into the light of consciousness. In music, the most elusive moods, by being embodied in ordered sounds, remain no longer subterranean, but are objectified and lifted into clearness. In the novel or drama, the writer is able not only to enact his visions of life in the imagination, but, by bodying them forth in external words and acts, to possess them for reflection. In painting, all that is seen and wondered at in nature is seen with more delicacy and discrimination and felt with greater freedom; or the vague fancies which a heated imagination paints upon the background of the mind come out more vivid and better controlled, when put with care upon a canvas.

Even ordinary expression, of course, arrests and clarifies experience, enabling us to commune with ourselves; but since its purpose is usually beyond itself, this result is hasty and partial, limited to what is needful for the practical end in view. In art alone is this value complete. For there, life is intentionally held in the medium of expression, put out into color and line and sound for the clear sight and contemplation of men. The aim is just to create life upon which we may turn back and reflect.

This effect of artistic expression upon experience has usually been called "intuition." Because of its connotation of mysterious knowledge, intuition is not a wholly satisfactory word, yet is probably as good as any for the purpose of denoting what artists and philosophers of art have had in mind and what we have been trying to describe. Other terms might also serve–vision, sympathetic insight (sympathetic, because it includes the value of experience; insight, because it involves possessing experience as a whole and ordered, and as an object for reflection). Intuition is opposed, on the one hand, to crude unreflecting experience that never observes itself as a whole or attains to clearness and self-possession; and, on the other hand, to science, which gives the elements and relations of an experience, the classes to which it belongs, but loses its uniqueness and its values. Science elaborates concepts of things, gives us knowledge about things; art presents us with the experience of things purified for contemplation. Scientific truth is the fidelity of a description to the external objects of experience; artistic truth is sympathetic vision–the organization into clearness of experience itself.

Compare, for illustration, life as we live it from day to day with our delineation of it as we recall it and tell it to an intimate companion; and then compare that with the analysis and classification of it which some psychologist or sociologist might make. Or compare the kind of knowledge of human nature that we get from Shakespeare or Moliere with the sort that we get from the sciences. In the one case, knowledge attends a personal acquaintance with the experience, a bringing of it home, a feeling for its values, a realization of the inner necessity of its elements; in the other, it is a mere set of concepts. Or finally, compare the knowledge of the human figure contained in an anatomist's manual with a painting of it, where we not only see it, but in the imagination touch it and move with it, in short live with it.

Intuition is the effect of artistic appreciation no less than of artistic creation. If the artist's expression of his feelings and ideas results in intuition, our appreciation of his work must have the same value, for appreciation is expression transferred from the artist to the spectator. By means of the colors, lines, words, tones that he makes, the artist determines in us a process of expression similar to his. Out of our own minds we put into the sense-symbols he has woven ideas and feelings which provide the content and meaning he intends. Hence all aesthetic appreciation is self-expression. This is evident in the case of the more lyrical types of art. The lyric poem is appreciated by us as an expression of our own inner life; music as an expression of our own slumberous or subconscious moods. Yet even the more objective types of art, like the novel or the drama, become forms of self-expression, for we have to build up the worlds which they contain in our own imagination and emotion. We have to live ourselves out in them; we can understand them only in terms of our own life.

In the appreciation of the more objective types of art, the personality expressed is not, of course, the actual personality; but rather the self extended and expanded through the imagination. The things which I seem to see and enjoy in the landscape picture I may have never really seen; I may have never really moved through the open plain there, as I seem to move, toward the mountain in the distance. The acts described in the novel or portrayed on the stage I do not really perform; the opinions uttered by the persons I do not hold. And yet, in order to appreciate the picture, it must be *as if* I really saw the mountain and moved towards it; in order to appreciate the novel or the play, I must make the acts and opinions mine. And this I can do; for, as it is a commonplace to note, each one of us has within him capacities of action and emotion and thought unrealized–the actual self is only one of many that might have been–hundreds of possible lives slumber in our souls. And no matter which of these lives we have chosen for our own, or have had forced upon us by our fate, we always retain a secret longing for all the others that have gone unfulfilled, and an understanding born of longing. Some of these we imagine distinctly–those that we consciously rejected or that a turn of chance might have made ours; but most of them we ourselves have not the power even to dream. Yet these too beckon us from behind, and the artist provides us with their dream. Through art we secure an imaginative realization of interests and latent tendencies to act and think and feel which, because they are contradictory among themselves or at variance with the conditions of our existence, cannot find free play within our experience. That same sort of imaginative enlarged expression of self that we get vicariously by participating in the life of our friends we get also from art.[1]

Yet in appreciation, as in creation, expression results in intuition. Appreciation is no mere imagining, transitory and lawless like a daydream. The activity of the imagination is so organized in a permanent and perspicuous form that we not only live it, but possess it as an object. The activities engaged in building up the work of art in my own mind are not the whole of me; judgment remains free to watch and synthesize those that are being crystallized there. In looking at a portrait, for example, the process of interpreting the life represented is ancillary to a total judgment of character. In the novel or drama, no matter with what abandon I put myself into the persons and situations, the expression of them in outward words and acts, and the organization which the artist has imposed upon them, makes of them permanent objects for reflection, not mere modes of feeling and imagining to endure. Self-expression that does not attain to objectivity is incomplete as art. Even music and lyric poetry are something more than mere feeling. In all genuine art, experience takes on permanence and form–a synthesis, a total meaning, supervenes within the flux of impressions and ideas and

---

1. Compare Santayana: *The Sense of Beauty*, p. 186.]

moods, not excluding, but embracing and controlling them. That is intuition.

The insight into experience which art provides is the more valuable because it is communicable; to possess it alone would be a good, but to share it is better. All values become enhanced when we add to them the joy of fellow feeling. The universality of aesthetic expression carries with it the universality of aesthetic insight. Merely private and unutterable inspirations are not art. Beauty does for life what science does for intelligence; even as the one universalizes thought, so the other universalizes values. In expressing himself, the artist creates a form into which all similar experiences can be poured and out of which they can all be shared. When, for example, we listen to the hymns of the church or read the poems of Horace, the significance of our experience is magnified because we find the feelings of millions there; we are in unison with a vast company living and dead. No thing of beauty is a private possession. All artists feed on one another and into each experience of art has gone the mind-work of the ages.

But there are two types of universality, one by exclusion, the other by inclusion. Communists like Tolstoy demand that art express only those feelings that are already common, the religious and moral; they would exclude all values that have not become those of the race. But this is to diminish the importance of art; for it is art's privilege to make feelings common by providing a medium through which they can be communicated rather than merely to express them after they have become common. Understanding is more valuable when it encompasses the things that tend to separate and distinguish men than when it is limited to the things that unite them. There is nothing so bizarre that art may not express it, provided it be communicable.

The life of the imagination, which is the life of art, is, moreover, the only life that we can have in common. Sharing life can never mean anything else than possessing the life of one another sympathetically. Actually to lead another's life would involve possessing his body, occupying his position, doing his work, and so destroying him. But through the sympathetic imagination we can penetrate his life and leave him in possession. To do this thoroughly is possible, however, only with the life of a very few people, with intimates and friends. With the mass, we can share only ideal things like religion or patriotism, but these also are matters of imagination. Now art enlarges the scope of this common life by creating a new imaginary world to which we can all belong, where action, enjoyment, and experience do not involve competition or depend on possession and mastery.

Finally, the intuitions that art provides are relatively permanent. Art not only extends life and enables us to share it, but also preserves it. Existence has a leak in it, as Plato said; experience flows in and then flows out forever. The individual passes from one act to another, from one phase of life to another, childhood, then youth, then old age. So the race; one generation follows another, and each type of civilization displaces a predecessor. Against this flux, our belief in progress comforts us; maturity is better than youth, we think, and each generation happier and more spiritual than the last. Yet the consolations of progress are partial. For even if we always do go on to something better in the future, the past had its unique value, and that is lost ineluctably. The present doubtless repeats much of the form of the past–the essential aspects of human nature remain the same; but the subtle, distinctive bloom of each stage of personal life, and of each period of the world's history, is transient. We cannot again become children, nor can we possess again the strenuous freedom of the Renaissance or the unclouded integrity of personality of the Greeks.

In the life of the individual, however, the flux is not absolute; for through memory we preserve something of the unique value of our past. Its vividness, its fullness, the sharp bite of its reality go; but a subtilized essence remains. And the worth that we attach to our personality depends largely upon it; for the instinct of self- preservation penetrates the inner world; we strive not only to maintain our physical existence in the present, but our psychic past as well. In conserving the values of the past through memory we find a satisfaction akin to that of protecting our lives from danger. Through memory we feel childhood's joys and youth's sweet love and manhood's triumphs still our own, secure against the perils of oblivion.

Now art does for the race what memory does for the individual. Only through expression can the past be preserved for all men and all time. When the individual perishes, his memories go with him; unless, therefore, he puts them into a form where they can be taken up into the consciousness of other men, they are lost forever. And just as the individual seeks a vicarious self-preservation through identifying himself with his children and his race, and finds compensation for his own death in their continuance, so he rejoices when he knows that men who come after will appreciate the values of his life. We of the present feel ourselves enriched, in turn, as by a longer memory, in adding to the active values of our own lives the remembered values of the past. Their desire to know themselves immortal is met by our desire to unite our lives with all our past. Art alone makes this possible. History may tell us what men did, but only the poet or other artist can make us relive the values of their experience. For through expression they make their memories, or their interpretations of other men's memories, ours. Art is the memory of the race, the conserver of its values.

The distinguishing characteristics of aesthetic expression observed by us–the pleasurableness of the medium, the enhanced unity–serve intuition as that has been described by us. One of the strongest objections against the theory of art as intuition, as that theory has been developed by Croce, for example, is that it provides no place for charm. Yet without charm there is no complete beauty, and any interpretation of the facts of the aesthetic experience which neglects this element is surely inadequate. But charm although an indispensable, is not an independent, factor in the experience of art; for it serves intuition. It does so in two ways. The charm of the medium, by drawing attention to itself, increases the objectivity of the experience expressed. Even when the experiences felt into color and line and sound are poignantly our own, to live pleasantly in any one of these sensations is to live as an object to oneself, the life sharing the externality of the medium–we put our life out there more readily when it is pleasant there. And the charm of the medium serves intuition in another way. When the activities of thought and feeling and imagination released by the work of art are delightful, they become more delightful still if the medium in which they function is itself delightful. To imagine

Charm'd magic casements, opening on the foam
Of perilous seas, in fairy lands forlorn

is a pleasure by itself, but more pleasurable, and therefore more spontaneous, because of the melody of sound in which it is enveloped. And when the activities expressed are not pleasant, the expression of them in a delightful medium helps to induce us to make them our own and accept them notwithstanding. The medium becomes a charming net to hold us, and because of its allurements we give ourselves the more freely to its spirit within. The following, for example, is not an agreeable thought:

To-morrow, and to-morrow, and to-morrow,
Creeps in this petty pace from day to day,
To the last syllable of recorded time;
And all our yesterdays have lighted fools
The way to dusty death.

Yet the expression of this thought is pleasant, among other reasons, because of the rhythmic charm of language. We shall come back to this fact in our chapter on "The Problem of Evil in Aesthetics." There is no contradiction between the fair form of a work of art and its content, however repellent. For if we value the sympathetic knowledge of life, we shall be glad of any means impelling us to undertake what alone can give this–a friendly dwelling with life itself. Thus the decorative and the expressive functions of art are reconciled–pleasure and intuition meet.

Just as from time to time pleasure in sensation has been one-sidedly thought to be the purpose of art, so likewise the unity characteristic of beautiful things. Indeed, beauty and order have become almost synonymous in popular thought. And, to be sure, this unity, as we have already remarked, has its own value; the mind delights in order just for its own sake, and the artist, who is bent on making something worthful on its own account, strives to develop it for that reason. And yet unity is no more independent of expression and intuition than sensation is; it too enters into their service. Many forms of unity in works of art are themselves media of expression–the simplest and most striking example is perhaps the rhythmical ordering of sounds in poetry and music, the emotional value of which everybody appreciates. In a later chapter, I shall try to show that the same is true of harmony and balance. In another way, also, unity serves intuition. For the existence of order in an experience is indispensable to that wholeness of view, that mastery in the mind, which is half of intuition. The merely various, the chaotic, the disorganized, cannot be grasped or understood. In order that an experience may be understood, its items must be strung together by some principle in terms of which they may demand each other and constitute a whole. Organization *is* understanding. Every work of art, every beautiful thing, is organized, and, as we have observed, organized not merely in the thought or other meaning expressed, but throughout, in the sensuous medium as well.

So far the value which we have discovered in artistic expression has been that of delightful and orderly sympathetic vision. This is supplemented from still another source of value. Through artistic expression pent-up emotions find a welcome release. No matter how poignant be the experience expressed, the weight, the sting of it disappears through expression. For through expression, as we have seen, the experience is drawn from the dark depths of the self to the clear and orderly surface of the work of art; the emotions that weighed are lifted out and up into color and line and sound, where the mind can view and master them. Mere life gives place to the contemplation of life; and contemplation imposes on life some of the calm that is its own. The most violent and unruly passions may be the material of art, but once they are put into artistic form they are mastered and refined. "There is an art of passion, but no passionate art" (Schiller). Through expression, the repression, the obstruction of feeling is broken down; the mere effort to find and elaborate a fitting artistic form for the material diverts the attention and provides other occupation for the mind; an opportunity is given to reflect upon and understand the experience, bringing it somehow into harmony with one's total life,–through all these means procuring relief. It is impossible to cite the famous passage from Goethe's "Poetry and Truth" too often:–

> And thus began that bent of mind from which I could not deviate my whole life through; namely, that of turning into an image, into a poem, everything that delighted or troubled me, or otherwise occupied my attention, and of coming to some certain understanding with myself thereupon.... All the works therefore that have been published by me are only fragments of one great confession.

This effect of artistic expression belongs, of course, to other forms of expression. Every confession, every confidential outpouring of emotion, is an example. We have all verified the truth that to formulate feeling is to be free with reference to it; not that we thereby get rid of it, but that we are able to look it in the face, and find some place for it in our world where we can live on good terms with it. The greatest difficulty in bearing with any disappointment or sorrow comes not from the thing itself–for after all we have other things to live for–but from its effect upon the presuppositions, so to speak, of our entire existence. The mind has an unconscious set of axioms or postulates which it assumes in the process of living; now anything that seems to contradict these, as a great calamity does, by destroying the logic of life, makes existence seem meaningless and corrupts that faith in life which is the spring of action. In order for the health of the mind to be restored, the contradictory fact must be somehow reconciled with the mind's presuppositions, and the rationality of existence reaffirmed. But an indispensable preliminary to this is that we should clearly envisage and reflect upon the fact, viewing it in its larger relations, where it will lose its overwhelming significance. Now that is what expression, by stabilizing and clarifying experience, enables us to do.

A great many works of art besides Goethe's, not merely of lyric poetry, but also of the novel and drama, among them some of the greatest, like the *Divine Comedy*, so far as they spring intimately from the life of the artist, are "fragments of a great confession," and have had the sanitary value of a confession for their creators. It is not always possible to trace the personal feelings and motives lying behind the artist's fictions; for the suffering soul covers its pains with subtle disguises; yet even when we do not know them, we can divine them. We are certain, for example, that Watteau's gay pictured visions were the projection–and confession–of his own disappointed dreams. The great advantage of art over ordinary expression, in this respect, is its universality. Art is the confessional of the race. The artist provides a medium through which all men can confess themselves and heal their souls. In making the artist's expression ours, we find an equal relief. Who does not feel a revival of some old or present despair of his own when he reads:

Un grand sommeil noir
Tombe sur ma vie;
Dormez toute espoir,

Dormez toute envie!
Je ne vois plus rien,
Je perds la memoire
Du mal et du bien....
Oh, la triste histoire!

yet who does not at the same time experience its assuagement? And this effect is not confined to lyrical art, for so far as, in novel and drama, we put ourselves in the place of the dramatis persona, we can pour our own emotional experiences into them and through them find relief for ourselves. Just so, Aristotle recognized the cathartic or healing influence of art, both in music and the drama–"through pity and fear effecting the proper purgation of these emotions"[2].

The delightsomeness of the work of art and its self-sufficient freedom, standing in contrast with the drab or difficult realities of nature and personal striving, serve also to make of beauty a consoler and healer. In place of a confused medley of sense impressions, art offers orderly and pleasant colors or sounds; instead of a real life of duties hard to fulfill and ambitions painfully accomplished, art provides an imagined life which, while imitating and thus preserving the interest of real life, remains free from its hazards and burdens. I would not base the value of art on the contrast between art and life; yet it is unlikely, I think, if life were not so bound and disordered, that art would seem so free and perfect; and it is often true that those who suffer and struggle most love art best. The unity of the work of art, in which each element suggests another within its world, keeping you there and shutting you out momentarily from the real world to which you must presently return, and the sensuous charm of the medium, fascinating your eyes and ears, bring forgetfulness and a temporary release.

To sum the results of the last two chapters. Art is expression, not of mere things or ideas, but of concrete

2. *Poetics*, 6, 2. *Politics*, 5,7.

experience with its values, and for its own sake. It is experience held in a delightful, highly organized sensuous medium, and objectified there for communication and reflection. Its value is in the sympathetic mastery and preservation of life in the mind.

Chapter IV

The Analysis of the Aesthetic Experience: The Elements of the Experience

Thus far we have sought to define art, to form a concrete idea of the experience of art, and to place it in its relations to other facts. We shall now pass from synthetic definition to psychological analysis. We want to pick out the elements of mind entering into the experience of art and exhibit their characteristic relations. In this chapter we shall concern ourselves chiefly with the elements, leaving the study of most of the problems of structure to the following chapter.

Every experience of art[1] contains, in the first place, the sensations which are the media of expression. In a painting, for example, there are colors; in a piece of music, tones; in a poem, word-sounds. To this material, secondly, are attached vague feelings. It is characteristic of aesthetic expressions, as we have observed, that their media, quite apart from anything that they may mean or represent, are expressive of moods—the colors of a painting have a *stimmung,* so have tones and words, when rhythmically composed. The simplest aesthetic experiences, like the beauty of single musical tones or colors, are of no greater complexity; yet almost all works of art contain further elements; for as a rule the sensations do not exist for their own sakes alone, but possess a function, to represent things. The colors of a landscape painting are not only interesting to us as beautiful colors, but as symbols of a

1. Throughout this discussion, I use "experience of art," "aesthetic experience," and "beauty" with the same meaning.

landscape; the words of a ballad charm and stimulate us not only through their music, but because of actions or events which they bring before the mind. This involves, psychologically speaking, that certain ideas–of trees and clouds in the painting, of men and their deeds in the poem–are associated to the sense elements and constitute their meaning. Such ideas or meanings are the third class of elements in the aesthetic experience. But these ideas, in their turn, also arouse emotions, only not of the indefinite sort which belong to the sense elements, but definite, like the emotions aroused by things and events in real life. For example, Rembrandt's "Man with the Gold Helmet" will not only move us in a vague way through the character and rhythm of its lines and colors, but will, in addition, stimulate sentiments of respect and veneration, similar to those that we should feel if the old warrior were himself before us. In such definite feelings we have, then, a fourth class of mental elements. A fifth class will make our list complete. It consists of images from the various sense departments–sight, hearing, taste, smell, temperature, movement–which arise in connection with the ideas or meanings, making them concrete and full. For example, some of the colors in a landscape painting will not only give us the idea that there is sunlight there, but will also arouse faint images of warmth, which will make the idea more vivid; other colors, representing the clouds, will produce faint sensations of softness; still others, representing flowers, may produce faint odors.

Let us study sensation as an element in beauty, first. Sensation is the door through which we enter into the experience of beauty; and, again, it is the foundation upon which the whole structure rests. Without feeling for the values of sensation, men may be sympathetic and intelligent, but they cannot be lovers of the beautiful. They may, for example, appreciate the profound or interesting ideas in poetry, but unless they can connect them with the rhythm-values of the sounds of the words, they have only an intellectual or emotional, not an aesthetic experience.

Yet, despite the omnipresence and supreme worth of sensation in beauty, not all kinds are equally fit for entrance into the experience. From the time of Plato, who writes of "fair sights and sounds" only, vision and hearing have been recognized as the preeminently aesthetic senses. These senses provide the basis for all the arts–music and poetry are arts of sound; painting, sculpture, and architecture are arts of vision. And there are good reasons for their special fitness. Most cogent of all is the fact that vision and hearing are the natural media of expression; sounds, be they words or musical tones, convey thoughts and feelings; so do visual sensations–the facial expression or gesture seen communicates the inner life of the speaker; and even abstract colors and space-forms, like red and the circle, have independent feeling-tones. A taste or a temperature sensation may be pleasant or unpleasant, but has no meaning, either by itself, as a color or a tone has, or through association, as a word has. It has no connection with the life of feeling or of thought. Its chief significance is practical–sweet invites to eating, cold impels to the seeking of a warm shelter, touch is a preliminary to grasping. All the so-called lower senses are bound up with instincts and actions. Of course sights and sounds have also a significance for instinct–the color and form and voice of the individual of the opposite sex, for example. But, before acting on the prompting of instinct, the lover may pause and enjoy the appealing color and form; he may connect his feelings with them and hold on to and delight in the resulting experience–an emotional appreciation of the object may intervene between the stimulus and the appropriate action, and even supplant it. In this way, vision and hearing may free themselves from the merely practical and become autonomous embodiments of feeling. The distance between the seen or heard object and the body is important. The objects of touch and taste, on the other hand, have to be brought into contact with the body; the practical reaction then follows; there is no time during which it may be suspended.

Important also, especially for the beauty of art, is our greater power to control sensations of vision and hearing. Only colors and sounds can be woven into complex and stable wholes. Tastes and odors, when produced simultaneously or in succession, do not keep their distinctness as colors and sounds do, but blur and interfere with each other. No one, however ingenious, could construct a symphony of odors or a picture of tastes. Nevertheless, the possibility of controlling colors and sounds and of creating stable and public objects out of them, is only a secondary reason for their aesthetic fitness. Even if one could construct instruments for the orderly production of tastes and odors–and simple instruments of this kind have been devised–one could not make works of art out of them; for a succession of such sensations would express nothing; they would still be utterly without meaning. The fundamental reason for the superiority of sights and sounds is their expressiveness, their connection with the life of feeling and thought. They take root in the total self; whereas the other elements remain, for the most part, on the surface.

Under favorable conditions, however, all sensations may enter into the sthetic experience. Despite the close connection between the lower senses and the impulses serving practical life, there is a certain disinterestedness in all pleasant sensations. Fine wines and perfumes offer tastes and odors which are sought and enjoyed apart from the satisfaction of hunger; in dancing, movement sensations are enjoyed for their own sake; in the bath, heat and cold. But, as we have seen, it is not sufficient for a sensation to be free from practical ends in order to become aesthetic; it must be connected with the larger background of feeling; it must be expressive. Now, under certain circumstances and in particular cases, this may occur, even in the instance of the lower senses. The perfume of flowers, of roses and of violets, has a strong emotional appeal; it is their "soul" as the poets say. The odor of incense in a cathedral may be an important element in devotion, fusing with the music and the architecture. Or recall the odor of wet earth and reviving vegetation during a walk in the woods on a spring morning. Even sensations of taste may become aesthetic. An oft-cited example is the taste of wine on a Rhine steamer. Guyau, the French poet-philosopher, mentions the taste of milk after a hard climb in the Pyrenees. A drink of water from a clear spring would serve equally well as an example familiar to all. The warmth of a fire, of sunlight, of a cozy room, or the cold of a star-lit winter night have an emotional significance almost, if not quite, equal to that of the visual sensations from these objects. Touch seems to be irretrievably bound up with grasping and using, but the touch of a well-loved person may be a free and glowing experience, sharing with sight in beauty. The movement sensations during a run in the open air or in dancing are not only free from all practical purpose, but are elements in the total animation. And other examples will come to the mind of every reader.

As our illustrations show, the lower senses enter into the beauty of nature only; they do not enter into the beauty of art. Their beauty is therefore vague and accidental. It usually depends, moreover, upon some support from vision, with the beauty of which it fuses. Apart from the picturesque surroundings seen, the mountain milk and the Rhine wine would lose much of their beauty; the warmth of sunlight or of fire, without the brightness of these objects, the odor of flowers without their form and color, would be of small aesthetic worth. Through connection with vision the lower senses acquire something of its permanence and independence. People differ greatly in their capacity to render the lower senses aesthetic; it is essentially a matter of refinement, of power to free them from their natural root in the practical and instinctive, and lift them into the higher region of sentiment. But every kind of sensation, however low, may become beautiful; this is not to degrade beauty, but to ennoble sensation.

From a psychological standpoint, sensation is the datum of the aesthetic experience, the first thing there, while its power to express depends upon a further process which links it up with thoughts and feelings. We must inquire, therefore, how this linkage takes place–how, for example, it comes about that the colors of a painting are something more than mere colors, being, in addition, embodiments of trees and sky and foliage, and of liveliness and gayety and other feelings appropriate to a spring landscape. Let us consider the linkage with feeling first.

There are two characteristics of aesthetic feeling in its relation to sensations and ideas which must be taken into account in any explanation; its objectification in them and the universality of this connection. Expression is embodiment. We find gayety in the colors of the painting, joy in the musical tones, happiness in the pictured face, tenderness in the sculptured pose. We hear the feeling in the sounds and see it in the lines and colors. The happiness seems to belong to the face, the joy to the tones, in the same simple and direct fashion as the shape of the one or the pitch of the others. The feelings have become true attributes. It is only by analysis that we pick them out, separate them from the other elements of idea or sensation in the whole, and then, for the purpose of scientific explanation, inquire how they came to be connected. And this connection is not one that depends upon the accidents of personal experience. It is not, for example, like the emotional significance that the sound of the voice of the loved one has for the lover, which even he may some day cease to feel, and which other men do not feel at all. It is rather typified by the emotional value of a melody, which, through psychological processes common to all men, becomes a universal language of feeling. The work of art is a communicable, not a private expression.

As we have observed, the elements of feeling in the aesthetic experience are of two broad kinds–either vague, when directly linked with the sensuous medium, or else definite, when this linkage is mediated by ideas through which the medium is given content and meaning. The former kind, which I shall consider first, comprises all cases of the emotional expressiveness of the medium itself,–of tones and word-sounds and their rhythms and patterns, of colors and lines and space-forms and their designs. The detailed study of this expressiveness I shall leave to the chapters on the arts; here I wish merely to indicate the kind of psychological process involved.

In many cases the psychological principle of association operates. The tender expressiveness of certain curved lines, like those of the Greek amphora, for example, is due, partially at least, to association with lines of the human body, with which normally this feeling is associated. The associated object, together with its feeling tone, are sufficiently common to the experience of all men to account for the universality of the emotion, and the isolation of the stimulus–abstract line–from its usual context of color and bulk accounts for the vagueness. Sometimes, on the other hand, expressiveness seems to be due to a direct psychological relation between the sense-stimulus and the emotion. This is almost certainly the case with rhythms, and, as I shall argue in the chapters on painting and music, is at least partially true of colors and tones. The expressiveness is at once too immediate and too universal to depend upon association with definite things and events, or personal, emotional crises. A rhythm, for example, may be exciting the first time it is heard; one does not have to wait to hear it at a battle-charge; a melody may be sad even when one has never heard it sung by chance at parting. Of course the fact that associations are not remembered is no proof that they do not operate; but it is difficult to conceive of any which could operate in these cases. For this reason, I think, we must suppose that certain sense-stimuli and combinations of stimuli not only produce in the sensory areas of the brain the appropriate sensations, but that their effects are prolonged, overflowing into the motor channels and there causing a total reaction of the organism, the conscious aspect of which is a vague feeling. The organic resonance is too slight and diffuse to produce a true emotion; hence only a mood results.

In all the representative arts the vague expressiveness of the medium is reinforced through emotions aroused by ideas which interpret sensation as an element of a thing. The green in the painting is not only green, but green of the sea; the red is not only red, but red of the sky; the curved line is not a mere curve, it is the outline of a wave. The totality of colors and lines is not a mere color and line composition, but a marine landscape. The feeling tones of the elements of this complex and of the complex itself are not only those of the colors and lines as such, but of the interpretative ideas as well; which in turn are the same as those of the corresponding real things. The psychological process is here simple enough. The feeling tone of the sea is carried by the idea of the sea, which now fuses with the green color and wavy lines of the painting.

But in order fully to explain the phenomena of aesthetic expression, it is not sufficient to show how the connection between feeling and sensation and idea takes place; it is necessary, in addition, to explain the nature of this connection. The feeling is not experienced by us as what it is–our reaction to the sensations or represented objects–but rather as an objective quality of them. The sounds are sad, the curve tender, the sea placid and reposeful. Why is this?

The explanation is, I think, as follows. Despite their usual subjectivity, feelings tend to be located in the objective world whenever they are in conflict with or not directly rooted in the personal life or character of the individual. In listening to music, for example, feelings of despair and terror may be aroused in me who am perhaps secure and happy; and even if the feelings are joyous, they are not occasioned by any piece of personal good fortune–my situation in life is the same now as before. Hence, finding no lodgment in the ego, and having to exist somewhere, they seek a domicile in the sounds evoking them. And, in general, works of art arouse but offer no personal occasions for feeling, and therefore absorb it into themselves.

The process of objectification may, however, go further. It often happens in the aesthetic experience that feelings are not objectified alone, but carry with them the idea of the self–

I come to feel *myself* as joyous or despairing in the sounds. The extent to which the idea of the self thus follows the objectified feelings depends largely upon the amount of their reverberation throughout the organism. When this is small, and the feelings are vague and tenuous, as in color appreciation, there is little or no definite projection of the idea of the self; when, on the other hand, it is large and the emotions are strong, as oftentimes in music, where breathing, circulation, hand and foot are affected, then I myself seem to be there,–striving, pursuing, struggling, in the sounds. I am where my body is. The projection of the idea of the self is facilitated for the same reason when the body is actually employed in the creation of the work of art, as in singing and acting. It also occurs more readily when the life expressed in the work of art is akin to the spectator's. Thus, an emotional and suggestible woman, in watching a fine performance of "Magda," inevitably puts herself in the place of the heroine if she has herself lived through a similar experience. But when the life expressed is strikingly foreign to our own, the projection of the idea of self is more difficult; the duality between subject and object tends to remain.

These phenomena have excited special attention when, as in painting and sculpture and the drama, a human being is represented. Suppose, for example, I see a statue of a runner ready to start. I not only see the form and color of the marble and recognize them as a man's; I also feel emotions of excitement, tension, and expectation such as I should myself feel were I too posed and waiting to run a race. And these emotions I experience as the man's, and as his, not in a vague way, but as definitely present in his sculptured form, even in particular parts of it,–in the swelling chest and tightened limbs. Or consider another case. Suppose I see Franz Hals' "Laughing Cavalier." I feel jollity in the face, as the cavalier's. Yet in both cases I may feel the emotions as also my own–as if I too were about to run or were laughing. And the projection of the idea of the self will occur most readily if I am myself a runner or a jolly person. In both instances, moreover, the process will be mediated by impulses to movements that are the normal accompaniments of the emotions in question. If I observe myself carefully, I may find that my own chest is tending to swell and my own limbs to tighten, in imitation of the runner's, or my own pupils to dilate and the muscles of my face to wrinkle and to part, in imitation of the Dutchman's. And these movement-impulses I objectify. I not only see jollity in the face, but laughter as well; in the statue, not only excitement, but running. And again–where my body is, there am I; so I am jolly with the cavalier and excited with the runner. The psychology of this process is simple enough. In my experience there is a plain connection between the sight of a movement and sensations attendant upon movement, and further, a connection between some of these movements, namely, the expressive movements, and the emotions which they express. In accordance with the law of association by contiguity, whenever any one of several mental elements usually connected together is present in the mind, the others tend to arise also. So here. Seeing the semblance of tight muscles and a smiling face, I feel the emotions which have these visual associates, experience the correlated movement-sensations, project them all into the object which initiated the process.

In recent years, a great deal has been made of these movement-sensations in explaining aesthetic feeling. Yet in the case of all people who are not strongly of the motor type, people in whose mental make-up movement plays a minor part in comparison with vision and other sensations, they play a secondary role, or even hardly any role at all. Most spectators, indeed, instead of actually making slight movements imitative of the movements seen or represented, and experiencing the corresponding sensations, make no movements at all and simply experience movement images; this substitution of image for movement probably occurs in the minds of all except the most imitative. Most people, even of the motor type, do not smile when they see the "Laughing Cavalier" or start to run when they see the statue of the runner;

careful observation of themselves would disclose only faint movement images which seem to play about their lips or limbs–mere images of movement have supplanted movements. And many visualists would not find any images at all. However, although the mistake has been committed by some investigators of supposing that everybody experiences movement because they themselves, being of the motor type, do, it cannot be denied, I think, that such people attain to a vividness of aesthetic living not reached by others. They appreciate beauty with their bodies as well as with their souls. And in their case too, as has been shown, aesthetic appreciation is more strongly histrionic–they not only put themselves into the work of art, but the idea of themselves as well.

Following the German school of einfuehlung, I have insisted throughout this discussion on the importance of feeling in the aesthetic experience; yet I do not think the voice of those people can be neglected who claim that their experience with works of art is of slight or no emotional intensity. There are people who would report that they feel no jollity when they see the "Laughing Cavalier," or anguish when they read the Ugolino Canto in the Inferno; yet such people often have a highly developed aesthetic taste. How can this difference be accounted for?

Starting with the emotional appreciation of art as primary, we can account for it in this wise. It is a familiar phenomenon in the mental life for a concept or idea of an emotional experience to take the place of that experience. What man has not rejoiced when the simple and cold judgment, "I suffered then," has come to supplant a recurring torment? Or who that has lived constantly with a sick person has not observed how, looking on the face of pain, inevitably the mere comment, "he is in distress," comes to supplant the liveliest sympathetic thrill? There are many reasons for this. The idea or judgment is a less taxing thing than an emotion, and so is substituted for it in the mind, which everywhere seeks economy of effort. The idea is also more efficient from a practical point of view, because it leads directly to action and does not divert and waste energy in diffused and useless movements. The physician simply recognizes the states of mind of his patients, he does not sympathize with them. Finally our own reactions to an objectified emotion may interfere with the emotion. If, for example, we see an angry man, our own fear of him may entirely supplant our sympathetic feeling of his anger. In general, in our dealings with our fellow men, we are too busy with our attitudes and plans with reference to them, and too much concerned with economizing our emotional energy, to get a sympathetic intuition of their inner life, and so are content with an intellectual recognition of it. Now this habit of substituting the more rapid and economical process of judgment for the longer and more taxing one of sympathy, is carried over into the world of art.

Nevertheless, the world of art is a region especially fitted for *einfuehlung*. For there the need for quick action, which in life tends to syncopate emotion, does not exist. The characteristic attitude of art is leisurely absorption in an object, giving time for all the possibilities of feeling or other experience to develop. Moreover, in art there is not the same saving need for the substitution of idea for feeling as in real life. For in art, feeling is not so strong as in life; even when the artist expresses his own personal experience, he lightens its emotional burden through expression, and we, when we make his experience ours, find a similar relief. The emotion is genuine, only weakened in intensity. In other cases, where the artist constructs a world of fictitious characters and events, our knowledge that they are not real suffices to diminish the intensity of the emotions aroused. For emotions have the practical function of inciting to action, and when action is impossible, as in the purely ideal world of the artist, they cannot keep their natural intensity. We cannot feel so strongly over the mere idea of an event as over a real event. Were it otherwise, who could stand the strain of *Hamlet* or *Othello*?

Throughout this discussion of the elements of the experience of art, I have used the terms emotion and feeling with an inclusive meaning, to cover impulses as well as feelings in the narrower sense. For in the aesthetic experience, there are impulses–impulses to move when action is represented in picture and statue, impulses to act, as when, in watching a play, we put ourselves in the place of the persons. But such impulses are always checked through the realization that they come from sources unrelated to our purposes, and fail to get the reenforcement or consent of the total self necessary to action. In reading or singing the "Marseillaise," to cite an example from poetry, I experience all kinds of impulses–to shoulder a musket, to march, to kill–but no one of them is carried out. Now an inhibited impulse is scarcely distinguishable from an emotion. With few exceptions, the impulses in art do not issue in resolves, decisions, determinations to act; or, if they do, the determinations refer to acts to be executed in the future, in an experience distinct and remote from the sthetic–the "Marseillaise" has doubtless produced such resolutions in the minds of Frenchmen; and there is much art that is productive in that way, providing the "birth in beauty" of which Plato wrote. In art, impulses result in immediate action only when action is itself the medium of expression, as in the dance, where impulses to movement pass over into motion. Of course such actions still remain aesthetic since they serve no practical end and are valued for themselves.

If the question were raised, which is more fundamental in the aesthetic experience, idea or emotion? the answer would have to be, emotion. For there exists at least one great art where no explicit ideas are present, music, whereas art without emotion does not exist. Take away the emotional content from expression and you get either a mere play of sensations, like fireworks, or else pseudo-science, like the modern naturalistic play. However, the supreme importance of the idea in art cannot be denied. Every complex work of art, save music, is an expression of ideas as well as of feelings, and even in music there exists the tendency for feeling to seek definition in ideas–do we not say a musical idea? And do we not find the masters of so abstract an art as ornament employing their materials to represent symbolic conceptions? I wish to call the attention of the reader to certain very general considerations touching the nature and function of ideas in the aesthetic experience, leaving the study of the concrete problems to the more special chapters.

First, the relation of the idea to the sense medium of the expression. Here, I think, we find something comparable to the process of *einfuehlung*. For in art, ideas, like feelings, are objectified in sensation. Only sensations are given; out of the mind come ideas through which the former are interpreted and made into the semblance of things. Consider, for example, Rembrandt's "Night-Watch." A festal mood is there in the golds and reds, and gloom in the blacks; but there also are the men and drums and arms. If we wished to push the analogy with *einfuehlung*, we might coin a corresponding term–*einmeinung*, "inmeaning." In all the representative arts, this is a process of equal importance with infeeling; for the artist strives just as much to realize his ideas of objects in the sense material of his art as to put his moods there.

When, moreover, we consider that the expression of the more complex and definite emotions is dependent upon the expression of ideas of nature and human life, we see that the process is really a single one. Feeling is a function of ideas; if, then, we demand sincerity in the one, we must equally demand conviction in the other. The poet could not convey to us his pleasure at the sight of nature or his awe of death unless he could somehow bring us into their presence. The painter could not express the moods of sunlight or of shadow until he had invented a technique for their representation. Clear and confident seeing is a condition of feeling. Hence every advance in the imitation of nature is an advance in the power of expression. The demand for fidelity of representation, for "truth to nature," so insistently made by the common man in his criticism of art, is justified even from the point of view of expressionism.

Yet this fidelity of representation does not involve exact reproduction of nature. The limitations of the media of the arts definitely exclude this. No painter can reproduce on a canvas the infinite detail of any object or exactly imitate its colors and lines. In the single matter of brightness, for example, his medium is hopelessly inadequate; even the light of the moon is beyond his power, not to speak of the light of the sun; he has to substitute a relative for an absolute scale of values. The sculptor cannot reproduce the color or hair of the human body. However, this failure exactly to imitate nature does not prevent the artist from suggesting to us ideas of the objects in which he is interested. If the outline of the marble be that of a man, we get the idea of a man; if the color and shape be that of a tree, we get the idea of a tree. Our acceptance of these ideas is, of course, only partial; for we are equally susceptible to the negative suggestions of the whiteness of the marble and the smallness of the outline of the tree. Every work of art represents a sort of compromise between reality and unreality, belief and disbelief.

Nevertheless, despite this compromise, the purpose of art is uncompromisingly attained. For art does not seek to give us nature over again, but to express its feeling tones, and these are conveyed when we get an idea of the corresponding object, even if that idea is inadequate from a strictly scientific point of view. We do not react emotionally to the infinite detail of any object, but only to its presence as a whole and to certain salient features. The artist succeeds when he constructs a humanized image of the object–one which arouses and becomes a center for feeling. This image, when made of a few elements, may be far more telling than a much more accurate copy; for there is no diffusion of interest to irrelevant aspects. How effective a medium for expression are the few and simple lines of Beardsley's draftsmanship! The amount of detail necessary to convey an emotionally effective idea is relative to the technique of the different arts and varies also with the suggestibility and discrimination of the observer. Here no a priori principles can be laid down for what only the experimental practice of the artist can determine.

Moreover, the negative suggestions of a work of art, although they are effective in preventing entire belief in the reality of the idea expressed, do not hinder the communication and appreciation of the attached feelings. Just so long as the belief attitude is not wholly extinguished, this is the case; and the skillful artist takes care of that. Of course, an attitude of self-surrender, of willingness to accept suggestions, has to be present and we cooperate with the artist in creating it. Aesthetic belief implies sufficient abandon that we may react emotionally to a suggestion, but not enough that we may react practically. We let the idea tell upon our feelings; we do not let it incite us to action. The aesthetic plausibility of an idea depends largely upon its initial plausibility with the artist. There is nothing more contagious than belief. To utter things with an accent of conviction is half the battle in getting oneself believed. If the artist pretends to believe something and expresses himself with an air of assurance, we accept it, no matter how preposterous it may be from the practical or scientific point of view. Think of Rabelais!

A work of art is a logical system. It presupposes certain assumptions, postulates, conventions, which we must accept if we are to live in its world. Now, in order that we may accept them, the artist must first have vividly accepted them himself. Only if they have become a very part of him, can they become at all valid for us. The failure of classicistic art in a non-classical age, of "Pre-Raphaelitism" after Raphael, is a failure in this–the artist has never lived even imaginatively in the world he depicts. His belief is an artifice and a sham, and he cannot impose upon us with his pretense. But once we have accepted the artist's postulates, then we are prepared to follow him in his conclusions. In the Homeric world, we shall not balk at the intercourse between gods and men; in mediaeval painting and drama, we shall accept miracle; in *Alice in Wonderland*, we shall accept any dream-like enchantment. But we demand that the conclusions shall follow from the premises, that the whole be consistent. We cannot tolerate miracle in a realistic novel or drama, or glaring inaccuracy of fact in a historical novel, because they are in contradiction to the laws of reality tacitly assumed. The final demand which we make of any work, of art is that it live. What can be made to live for us may be beautiful to us. But nothing can draw our life into itself which has not drawn the artist's, or which is untrue to its own inner logic.

One of the most life-creating elements of a work of art is imagery. Everywhere in art the tendency exists for ideas to be filled out, rendered concrete and vivid, through images. In looking at a painting of a summer landscape, for example, we not only recognize the colors as meaning sunlight, but actually experience them as warm; in looking at a statue we not only recognize its surface as that of the body of a woman, but we feel its softness and smoothness; which involves that the ideas of sunlight and a human body, employed in interpreting the sensations received from these works of art, are developed back into the original mass of images from which they were derived. However, although ideas are formed from images, they are not images,—as our ordinary employment of them in recognizing objects attests. We may and usually do, for example, recognize a mirror as smooth without experiencing it as smooth—the image equivalent of the idea remains latent. Our ordinary experience with objects is too hasty and too intent on practical ends for images to develop. On the other hand, the leisurely attitude characteristic of the aesthetic experience is favorable to the recall of images; hence, just as in the aesthetic perception of objects we put our feelings into them, so equally we import into them the relevant images. The aesthetic reaction tends to be total. Our demand for feeling in art also requires the image; for feelings are more vividly attached to images than to abstract ideas. It is a fact familiar in the experience of everybody that the strength of the emotional tone of an object is a function of the clearness of the image which we form of it on recall. We can preserve the feeling tone of a past event or an absent object only if we can keep a vivid image of it; as our image of it becomes vague, our interest in it dissipates. Everywhere in our experience the image mediates between feeling and idea. So in art. Images have no more an independent and self-sufficient status in art than sensations have; like the latter they are a means for the expression of feeling. In the painting of sunlight, for example, the images of warmth carry joyousness and a sense of ease; in the statue, the tactile images convey the emotional response to the represented object. In literature the expressiveness of images is perhaps even more impressive. Consider how longing is aroused by the tactile, gustatory, and thermal images in the oft-quoted lines of Keats:

O, for a draught of vintage! that hath been
Cool'd a long age in the deep-delved earth.

Examples might be multiplied indefinitely.

In literature alone of the arts, images from all departments of sense can be aroused. Visual images play a greater role there than in painting and sculpture, for the reason that, in the latter, visual sensations take their place–we do not image what we can see. In sculpture, the greater part of the imagery is of touch and motion–in the imagination, we feel the surfaces and move with the represented motions; the whiteness or blackness of the materials prevents the arousal of the image of the color of the body. In painting, besides the temperature images already mentioned, there are touch images–in still-life, for example, when silks and furs are represented; images of odors, in flower pieces; of motion, in pictures which depict motion, as in the racing horses of Degas; of taste, in pictures of wine and fruit. Of course the kind and amount of imagery depend upon the imaginal type to which the spectator belongs and the wealth of the imaginal furnishing of his mind. In any art, moreover, the chief and requisite thing is expression through the sense medium, which should never be obscured by expression through associated images. It is not the primary business of a flower painter to arouse images of perfume, but to compose colors and lines; nor the function of the musician to arouse the visual images which accompany the musical experience of many people, but to compose sounds. In sculpture, on the other hand, images of touch and movement play an almost necessary part, for they are constituent elements in the representation of form and motion; yet it is not indispensable to the appreciation of sculpture that images of the sweet odor of the human body be awakened. The image is seldom the basis of aesthetic appreciation; it is more often its completion. But we shall go into these matters more in detail in our special chapters.

In the representative arts, particularly painting and sculpture, the associated images are fused with the visual sensations which constitute the medium. I see the softness and sweet-odorousness of the painted rose petal, just as I see the real rose soft and sweet; I see the surface of the statue firm and shapely, just as I see the human body so. This is because the ideas of the things represented in painting and sculpture seem to be actually present in the visual sensations which they interpret; the flower and the man seem to be there before me. In these arts, aesthetic perception is a fusion of image with sensation in much the way that normal perception is. In literature and music, on the other hand, the connection between the sense medium of the art and the associated images is less close; and for the reason that the sounds are no part of the things which they bring before the mind. In looking at a picture of a rose, I see the red as an element of the rose represented; whereas, in reading about a rose, I only seem to hear a voice describing it. In the latter case, therefore, the olfactory and visual images have a certain remoteness and independence of the word-sounds; I do not actually see and smell them in the sounds. However, in the case of familiar words with a strong emotional significance, the fusion of image with sound may be almost complete. Who, for example, does not see a sweet and red image of a rose into the word-sounds when he reads:

Oh, my love's like a red, red rose
That's newly sprung in June.

Or, when Dante describes the *selva oscura*, who does not see the darkness in the word *oscura*? In all such cases a strong feeling tone binds together the word-sound with the image. This fusion is most striking in poetry because of the highly emotional material with which it works.

The ideas and images associated with a work of art depend very largely on the education, experience, and idiosyncrasy of the spectator. The scholar, for example, will put tenfold more meaning into his reading of the *Divine Comedy* than the untrained person. Or compare Pater's interpretation of the "Mona Lisa" with Muther's. Can we say that certain ideas and images belong properly to the work of art, while others do not? With regard to this, we can, I think, set up two criteria. First, the intention of the artist–whatever the artist meant his work to express: that it expresses. Yet, since this can never be certainly and completely discovered, there must always remain a large region of undetermined interpretation. Now for judging the relevancy of this penumbra of meaning and association the following test applies–does it bring us back to the sensuous medium of the work of art or lead us away? Anything is legitimate which we actually put into the form of the work of art and keep there, while whatever merely hangs loose around it is illegitimate. For example, if while listening to music we give ourselves up to personal memories and fancies, we are almost sure to neglect the sounds and their structure; we cannot objectify the former in the latter; with the result that the composition is largely lost to us. Naturally, no hard and fast lines can be drawn, especially in the case of works of vague import like music; yet we can use this criterion as a principle for regulating and inhibiting our associations. It demands of us a wide-awake and receptive appreciation. The genuine meanings and associations of a work of art are those which are the irresistible and necessary results of the sense stimuli working upon an attentive percipient; the rest are not only arbitrary, but injurious.

To this, some people would doubtless object on the ground that art was made for man and not man for art. The work of art, they would claim, should interpret the personal experience of the spectator; hence whatever he puts into it belongs there of right. There are, however, two considerations limiting the validity of this assertion. First, the work of art is primarily an expression of the artist's personality and, second, its purpose is to provide a common medium of expression for the experience of all men. If interpretation remains a purely individual affair, both its relation to the artist and the possibility of a common aesthetic experience through it are destroyed. For this reason we should, I believe, deliberately seek to make our appreciations historically sound and definite. And in the social and historical appreciation resulting, we shall find our own lives–not so different from the artist's and our fellows'–abundantly and sufficiently expressed.

Chapter V

The Analysis of the Aesthetic Experience: The Structure of the Experience

In our discussion of first principles, we set down a high degree of unity as one of the distinguishing characteristics of works of art. In this we followed close upon ancient tradition; for the markedly structural character of beauty was noticed by the earliest observers. Plato, the first philosopher of art, identified beauty with simplicity, harmony, and proportion, and Aristotle held the same view. They were so impressed with aesthetic unity that they compared it with the other most highly unified type of thing they knew, the organism; and ever afterwards it has been called "organic unity." With the backing of such authority, unity in variety was long thought to be the same as beauty; and, although this view is obviously one-sided, no one has since succeeded in persuading men that an object can be beautiful without unity.

Since art is expression, its unity is, unavoidably, an image of the unity of the things in nature and mind which it expresses. A lyric poem reflects the unity of mood that binds together the thoughts and images of the poet; the drama and novel, the unity of plan and purpose in the acts of men and the fateful sequence of causes and effects in their lives. The statue reflects the organic unity of the body; the painting, the spatial unity of visible things. In beautiful artifacts, the basal unity is the purpose or end embodied in the material structure.

But the unity of works of art is not wholly derivative; for it occurs in the free arts like music, where nothing is imitated, and even in the representative arts, as we have observed, it is closer than in the things which are imaged. Aesthetic unity is therefore unique and, if we would understand it, we must seek its reason in the peculiar nature and purpose of art. Since, moreover, art is a complex fact, the explanation of its unity is not simple; the unity itself is very intricate and depends upon many cooperating factors.

In the case of the imitative arts, taking the given unity of the objects represented as a basis, the superior unity of the image is partly due to the singleness of the artist's interest. For art, as we know, is never the expression of mere things, but of things so far as they have value. Out of the infinite fullness of nature and of life, the artist selects those elements that have a unique significance for him.

Music, when soft voices die,
Vibrates in the memory;
Odors, when sweet violets sicken,
Live within the sense they quicken;
Rose leaves, when the rose is dead,
Are heaped for the beloved's bed;
And so thy thoughts when thou art gone,
Love itself shall slumber on.

Observe how, out of the countless things which he knows, the poet has chosen those which he feels akin to his faith in the immortality of love. The painter would not, if he could, reproduce all the elements of a face, but only those that are expressive of the interpretation of character he wishes to convey. The novelist and the dramatist proceed in a like selective fashion in the treatment of their material. In the lives of men there are a thousand actions and events–casual spoken words, recurrent processes such as eating and dressing, hours of idleness and futility which, because repetitious, habitual, or inconsequential, throw no light upon that alone in which we are interested,–character and fortune. To describe a single example of these facts suffices. In the novel and drama, therefore, the personalities and life histories of men have a simplicity and singleness of direction not found in reality. The artist seeks everywhere the traits that individualize and characterize, and neglects all others.

Moreover, since the aim of art is to afford pleasure in the intuition of life, the artist will try to reveal the hidden unities that so delight the mind to discover. He will aim to penetrate beneath the surface of experience observed by common perception, to its more obscure logic underneath. In this way he will go beyond what the mere mechanism of imitation requires. The poet, for example, manifests latent emotional harmonies among the most widely sundered things. The subtle novelist shows how single elements of character, apparently isolated acts or trivial incidents, are fateful of consequences. He discloses the minute reactions of one personality upon another. Or he enters into the soul of man himself, into his private and individual selfhood, and uncovers the hidden connections between thought and feeling and impulse. Finally, he may take the wider sweep of society and tradition into view and track out their part in the molding of man and his fate. In the search for unity, the artist is on common ground with the man of science; but with this difference: the artist is concerned with laws operating in concrete, individual things in which he is interested; while the scientist formulates them in the abstract. For the artist, unity is valuable as characterizing a significant individual; for the scientist, it is valuable in itself, and the individual only as an example of it.

This same purpose of affording pleasure in sympathetic vision leads the artist not only to present the unity of life, but so to organize its material that it will be clear to the mind which perceives it. Too great a multitude of elements, elements that are not assorted into groups and tied by relations or principles, cannot be grasped. Hence the artist infuses into the world which he creates a new and wholly subjective simplicity and unity, to which there is no parallel in nature. The composition of elements in a picture does not correspond to any actual arrangement of elements in a landscape, but to the demands of visual perspicuity. The division of a novel into chapters, of the chapters into paragraphs, of the paragraphs into sentences, although it may answer in some measure to the objective divisions of the life-story related, corresponds much more closely to the subjective need for ready apprehension. The artist meets this need halfway in the organization of the material which he presents. Full beauty depends upon an adaptation of the object to the senses, attention, and synthetic functions of the mind. The long, rambling novel of the eighteenth century is a more faithful image of the fullness and diversity of life, but it answers ill to the limited sweep of the mind, its proneness to fatigue, and its craving for wholeness of view.

But even all the reasons so far invoked–the necessity for significance, the interest in unity, the demand for perspicuity–do not, I think, suffice to explain the structure of works of art. For structure has, oftentimes, a direct emotional appeal, which has not yet been taken into account, and which is a leading motive for its presence. Consider, for example, symmetry. A symmetrical disposition of parts is indeed favorable to perspicuity; for it is easier to find on either side what we have already found on the other, the sight of one side preparing us for the sight of the other; and such an arrangement is flattering to our craving for unity, for we rejoice seeing the same pattern expressed in the two parts; yet the experience of symmetry is richer still: it includes an agreeable feeling of balance, steadfastness, stability. This is most evident in the case of visual objects, like a Greek vase, where there is a plain division between right and left similar halves; but it is also felt in music when there is a balance of themes in the earlier and later parts of a composition, and in literature in the well-balanced sentence, paragraph, or poem. To cite the very simplest example, if I read, "on the one hand ... on the other hand," I have a feeling of balanced tensions precisely analogous to what I experience when I look at a vase. Structure is not a purely intellectual or perceptive affair; it is also motor and organic, and that means emotional. It is felt with the body as well as understood by the mind. I have used the case of symmetry to bring out this truth, but I might have used other types of unification, each of which has its unique feeling tone, as I shall show presently, after I have analyzed them.

Keeping in mind the motives which explain the structure of works of art, I wish now to distinguish and describe the chief types. There are, I think, three of these, of which each one may include important special forms–unity in variety, dominance, and equilibrium.

Unity in variety was the earliest of the types to be observed and is the most fundamental. It is the organic unity so often referred to in criticism. It involves, in the first place, wholeness or individuality. Every work of art is a definite single thing, distinct and separate from other things, and not divisible into parts which are themselves complete works of art. No part can be taken away without damage to the whole, and when taken out of the whole, the part loses much of its own value. The whole needs all of its parts and they need it; "there they live and move and have their being." The unity is a unity of the variety and the variety is a differentiation of the unity. The variety is of equal importance with the unity, for unity can assert itself and work only through the control of a multiplicity of elements. The analogy between the unity of the work of art and the unity of the organism is still the most accurate and illuminating. For, like the work of art, the body is a self-sufficient and distinctive whole, whose unified life depends upon the functioning of many members, which, for their part, are dead when cut away from it.

The conception of unity in variety as organic represents an ideal or norm for art, which is only imperfectly realized in many works. There are few novels which would be seriously damaged by the omission of whole chapters, and many a rambling essay in good standing would permit pruning without injury, unless indeed we are made to feel that the apparently dispensable material really contributes something of fullness and exuberance, and so is not superfluous, after all. The unity in some forms of art is tighter than in others; in a play closer than in a novel; in a sonnet more compact than in an epic. In extreme examples, like *The Thousand and One Nights,* the *Decameron,* the *Canterbury Tales,* the unity is almost wholly nominal, and the work is really a collection, not a whole. With all admissions, it remains true, however, that offenses against the principle of unity in variety diminish the aesthetic value of a work. These offenses are of two kinds–the inclusion of the genuinely irrelevant, and multiple unity, like double composition in a picture, or ambiguity of style in a building. There may be two or more parallel lines of action in a play or a novel, two or more themes in music, but they must be interwoven and interdependent. Otherwise there occurs the phenomenon aptly called by Lipps "aesthetic rivalry"–each part claims to be the whole and to exclude its neighbor; yet being unable to do this, suffers injury through divided attention.

Unity in variety may exist in any one or more of three modes–the harmony or union of cooperating elements; the balance of contrasting or conflicting elements; the development or evolution of a process towards an end or climax. The first two are predominantly static or spatial; the last, dynamic and temporal. I know of no better way of indicating the characteristic quality of each than by citing examples.

Aesthetic harmony exists whenever some identical quality or form or purpose is embodied in various elements of a whole–sameness in difference. The repetition of the same space-form in architecture, like the round arch and window in the Roman style; the recurrence of the same motive in music; the use of a single hue to color the different objects in a painting, as in a nocturne of Whistler: these are simple illustrations of harmony. An almost equally simple case is gradation or lawful change of quality in space and time–the increase or decrease of loudness in music of saturation or brightness of hue in painting, the gentle change of direction of a curved line. In these cases there is, of course, a dynamic or dramatic effect, if you take the elements in sequence; but when taken simultaneously and together, they are a harmony, not a development. Simplest of all is the harmony between like parts of regular figures, such as squares and circles; or between colors which are neighboring in hue. Harmonious also are characters in a story or play which are united by feelings of love, friendship, or loyalty. Thus there is harmony between Hamlet and Horatio, or between the Cid and his followers.

Aesthetic balance is the unity between elements which, while they oppose or conflict with one another, nevertheless need or supplement each other. Hostile things, enemies at war, business men that compete, persons that hate each other, have as great a need of their opponents, in order that there may be a certain type of life, as friends have, in order that there may be love between them; and in relation to each other they create a whole in the one case as in the other. There is as genuine a unity between contrasting colors and musical themes as there is between colors closely allied in hue or themes simply transposed in key. Contrasting elements are always the extremes of some series, and are unified, despite the contrast, because they supplement each other. Things merely different, no matter how different, cannot contrast, for there must be some underlying whole, to which both belong, in which they are unified. In order that this unity may be felt, it is often necessary to avoid absolute extremes, or at least to mediate between them. Among colors, for example, hues somewhat closer than the complementary are preferred to the latter, or, if the extremes are employed, each one leads up to the other through intermediate hues. The unity of contrasting colors is a balance because, as extremes, they take an equal hold on the attention. The well-known accentuation of contrasting elements does not interfere with the balance, because it is mutual. A balanced unity is also created by contrasts of character, as in Goethe's *Tasso*, or by a conflict between social classes or parties, as in Hauptmann's *Die Weber*. Balanced, finally, is the unity between the elements of a painting, right and left, which draw the attention in opposite directions. The third type of unity appears in any process or sequence in which all the elements, one after another, contribute towards the bringing about of some end or result. It is the unity characteristic of all teleologically related facts. The sequence cannot be a mere succession or even a simple causal series, but must also be purposive, because, in order to be aesthetic, the goal which is reached must have value. Causality is an important aspect of this type of unity, as in the drama, but only because a teleological series of actions depends upon a chain of causally related means and ends. The type is of two varieties: in the one, the movement is smooth, each element being harmoniously related to the last; in the other, it is difficult and dramatic, proceeding through the resolution of oppositions among its elements. The movement usually has three stages: an initial phase of introduction and preparation; a second phase of opposition and complication; then a final one, the climax or catastrophe, when the goal is reached; there may also be a fourth,–the working out of the consequences of this last. Illustrations of this mode of unity are: the course of a story or a play from the introduction of the characters and the complication of the plot to the denouement or solving of the problem; the development of a character in a novel from a state of simplicity or innocence through storm and stress into maturity or ruin; the evolution of a sentiment in a sonnet towards its final statement in the last line or two; the melody, in its departure from the keynote, its going forth and return; the career of a line.

As I have indicated before, each type of unity has its specific emotional quality. The very word harmony which we use to denote the first mode is itself connotative of a way of being affected, of being moved emotionally. The mood of this mode is quiet, oneness, peace. We feel as if we were closely and compactly put together. If now, within the aesthetic whole, we emphasize the variety, we begin to lose the mood of peace; tensions arise, until, in the case of contrast and opposition, there is a feeling of conflict and division in the self;

yet without loss of unity, because, if the whole is aesthetic, each of the opposing elements demands the other; hence there is balance between them, and this also we not only know to be there, but feel there. The characteristic mood of the evolutionary type of unity is equally unique–either a sense of easy motion, when the process is unobstructed, or excitement and breathlessness, when there is opposition.

The different types of unity are by no means exclusive of each other and are usually found together in any complex work of art. Symmetry usually involves a combination of harmony and balance. The symmetrical halves of a Greek vase, for example, are harmonious in so far as their size and shape are the same, yet balanced as being disposed in opposite directions, right and left. Rhythm is temporal symmetry, and so also represents a combination of harmony and balance. Static rhythm is only apparent; for in every seeming case, the rhythm really pervades the succession of acts of attention to the elements rather than the elements themselves; a colonnade, for example, is rhythmical only when the attention moves from one column to another. There is harmony in rhythm, for there is always some law–metrical scheme in poetry, time in music, similarity of column and equality of interval between them in a colonnade–pervading the elements. But there is also balance; for as the elements enter the mind one after the other, there is rivalry between the element now occupying the focus of the attention and the one that is about to present an equal claim to this position. Because of its intrinsic value, we tend to hold on to each element as we hear or see it, but are forced to relinquish it for the sake of the one that follows; only for a moment can we keep both in the conscious span; the recurrence and overcoming of the resulting tension, as we follow the succession through, creates the pulsation so characteristic of rhythm. The opposition of the elements as in turn they crowd each other out does not, however, interfere with the harmony, for they have an existence all together in memory, where the law binding them can be felt,–a law which each element as it comes into consciousness is recognized as fulfilling. Since we usually look forward to the end of the rhythmical movement as a goal, rhythm often exists in combination with evolution, and is therefore the most inclusive of all artistic structural forms. In a poem, for example, the metrical rhythm is a framework overlying the development of the thought. Dramatic unity is found combined with balance even in the static arts, as, for example, in the combination of blue and gold, where the balance is not quite equal, because of a slight movement from the blue to the more brilliant and striking gold. I have already shown how harmony, opposition, and evolution may be combined in a melody. In the drama, also, all three are present. There is a balance of opposing and conflicting wills or forces; this is unstable; whence movement follows, leading on to the catastrophe, where the problem is solved; and throughout there is a single mood or atmosphere in which all participate, creating an enveloping harmony despite the tension and action. And other illustrations of combinations of types will come to the mind of every reader.

Each form of unity has its difficulties and dangers, which must be avoided if perfection is to be attained. In harmony there may be too much identity and too little difference or variety, with the result that the whole becomes tedious and uninteresting. This is the fault of rigid symmetry and of all other simple geometrical types of composition, which, for this reason, have lost their old popularity in the decorative and pictorial arts. In balance, on the other hand, the danger is that there may be too great a variety, too strong an opposition; the elements tend to fly apart, threatening the integrity of the whole. For it is not sufficient that wholeness exist in a work of art; it must also be felt. For example, in Pre-Raphaelite paintings and in most of the Secession work of our own day, the color contrasts are too strong; there is no impression of visual unity. In the dramatic type of unity there are two chief dangers–that the evolution be tortuous, so that we lose our way in its bypaths and mazes; or, on the other hand, that the end be reached too simply and quickly; in the one case, we lose heart for the journey because of the obstacles; in the other, we lose interest and are bored for want of incidents.

We come now to the second great principle of aesthetic structure– Dominance. In an aesthetic whole the elements are seldom all on a level; some are superior, others subordinate. The unity is mediated through one or more accented elements, through which the whole comes to emphatic expression. The attention is not evenly distributed among the parts, but proceeds from certain ones which are focal and commanding to others which are of lesser interest. And the dominant elements are not only superior in significance; they are, in addition, representative of the whole; in them, its value is concentrated; they are the key by means of which its structure can be understood. They are like good rulers in a constitutional state, who are at once preeminent members of the community and signal embodiments of the common will. Anything which distinguishes and makes representative of the whole serves to make dominant. In a well-constructed play there are one or more characters which are central to the action, in whom the spirit and problem of the piece are embodied, as Hamlet in *Hamlet* and Brand in *Brand*; in every plot there is the catastrophe or turning point, for which every preceding incident is a preparation, and of which every following one is a consequent; in a melody there is the keynote; in the larger composition there are the one or more themes whose working out is the piece; in a picture there are certain elements which especially attract the attention, about which the others are composed. In the more complex rhythms, in meters, for example, the elements are grouped around the accented ones. In an aesthetic whole there are certain qualities and positions which, because of their claim upon the attention, tend to make dominant any elements which possess them. In space-forms the center and the edges are naturally places of preeminence. The eye falls first upon the center and then is drawn away to the boundaries. In old pictures, the Madonna or Christ is placed in the center and the angels near the perimeter; in fancy work it is the center and the border which women embroider. In time, the beginning, middle, and end are the natural places of importance; the beginning, because there the attention is fresh and expectant; towards the middle, because there we tend to rest, looking backward to the commencement and forward to the end; the end itself, because being last in the mind, its hold upon the memory is firmest. In any process the beginning is important as the start, the plan, the preparation; the middle as the climax and turning point; the end as the consummation. Of course by the middle is not meant a mathematical point of division into equal parts, but a psychological point, which is usually nearer the end, because the impetus of action and purpose carry forward and beyond. Thus in a plot the beginning stands out as setting the problem and introducing the characters and situation; then the movement of the action, gathering force increasingly as it proceeds, breaks at some point well beyond the middle; in the last part the problem is solved and the consequences of the action are revealed. Large size is another quality which distinguishes and tends to make dominant, as in the tower and the mountain. In one of Memling's paintings, "St. Ursula and the Maidens," which, when I saw it, was in Bruges, the lady is represented twice as tall as the full grown girls whom she envelops in her protecting cloak; yet, despite the unnaturalness, we do not experience any incongruity; for it is rational to our feeling. Intensity of any sort is another property which creates dominance–loudness of sound in music; concentration of light in painting, as in Rembrandt; stress in rhythm; depth and scope of purpose and feeling, as in the great characters of fiction. The effectiveness of intensity may be greatly increased through contrast–the pianissimo after the fortissimo; the pathos of the fifth act of *Hamlet* set off by the comedy of the first scene. Sometimes all the natural qualifications of eminence are united in a single work: in old paintings, for example, the Christ Child, spiritually the most significant element of the whole, will be of supernatural size, will occupy the center of the picture, will have the light concentrated upon him, and will be dressed in brightly gleaming garments.

As I have already indicated, there may be more than one dominant element; for instance, two or more principal characters in a novel or play–Lord and Lady Macbeth, Sancho and Don Quixote, Othello and Desdemona, Brand and his wife. In this case, there must be either subordination among them, a hierarchical arrangement; or else reciprocity or balance, as in the illustrations cited, where it is difficult to tell which is the more important of the two; otherwise they would pull the whole apart. The advantage of several dominant elements lies in the greater animation, and when the work is large, in the superior organization, which they confer. In order that there may be perspicuity, it is necessary, when there are many elements, that they be separated into minor groups around high points which individualize and represent them, and so take their place in the mind, mediating between them and unity when a final synthesis of the whole is to be made.

The third great principle of aesthetic structure is equilibrium or impartiality. This is a principle counteracting dominance. It demands, despite the subordination among the elements, that none be neglected. Each, no matter how minor its part in the whole, must have some unique value of its own, must be an end as well as a means. Dominance is the aristocratic principle in art, the rule of the best; this is the democratic principle, the demand for freedom and significance for all. Just as, in a well-ordered state, the happiness of no individual or class of individuals is sacrificed to that of other individuals or classes; so in art, each part must be elaborated and perfected, not merely for the sake of its contribution to the whole, but for its own sake. There should be no mere figure-heads or machinery. Loving care of detail, of the incidental, characterizes the best art.

Of course this principle, like the others, is an ideal or norm, which is only imperfectly realized in many works of art. Many a poet finds it necessary to fill in his lines and many a painter and musician does the like with his pictures or compositions. There is much mere scaffolding and many lay-figures in drama and novel. But the work of the masters is different. There each line or stroke or musical phrase, each character or incident, is unique or meaningful. The greatest example of this is perhaps the *Divine Comedy*, where each of the hundred cantos and each line of each canto is perfect in workmanship and packed with significance. There is, of course, a limit to this elaboration of the parts, set by the demands for unity and wholeness. The individuality of the elements must not be so great that we rest in them severally, caring little or nothing for their relations to one another and to the whole. The contribution of this principle is richness. Unity in variety gives wholeness; dominance, order; equilibrium, wealth, interest, vitality.

The structure of works of art is even more complicated than would appear from the description given thus far. For there is not only the unity of the elements among themselves, but between the two aspects of each element and of the whole–the form and content. This–the unity between the sense medium and whatever of thought and feeling is embodied in it–is the fundamental unity in all expression. It is the unity between a word and its meaning, a musical tone and its mood, a color and shape and what they represent. Since, however, it is indispensable to all expression, it is not peculiar to art. And to a large extent, even in the creative work of the artist, this unity is given, not made; the very materials of the artist consisting of elementary expressions–words, tones, colors, space-forms–in which the unity of form and content has already been achieved, either by an innate psycho-physical process, as is the case with tones and simple rhythms, or by association and habit, as is the case with the words of any natural language, or the object-meanings which we attach to colors and shapes. The poet does not work with sounds, but with words which already have their definite meanings; his creation consists of the larger whole into which he weaves them. Of course, even in the case of ordinary verbal expression, the thought often comes first before its clothing in words, when there is a certain process of choice and fitting; and in painting there is always the possibility of varying conventional forms; yet even so, in large measure, the elements of the arts are themselves expressions, in which a unity of form and content already exists.

In art, however, there are subtler aspects to the relation between form and content, and these have a unique aesthetic significance. For there, as we know, the elements of the medium, colors and lines and sounds, and the patterns of these, their harmonies and structures and rhythms, are expressive, in a vague way, of feeling; hence, when the artist employs them as embodiments of his ideas, he has to select them, not only as carriers of meaning, but as communications of mood. Now, in order that his selection be appropriate, it is clearly necessary that the feeling tone of the form be identical with that of the content which he puts into it. The medium as such must reexpress and so enforce the values of the content. This is the "harmony," as distinguished from the mere unity, of form and content, the existence of which in art is one of its distinguishing properties. I have already called attention to this in our second chapter. It involves, as we observed, that in painting, for example, the feeling tone of the colors and lines should be identical with that of the objects to be represented; in poetry, that the emotional quality of meter and rhythm should be attuned to the incidents and sentiments expressed. Otherwise the effect is ugly or comical.

When we come to the work of art, this harmony is already achieved. But for the artist it is something delicately to be worked out. Yet, just as in ordinary expression form and content often emerge in unison, the thought itself being a word and the word a thought; so in artistic creation, the mother mood out of which the creative act springs, finds immediate and forthright embodiment in a congenial form. Such a spontaneous and perfect balance of matter and form is, however, seldom achieved without long and painful experimentation and practice, both by the artist himself in his own private work, and by his predecessors, whose results he appropriates. Large traditional and oftentimes rigid forms, such as the common metrical and musical schemes and architectural orders, into which the personal matter of expression may aptly fall, are thus elaborated in every art. As against every looser and novel form, they have the advantages first, of being more readily and steadily held in the memory, where they may gather new and poignant associations; second, of coming to us already freighted with similar associations out of the past; and last, of compelling the artist, in order that he may fit his inspiration into them, to purify it of all irrelevant substance. Impatient artists rebel against forms, but wise ones either accommodate their genius to them, until they become in the end a second and equally spontaneous nature, or else create new forms, as definite as the old.

Chapter VI

Problem of Evil in Aesthetics: And its Solution Through the Tragic, Pathetic and Comic

When, in our third chapter, we defined the purpose of art, we indicated that it was broad enough to include the expression of evil, but we did not show in detail how this was possible. That is our present theme.

Art is sympathetic representation; the effort not only to reveal an object to us, but to unite us with it. The artist finds no difficulty in accomplishing this purpose with reference to one class of objects–those which, apart from portrayal, we call beautiful. To these we are drawn immediately because they serve directly the ends of life. Nature sees to it that we dwell with pleasure on the sight of healthy children, well-grown women, and bountiful landscapes. And to the representations of such objects we are attracted by the same instincts that attract us to the things themselves. No special power of art is required that we take delight in them; the task of the artist is half accomplished before he begins. Yet the scope of art is wider than this, for it represents evil as well as good. Death as well as life, sickness and deformity as well as health, suffering as well as joy, sin equally with goodness, come within its purview. And these also it not only reveals to us but makes good to know, so good in fact that they are perhaps the preferred objects of artistic representation. But instead of being able to rely on instincts that would draw us to these objects, art has to overcome those that would lead us away from them. It has to conquer our natural horror at death, pain at suffering, and revulsion against wickedness. How does it? That is the problem of evil in sthetics.

There are many means by which this problem is solved. In the first place, the mere fact that art is representation and not reality does much toward overcoming any feelings of moral or physical repugnance we might have toward the objects represented. These feelings exist for the sake of action; hence, when action is impossible–and we cannot act on the unreal–although they may still persist, they become less strong. Toward the merely imaginary, the practical and moral attitudes, which towards the real would lead to condemnation and withdrawal, lose their relevance and tend to disappear. That is one of the advantages of art over the more immediate perception of life. It is difficult to take a purely aesthetic attitude towards all of life, to seek only to get into sympathetic contact with it for the sake of an inner realization of what it is; much of it touches us too closely on the side of our practical and moral interests. A certain man, for example, does not belong to our set, or his ways are so bohemian that it would imperil our social position or the safety of our souls to get acquainted with him; so we reject him and cast him into the outer darkness of our disapproval–or he rejects us. Such a person, we feel, is to be avoided or haply, if we be saints, to be saved from himself; but not to be accepted and understood. And even if we succeed in freeing ourselves from the moral point of view, we are still preoccupied with the practical, if the man happens to interest us commercially; we have not the time nor the desire to see his nature as a whole. Not so in art. As a character in a novel, a man cannot be employed; nor can it be a hazard to keep company with him; and his soul is surely beyond our saving; the only thing left for us to do is to sympathize with and try to understand him, to enter into communion with his spirit. By freeing life from the practical and moral, art gives the imagination full sway. This, to be sure, is only a negative force working in the direction of beauty, yet is important none the less because it enables the more positive influences to function easily.

One of these is what I would call "sympathetic curiosity," which may encompass all images of life. Things which, if met with in life, would certainly repel, when presented in image, simply excite our curiosity to know. Of course some are impelled by the same interest to get into contact with all experience–*Homo sum: humani nihil alienum a me puto*–yet with the great majority the impulses to withdraw are too strong. But all have a desire for further knowledge when a mere idea of human life, however repellent, is presented; for the instinct of gregariousness, which creates a special interest in our kind, works with full force in the mind to strengthen curiosity. There is no part of human experience which it does not embrace. We can well forego knowledge of stars and trees, but we cannot remain ignorant of anything human. As the moth to the flame, we are led, even against our will, into all of life, even the most unpleasant. The charm possessed by the novel and unplumbed, by such stories as *Jude the Obscure*, or by the weird imaginings of a Baudelaire, comes from this source. It is no mere scientific curiosity, because it includes that "consciousness of kind," which makes us feel akin to all we know.

Sympathetic curiosity, however, seldom works alone, for other interests, less worthy and therefore often unavowed, usually cooperate to overcome our repugnances towards the unpleasant. Many of our repugnances are not simple and original like those felt towards death, darkness, and deformity, but highly complex products of education, which may be dissolved by a strong appeal to the more primitive instincts which they seek to repress. An artist may, for example, through a vivid portrayal, so excite the animal lust and cruelty which lurk hidden in all of us as to make the most morally reprehensible objects acceptable. Nature has taken many a revenge on civilization through art. Although no one should demand that these appeals be entirely excluded, yet when they operate alone, without the sublimation of insight, they are flagrantly unaesthetic in their influence, because they deprive the work of art of its freedom.

Another means which the artist may employ in order to win us is the appeal of sense. However repellent be the objects which he represents, if he can clothe them in a sensuous material which will charm us, he will have exerted a powerful countervailing force. We have already had occasion to observe this in our first chapter. Through the call of sense we are invited to enter and are made welcome at the very threshold of the work of art. Engaging lines, winsome colors and tones, and compelling rhythms can overcome almost any repugnance that we might otherwise feel for the subject-matter. Their primary appeals are superior to all the reservations of civilization. No wonder that the stern moralists who would keep beauty for the clean and holy have been afraid of art! Yet the delight of sense, because its emotional effect is diffused, does not interfere with the contemplative serenity of art, as unbridled passion does; it even quiets passion by diverting the attention to itself; hence may always be employed by the artist. A good example of the aesthetic fascination of sensation is Von Stuck's "Salome" in the Art Institute of Chicago. For all normal feeling, Salome dancing with the head of John the Baptist is a revolting object; yet how beautiful the artist has made his picture through the simple loveliness of gold and red!

It would be a mistake, however, to infer the indifference of the subject-matter in art. The creation of a work of art is based on a primary aesthetic experience of nature or human life, and not everything is capable of producing such an experience in all men. The subject must be one towards which the artist or spectator is able to take the sthetic attitude of emotional, yet free, perception. Some people are unable to lay aside their moral prepossessions towards certain phases of life or even towards representation of them; the idea affects them as would the reality. For such people even the genius of a Beardsley is too feeble to create an experience of beauty out of the material with which he works. Or again, some people cannot objectify their sensual egotistic impulses and feelings; for them the reading of a Boccaccio, for example, is only a substitute for such feelings, not a means of insight into them. It requires a robust intellectual attitude, a predominance of mind over feeling and instinct, aesthetically to appreciate some works of art. But for those who can receive it, the representation of any phase of life may afford an aesthetic experience, may create a thing good to know, if only it be mastered by the mind and embodied in a charming form.

The charm of sense together with the satisfaction of insight are sufficient to explain the conquest of evil by art. Yet further means have been employed–the special appeals of the tragic, pathetic, and comic.

What any one may mean by tragic is largely a matter of personal definition or tradition; yet there is, I think, a common essence upon which all would agree. First, tragedy always involves the manful struggle of a personality in the pursuit of some end, at the cost of suffering, perhaps of death and failure. The opposition may come from nature, as in *The Grammarian's Funeral*; from fate, as in the *Oedipus*; from social and political interests, as in *Antigone*; that is of little moment; it is important solely that the battle be accepted and waged unflinchingly to the issue. In this ultimate sense, most of human life is tragic; because it involves a continual warfare with circumstances, which the majority of people carry on with a silent heroism. Originally, only the glorious and spectacular conflicts of great personalities were deemed worthy of representation in art; but with the growth of sympathy the range of tragic portrayal has gradually been extended over almost the whole of human life. The peasant in his struggle for subsistence against a niggardly soil, or the patient woman who loses the bloom of her youth in the unremitting effort to maintain her children, are tragic figures.

Second, it is part of the essence of tragedy that the conflict should be recognized as necessary and its issue as inevitable. In one form or another, whether as Greek or Christian or naturalistic, fatality has remained an abiding element in the idea of tragedy. The purpose or passion or sentiment which impels the hero to undertake and maintain the struggle must be a part of his nature so integral that nothing else is possible for him. "*Ich kann nicht anders*" is the cry of every tragic personality. And the opposition which he meets from other persons, from social forces or natural circumstances, must seem to be equally fateful–must be represented as issuing from a counter determination or law no less inescapable than the hero's will. Even when the catastrophe depends upon some so-called accident, it must be made to appear necessary that our human purposes should sometimes be caught and strangled in the web of natural fact which envelops them.

The reasons for our acceptance of tragedy are not difficult to find and have been noted, with more or less clearness, by all students. We accept it much as the hero accepts his own struggle–he believes in the values which he is fighting for and we sympathetically make his will ours. Moreover, we discover a special value in his courage which, we feel, compensates for the evil of his suffering, defeat, or death. So long as we set any value on life, it is impossible for us not to esteem courage; for courage is at once the defense against attack of all our possessions and the source, in personal initiative and aggressive action, of newer and larger life. And any shrinking that we may feel against the sternness of the struggle is quenched both by the hero's example and by our recognition of its necessity. Since we are not participants of it, our protest would be futile, and even if we played a part in it, we should be as foolish as we should be weak, not to recognize that the will which opposes us is as inflexible as our own–"such is life"–that is our ultimate comment. An appreciation of tragedy involves, therefore, a sure discernment of the essential disharmony of existence, yet at the same time, a feeling for the moral values which it may create; neither the optimist nor the utilitarian can enter into its world.

There are, however, works of art in which sheer evil, without any compensating development of character, is portrayed; where indeed the struggle may even cause decay of character. In Zola's *The Dram Shop*, for example, the story is the tale of the moral decline, through unfortunate circumstances and vicious surroundings, of the sweet, pliant Gervaise. Instead of developing a resistance to circumstances which would have made them yield a value even in defeat, she lets herself go and is spoiled beneath them. She has no friend to help or guardian angel to save. We do not blame her, for, with her soft nature, she could not do otherwise than crumble under the hard press of fate; neither can we admire her, for she lacks the adamantine stuff of which heroes are made. This is pathos, not tragedy. And just as most of human life involves tragedy in so far as it develops a strength to meet the dangers which threaten it, so likewise it involves pathos, in so far as it seldom resists at every point, but gives way, blighted without hope. Many a man or woman issues from life's conflicts weaker, not stronger; broken, not defiant; petulant, not sweetened; and at the hour of death there are few heroes. Yet there may be beauty in the story of this human weakness and weariness. Whence comes it? How can the representation of this sheer evil become a good? The principle involved is a simple one. Announced first, as far as I know, by Mendelssohn, it has recently been much more scientifically and penetratingly analyzed by Lipps, although wrongly applied by him to the tragic rather than the pathetic.

It is a familiar and generally recognized experience, as Lipps has observed, that any threat or harm done to a value evokes in us a heightened appreciation of its worth. Parting is a sweet sorrow because only then do we fully realize the worth of what we are losing; the beauty of youth that dies is more beautiful because in death its radiance shines the brighter in our memory. A good in contemplation comes to take the place of a lost good in reality. Just as we hold on the more tightly to things that are slipping away from us in a vain effort to keep them, so to save ourselves from utter sorrow, we build up in the imagination a fair image of what we have lost, free of the dust of the world. This makes the peculiar charm of the delicate and fragile, of weak things and little things, of the transient and perishable; they awaken in us the tender, protective impulse while they last, and when they are gone they suffer at our hands an idealization which the strong and enduring can never receive. Our pity for them mediates an increased love of them; we mock at fate which deprives us of them by keeping them secure and fairer in our memory.

As in life, so in art. Beneath and around the pictured destruction and ruin there opens up to us a more poignant vision of the loveliness of what was or might have been. At the end of *The Dram Shop*, when Gervaise sinks into ruin, we inevitably revert to the beginning and see again, only more intensely, the gentle girl that she was, or else, going forward, we imagine what she might have been, if only she had been given a chance. The form of a possible good rises up from under the actual evil. The story of oppression becomes the praise of freedom; the picture of death, a vision of life. I know of no finer example of this in all literature than Sophocles' *Ajax*. Ajax has offended Athena, so he, the hero of the Grecian host, is seized with the mad desire to do battle with cattle and sheep. In lucid intervals he laments to his wife the shameful fate which has befallen him. How glorious his former prowess appears lost in so ridiculous a counterfeit! And his despair creates its magic.

In almost all so-called tragedies, true tragedy and pathos are intermingled; for we feel both pity and admiration, and the pity intensifies the admiration. The danger that threatens or the disaster that overwhelms the values which the hero embodies make us realize their worth the more. Throughout the *Antigone* we admire the heroine's tragic courage of devotion; but it is at the point when, just before her death, she laments her youth and beauty that shall go fruitless–

Alechron, anymenaion, oute ton gamon mepos
lachousan oute paideion tpophaes

that we feel the fullness of strength that was needed for the sacrifice. One might perhaps think this lament a blemish of weakness in a picture of fortitude; but the impression is just the opposite, I believe; for force is measured by what it overcomes.

There are so many different theories of tragedy that it would be impossible, were it worth while, to embark on a criticism of all of them. There are certain ones, however, which, because of their wide acceptance, demand some attention at our hands. First, it is often assumed that a tragedy should represent the good as ultimately triumphing, despite suffering and failure. But how can the good triumph when the hero fails and dies? Only, it is answered, if the hero represents a cause which may win despite or even because of his individual doom; and it is with this cause, not with him, that we chiefly sympathize. This was Hegel's view, who demanded that the tragic hero represent some universal interest which, when purged of the one-sidedness and uncompromising insistence of the hero's championing, may nevertheless endure and triumph in its genuine worth. In the *Antigone*, Hegel's favorite example, the cause of family loyalty finds recognition through the punishment of Creon for the girl's death; while at the same time the principle of the sovereignty of the state is upheld through her sacrifice. There are many tragedies which conform, at least partially, to this scheme; but not all, hence it cannot be a universal norm. In *Romeo and Juliet*, for example, although the death of the young people serves to bring about a reconciliation of their families, the real principle for which they suffered–the right of private choice in matters of love–is in no way furthered by the outcome of the play. And, although it is always possible to universalize the good which is sought by any will, it is not possible to deflect upon a principle the full intensity of our sympathy, away from the individual, concrete passion and action. Whenever a great personality is represented, it is his personal suffering and fortitude that win at once our pity and our admiration. For private sorrows, for the ruin of character, for the death of those whom we are made to love, there can be no complete atonement in the universal; because it is with the individual that we are chiefly concerned. No; the reconciliation lies where we have placed it–in tragedy, in the personal heroism of the strong character; in pathos, in the vision, not in the triumph, of the good.

The ordinary Protestant theological theory of tragedy is even more inadequate than the Hegelian. For, by assuming that there is no genuine loss in the world, that every evil is compensated for in the future lives of the heroes, it takes away the sting from their sacrifice and so deprives them of their crown of glory. It makes every adventure a calculation of prudence and every despair a farce. It is remote from the reality of experience where men stake all on a chance and, instead of receiving the good by an act of grace, wring it by blood and tears from evil.

On much the same level of thinking is the moralistic theory which requires that the misfortunes of the hero should be the penalty for some fault or weakness. This view, which has the authority of Aristotle, is also based on the doctrine of the justice of the world-order. It was pretty consistently carried out in the classical Greek drama; although there suffering is not exacted as an external retribution, but as the inevitable consequence of the turbulent passions of the characters; for even the punishment for offenses against the gods is of the nature of a personal revenge which they take. Later, of course, when the gods retreated into the background of human life, retributive justice was conceived more abstractly. Now, it must be admitted, I think, that this idea, so deeply rooted in the popular mind, has exerted a profound influence on the drama; yet it cannot be applied universally without sophistry. To be sure, in *Romeo and Juliet*, the young people were disobedient and headstrong; in *Lear*, the old father was foolishly trustful of his wicked daughters; these frailties brought about their ruin. But did they deserve so hard a fate as theirs? Did not Lear suffer as much for his folly as his daughters for their wickedness? This is always true in life, and Shakespeare holds the mirror up to nature–but is it consistent with the theory of retributive justice? One can usually trace back to some element of his nature, physical or moral, the misfortunes that befall an individual; even those which we call accidents, as Galton claimed, are often due to some inherent defect of attention which makes us fail to respond protectively at the right moment. If we take the self to include the entire organism, then it remains true that we cooperate as a partial cause in all that happens to us. Ophelia's weak and unresisting brain must share with the stresses which surrounded her the responsibility for her madness. In this sense, and in this sense only, do we deserve our fate, be it good or ill. Yet, when interpreted in this broadest meaning, retributive justice loses all ethical significance. And the cosmic disharmony appears all the more glaring. It ceases to be chargeable to an external fate or God, to the environment or convention, which might perhaps be mastered and remolded; and is seen pervading the nature of reality itself, no accidental circumstance, but essential evil, ineradicable. The greatest tragic poets see it thus. And then blame turns to understanding and resentment into pity.

Retributive justice, as the motive force of tragedy, has for us lost its meaning. We no longer feel the necessity of justifying the ways of God to man, because we have ceased to believe that there exists any single, responsible power. The good is not a preordained and automatically accomplished fact, but an achievement of finite effort, appearing here and there in the world when individuals, instead of contending against each other, cooperate for their mutual advantage.

In addition to the comic, there is much artistic representation of evil which can be classed neither as pathetic nor as tragic. Neither moral admiration nor idealization are aroused by the characters portrayed. They may be great criminals like Lady Macbeth or Iago, or the undistinguished and disorderly people of modern realistic literature, yet in either case we find them good to know. And we do so, not merely because we enjoy, as disinterested onlookers, the spectacle of human existence, but because the artist makes us enter into it and realize its values. For even that which from the moral point of view we pronounce evil is, so long as it maintains itself, a good thing from its own point of view. Every will, however blind and careless, seeks a good and finds it, if only in hope and the effort to attain. Through the intimacy of his descriptions and often against our resistance, the artist may compel us to adopt the attitude of the life which he is portraying, constraining us to feel the inner necessity of its choices, the compulsion of its delights. It is difficult to abandon ourselves thus to sympathy with what is wrong in life itself, because we have in mind the consequences and relations which make it wrong; yet we all do so at times, whenever we let ourselves go, charmed by its momentary offering. But in the world of art this is easier, because there the values, being merely represented, can have no sinister effects. When great personalities are portrayed, this abandon is readiest; for the strength or poignancy of their natures carries us away as by a whirlwind. Witness Lady Macbeth when she summons the powers of hell to unsex her for her murderous task, or Vanni Fucci in the *Inferno*, who mocks at God. For the instant, we become as they and feel their ecstasy of pride and power as our own. Yet the great artist can awaken this sympathy even for characters that are small and weak. In Gogol's *Dead Souls*, for example, there are no heroes. The most interesting characters are the country gentlemen who return to their estates planning to write books which will regenerate Russia. But the old habits of life in the remote district are too strong. So, instead of writing, they fall back into the routine of their ancestors and merely smoke and dream. Here are failure and mediocrity; yet so intimate is the artist's story that we not only understand it all, but feel how good it is–to dream our lives away. I do not doubt that in this story there are elements of pathos and comedy; yet, in general, the delineation is too objective for either; we neither laugh nor cry, but are simply borne on, unresisting, ourselves become a part of the silent tide of Russian life.

The problem of evil in aesthetics may finally be solved by the use of the comic. For in comedy we take pleasure in an object which, in the broadest sense, is evil. In order for an object to be comical there must be a standard or norm, an accepted system, within which the object pretends but fails to fit, and with reference to which, therefore, it is evil. There must be some points of contact between the object and the standard in order that there may be pretense, but not enough points for fulfillment. If we never had any definite expectations with reference to things, never made any demands upon them; if instead of judging them by our preconceived ideas, we took them just as they came and changed our ideas to meet them,–there would be nothing comical. Or, if everything fitted into our expectations and was as we planned it, then again there would be nothing comical. In a world without ideas, the comic could not exist. The comic depends upon our apperceiving an object in terms of some idea and finding it incongruous. The most elementary illustrations demonstrate this. The unusual is the original comic; to the child all strange things are comical–the Chinaman with his pigtail, the negro with his black skin, the new fashion in dress, the clown with his paint and his antics. As we get used to things, and that means as we come to form ideas of them into which they will fit, adjusting the mind to them, rather than seeking to adjust them to the mind, they cease to be comical. So fashions in dress or manners which were comical once, become matters of course and we laugh no longer. Enduringly comic are only those objects that persistently create expectations and as persistently violate them. Such objects are few indeed; but they exist, and constitute the perennial, yet never wearying, stock in trade of comedy. But the comic spirit does not have to depend upon them exclusively, for, as life changes, it constantly raises new expectations and offers new objects which at once provoke and fail to meet them. Everything, therefore, is potentially comical and, in the course of human history, few things can escape a laugh; some curious mind is sure, sooner or later, to bring them under a new idea against which they will be shown up to be absurd. The sanctities of religion, love, and political allegiance have not been exempt.

Why, if the comical object is always opposed to our demands, should we take pleasure in it? How can we be reconciled to things that are admittedly incongruous with our standards? Why are we not rather displeased and angry with them? Investigators have usually looked for a single source of pleasure in the comic, but of those which have been suggested at least two, I think, contribute something. First, by adopting the point of view of the standard as our own, identifying ourselves with it, and through the contrast of ourselves with the object, we may take pleasure in the resulting exaltation of ourselves. The pleasure in the comic is often closely akin to that which we feel in distinction of any kind. We feel ourselves superior to the object at which we laugh. There is pride in much of laughter and not infrequently cruelty, a delight in the absurdities of other men because they exalt ourselves as the representatives of the rational and normal. There is often a touch of malice even in the laughter of the child. Nevertheless, the pleasure in the comic is still contemplative, and so far aesthetic, because it is a pleasure in perception, not in action. No matter how evil be the comic object, we do not seek to destroy or remodel it; action is sublimated into laughter.

But the pleasure in the comic may arise through our taking the opposite point of view–that of the funny thing itself. Instead of upholding the point of view of the standard, we may identify ourselves with the object. If the comic spirit is oftentimes the champion of the normal and conventional, it is as often the mischief-maker and rebel. Whenever the maintaining of a standard involves strain through the inhibition of instinctive tendencies, to relax and give way to impulse causes a pleasure which centers itself upon the object that breaks the tension. The intrusive animal that interrupts the solemn occasion, the child that wittingly or not scoffs at our petty formalities through his naive behavior, win our gratitude, not our scorn. They provide an opportunity for the welcome release of nature from convention. And the greater the strain of the tension, the greater the pleasure and the more insignificant the object or event that will bring relief and cause laughter. The perennial comic pleasure in the risque is derived from this source. There is an element of comic pleasure in the perpetration of any mischievous or unconventional act. Those things which men take most seriously, Schopenhauer has said, namely, love and religion, and we might add, morality, are the most abundant sources of the comic, because they involve the most strain and therefore offer the easiest chances for a playful release. Even utter and absolute nonsense is comical because it undoes all Kant's categories of mind.

Hence, contrary to the theory of Bergson, the spontaneous as well as the mechanical and rigid may be comical. Sometimes the same object may be comical from both the points of view which we have specified; this is always true, as we shall see, in the most highly developed comedy. For example, we may laugh at the child's prank because it is so absurd from the point of view of our grown-up expectations as to reasonable conduct, and at the same time, taking the part of the child, rejoice at the momentary relief from them which it offers us. Our scorn is mixed with sympathy. And oftentimes the child himself will hold both points of view at once, laughing at his own absurdity and exulting nevertheless in his own freedom. This is the essence of slyness. It follows, moreover, that a thing which was comical for one of the reasons assigned may become comical for the other, by a simple change in the point of view regarding it. For the behavior which first pleased us because it was unconventional tends itself to become a new convention, with reference to which the old convention then becomes the object of a laughter which is scornful. The tables are turned: the rebel laughs at the king.

The foregoing explanation of why we find the comical pleasant also explains why so many of our other pleasures are intermixed with the comical–why so often we not only smile when we are pleased, but laugh. For, in the case of all except the most elementary enjoyments, our pleasures are connected with the satisfaction of definite expectations regarding the actions or events of our daily lives. But, owing to the dulling effect of habit, the pleasure attendant upon these satisfactions gradually becomes smaller and smaller or even negligible; until, as a result, only the novel and surprising events which surpass our expectations give us large pleasure; but these are comical. With the child, whose expectations are rigid and few in number because of his lack of discrimination and small experience, almost all pleasures, like almost all events, are of the nature of surprises. The child almost always laughs when he is pleased. The slang phrase "to be highly tickled" expresses with precision this close connection between laughter and pleasure. Moreover, as the complexity of life increases, its strains and repressions are multiplied, with the result that any giving way to an impulse contains a slight element of the mischievous or ridiculous; whence, for this reason too, the pleasant is also the comical. In fact, most of the pleasures of highly complex and reflective persons are tinged with laughter.

We expect art to accomplish three great results—reconciliation, revelation, and sympathy. So far we have shown how comic art may accomplish the first; we have yet to prove how it may accomplish the rest. In his book *Le Rire*, Bergson has expressed the view that comedy is explicitly falsifying and unsympathetic. As to the former charge, we can, I think, convince ourselves of the opposite if we examine certain of the more obvious methods of comedy, particularly those which might seem at first sight to lend support to his contention. One of the most common of these is exaggeration. The simplest example is caricature, where certain features of an object are purposely exaggerated. The effect is, of course, comical, because we expect the normal and duly-proportioned. What a manifest falsification, one might assert! Yet just the opposite is the actual result. For every good caricaturist selects for exaggeration prominent and characteristic traits, through which by the very emphasis that is placed upon them, the nature of the individual is better understood. Another favorite method is abstraction. Certain traits are presented as if they were the whole man. We get the typical comic figures of the novel and drama; the physician who is only a physician; the lawyer who injects the legal point of view into every circumstance of life; the lover or the miser who is just love or greed; the people who, as in Dickens, meet every situation with the same phrase or attitude, This, too, looks like a plain falsification of human nature, because, however strong be the professional bias or however overmastering the ruling passion, real people are always more complex and many-sided, having other modifying and counteracting elements of character which prevent their speech and actions from being completely monotonous and mechanical. Nevertheless, we can again acquit the comic writer of falsification, because we understand the method which he is employing, the trick of his trade. He deceives no one. On the contrary, he enables us to perceive the logic of certain elementary springs of character. Following the method of the experimentalist, he selects certain aspects from the total complexity of a phenomenon and shows how they work when isolated from the rest. And, like the man of science, he provides insight into the normal, because we can accept his results as at least partially or approximately true. Art of this kind is abstract and therefore less valuable than the portrayal of the concrete; yet only the dogmatist who insists on the restriction of art to the individual can reject it.

There is, however, a third common method of comical representation which neither exaggerates nor abstracts, but preserves the concreteness of the finest art–we may call it the method of contrast. It consists in exhibiting the contrast between the actual conduct of men and women and the standard,–either that which they themselves profess to live up to or our own, which we impose upon them. Their pretenses are unmasked or their absurdities shown up against the ideal of reasonableness. We behold the *bourgeois* who would be a gentleman remain *bourgeois* and the women who would be scholars remain women. Success in comedy of this kind depends upon possessing the ability to formulate the implicit assumptions underlying the behavior of the people portrayed or to make one's own standards with reference to them valid for the spectator. Here is no falsification, but, on the contrary, a vivid revelation of the truth; because, just as by placing two colors in contrast with one another the hue of each is intensified, so by setting man in relief against the background of what he ought to be, we perceive his real nature more sharply. As the child dressed like a grown-up appears all the more childish for his garb, so man appears the more human for his pretenses. To be sure, in order to increase the comical effect, this method is often employed in conjunction with that of exaggeration. The Athenian democracy was probably not quite so stupid as Aristophanes represents it; the average Britisher is not so philistine as Shaw paints him. Yet the measure of exaggeration may be small and we readily discount it. And finally, whereas in simple representation there is a revelation of the object only, in comical representation there is a two-fold revelation,–of the ideal and of the incongruous reality. The former is always indirectly revealed; for, as we know, the very existence of the comic depends upon it. The man who laughs, his notion of the right and the reasonable, his attitude towards the world and life, become manifest through the things which he laughs at. Only a man of a certain kind, with a certain sympathy and antipathy, could laugh as he laughs. The comic writer, however much of a scoffer and a skeptic, and however much he may deny it, is always an idealist. And it is for the revelation of themselves as much as for the revelation of the people whom they portray that we value the work of a Swift, a Voltaire, or a Thackeray.

Another charge which has been brought against the comic is that it is unsympathetic. Its attitude, it is said, is one of externality, opposed therefore to the intimacy necessary for the complete aesthetic reaction. Whereas simple aesthetic representation places us within the object itself, comical representation only exhibits a relation between it and an idea. We judge it from our point of view, not from its own. The pleasure in pride and superiority which we feel towards the comical object seems also inconsistent with sympathy; for sympathy would create a fellow feeling with it, and place us not above, but on a level with it. If we do sympathize, the comic object ceases to be comical and becomes pathetic. We can find the follies and sins of men comical just so long as we do not sympathize with the sufferings which they entail. There is nothing comical that may not also become pathetic; and the difference depends exactly on the presence or absence of sympathy. Nothing, for example, is more pathetic than death; yet if you keep yourself free of its sorrow, there is nothing more comical–that man, a little lower in his own estimation than the angels, should come to this, a lump of clay.

It is unquestionably true that a free, disinterested attitude is essential to comedy. You must not let yourself be carried away by any feeling; if you are over-serious you cannot laugh; you must keep to reflection and comparison. Yet this attitude is not utterly destructive of all feeling. Man is complex enough at once to feel and to reflect. He can pity as well as laugh. The pathetic and the comic are constantly conjoined–witness our feeling towards Don Quixote or towards any of the great characters of Thackeray–we do not know whether to laugh or to cry. And in the most effective comedy, the standard applied to the comical object is not foreign, but rather, as we have observed, the implicit standard of the object itself, discernible only by the most intimate acquaintance with it. The sting of laughter comes from our acceptance of it as valid for ourselves; we blush and join in the laugh at ourselves. The mischievous-comic, moreover, depends directly upon sympathy; for it requires that we take the point of view of the funny thing; our pleasure in it implies a secret sympathy for it–we hold it up to a standard, yet all the time are in sympathy with its rebellion. When we laugh at the prank of the child, love is mixed with the laugh. The dual nature of man as at once a partisan of convention and of the impulses that it seeks to regulate, is nowhere better illustrated than in the comic. Finally, disinterestedness is not peculiar to comedy; for it pervades all art. Feeling must be dominated by reflection; even pathos demands this, for, if we lose ourselves in sorrowful feeling, no fair image can arise and steady us.

There is, however, much comedy that is obviously unsympathetic, even hostile. There is satire, which condemns, as well as humor which pardons. The one blames the unexpected and unconventional, the other sympathizes with it. Comedy is either biting or kindly. The one is moralistic and reformatory in its aim, the other is aesthetic and contemplative. Because of its failure in sympathy, satirical comedy is incomplete as art. It provides insight and pleasure in the object, but no union with it. It does not attain to beauty, which is free and reconciling. Kindly comedy or humor, on the other hand, is full beauty, combining sympathy with judgment, abandon with reflection. Nevertheless, satire tends inevitably towards humor. For what we laugh at gives us pleasure, and what pleases us we must inevitably come to like, and what we like cannot long fail to win our sympathy. I do not think that even a Swift or a Voltaire could have been irreconcilably opposed to a world which offered them so much merriment. The satire, which begins in moral fervor, must end in understanding. The bond that binds us to our fellows is too strong to be broken by the aloofness of our condemnation. The same intelligence that discerns the incongruity between what men ought to be and what they are, cannot fail to penetrate the impelling reasons for the failure. Only in humor is sympathetic insight complete. Satire has the temporal usefulness of a practical expedient, humor the eternal value of beauty.

Chapter VII

The Standard of Taste

Our interest in art is seldom a matter of mere feeling or appreciation; usually it is a matter of judgment as well. Beginning in feeling, the sthetic experience passes over into comparison and estimation–into criticism, and there finds its normal completion. This, which is evidently true of the aesthetic life of artists and connoisseurs, is true also of average men. We all enjoy the beautiful in silence, but afterwards we want to talk about it to our friends. If conversation about art were suppressed, the interest in it would hardly survive. On this side, the enjoyment of art is intensely sociable, for to the civilized man sociability means discourse.

But, as Kant pointed out, it is characteristic of conversation about art that the participants try to reach agreement in their judgments without acknowledging common principles with reference to which disputes can be decided. And yet, since no man is content to hold an opinion all by himself, but each tries to persuade the others of the validity of his own judgment, it would seem as if there must be some axioms or postulates admitted by all. Hence what Kant called the antinomy of taste: Thesis–the judgment of taste is not based on principles, for otherwise we would determine it by proofs; antithesis–the judgment of taste is based on principles, for otherwise, despite our disagreements, we should not be quarreling about it.

In accordance with this situation, two opposed theories of criticism have always existed. On the one hand, in face of the apparent lawlessness of beauty, some thinkers have believed that there exist principles which can be applied to works of art to test their beauty with a certainty equal to that of the principles of logic in their application to inferences. Lessing, for example, in the *Hamburgische Dramaturgic* wrote that the laws laid down by Aristotle in the *Poetics* were as certain in their application to the drama as Euclid's *Elements* in geometry. This comparison is a forcible statement of belief in the existence of aesthetic standards, held by the entire classical tradition, and still held by those who are spiritually akin to it, although of course no one to-day would claim–and when it came to details Lessing himself did not claim–that the judgment of Aristotle or of any one else is infallible. To-day those who believe in the possibility of rational aesthetic criticism think that reflection upon the purpose and methods of the arts results in the formulation of broad principles by means of which judgments of taste can be appraised and a community of taste achieved. These principles, they would admit, are more difficult of application than the simpler logical rules, owing to the greater subtlety and complexity of art, yet, when found, have an equal validity within their own field.

On the other hand, the view that "there is no disputing about tastes" has never lacked adherents. According to this view, criticism can be only a report of personal, enthusiastic appreciation or repugnance without claim to universality. Anatole France, surely a master of such criticism, has expressed this conviction as follows: "L'estetique ne repose sur rien de solide. C'est un chateau en Pair. On veut l'appuyer sur Pethique. Mais il n'y a pas d'ethique. Il n'y a pas de sociologie" ... And again, in the same preface to *La Vie Litteraire:* "Pour fonder la critique, on parle de tradition et de consentement universel. Il n'y en a pas. L'opinion presque general, il est vrai, favorise certains oeuvres. Mais c'est en vertu d'un prejuge, et nullement par choix et par effet d'une preference spontane. Les oeuvres que tout le monde admire sont celles que personne n'examine." Although the classic view is, I think, nearer the truth, let us examine the arguments that may be advanced in favor of the impressionistic theory, as it has been called. What is there about aesthetic appreciation that makes it seemingly so recalcitrant to law?

First, every aesthetic experience is unique, and therefore, it is claimed, incomparable. Art is the expression of personality, and personality is always individual. But unique things are, in the end, incapable of classification, hence are not amenable to general laws or principles. Of course, works of art can be classified by following some abstract characteristic, arranged in a series according as this quality is realized in them to a greater or less degree; but, in so far as a work is beautiful, it contains at least one quality not possessed by other works, the quality that gives it its distinctive flavor,–which is, indeed, its beauty. The impressionist would admit, for example, that in intellectual power Keats's *Eve of St. Agnes* is inferior to Wordsworth's *Intimations*; also that it lacks the moral grandeur of the latter; but would claim, on the other hand, that in saying this, one is far from judging the beauty of Keats's poem, because that is completely lacking in Wordsworth. So far as the poem is beautiful, it is unique; hence you get no farther with it through comparison with some other poem. You either appreciate it absolutely or you do not; if you do, well and good; you may then write a prose poem about it, if you desire, and so communicate some of your feeling for it to another person; if you do not appreciate it, no one can blame you or quarrel with you; all that any one can do is to invite you to read again, and, perhaps through his eloquence, seek to inspire you with– his own enthusiasm. Every work of art is superlative. Just as the lover thinks his sweetheart the most beautiful woman in the world, so he who appreciates a work of art finds it supreme. And among superlatives there is no comparison, no better or worse.

From another point of view, moreover, the aesthetic experience seems unfavorable to comparison and classification. For a work of art demands a complete abandon of self, an entire absorption in it of attention and emotion.

Every picture has a frame, and every other work of art an ideal boundary to keep you in its world. Beyond the frame you shall not go; beyond the stage you shall not pass; beyond the outline of the statue you shall not look. And if you do pass beyond, you have lost the full intensity and flower of the experience; and whatever comparisons you then make will not concern its original and genuine beauty. Every work of art is jealous; to appreciate it aright, you must for the moment appreciate it singly, without thought of another. Finally, the impressionist or skeptic would maintain that an alleged aesthetic principle would necessarily be abstracted from extant works of art; hence could not be applied to new art. A thing which does not belong within a class cannot be judged by principles governing that class. In so far, therefore, as a work of art is original, it must frustrate any attempt to judge it by traditional, historical standards–and what other standards are there?

Although the two facts of the aesthetic experience–its uniqueness and claim to complete sympathy–upon which the skeptical opinion can be based, are undoubted, the inferences deduced from them do not follow. If they did follow, the aesthetic experience would be fundamentally different from every other type; it would be totally atomic and discrete, instead of fluid and continuous like the rest. But its apparent discreteness is due to a failure to distinguish between the silent, unobtrusive working of comparison and the more obvious and self-conscious working. When rapt in the contemplation of a work of art, I may seemingly have no thought for other works; relative isolation and circle-like self-completeness are characteristic of the aesthetic experience; yet, as a matter of fact, the completeness of my reaction and the measure of my delight and absorption are partly determined by the accordance of the given work of art with a certain expectation or set of mind with reference to objects of its sort. I can consent fully to the will of the artist only if he has first consented to my will as expressed in other works which I have enjoyed and praised. The situation in aesthetics is no different from that which exists in any other field of values; through many experiences of good things I come to form a type or standard of what such things should be like; and, if any new thing of the kind is presented to me, I cannot be so well pleased with it if it does not conform. The type may never be formulated by me explicitly, yet it will operate none the less. The formation of what is called good taste occurs by exactly this process. The first work of art that I see, if it please me, becomes my first measure. If I see a second, in order to win my approval, it will either have to satisfy the expectation aroused by the first, or else surpass it. In the latter case, a standard somewhat different from the old is created through the new experience; and, when I have acquired a large acquaintance with works of art, there grows up a standard which is the resultant of all of them–a type or schema no longer associated with particular works. Sometimes, however, it happens that the standard continues to be embodied in some one or few works which, because of outstanding excellence, serve as explicit paradigms governing judgment; such works are classics in the true sense. And the impressionist is certainly wrong in his contention that the aesthetic appreciation of a work of art excludes the recall of other works and conscious comparison with them. It is only when appreciation is of the more naive sort that this is the case. The trained observer, on seeing one of Vermeer's pictures, for example, cannot fail to think of other works of the same artist; and, if he is learned in the history of art, he may even recall the whole development of Dutch painting. For the moment, perhaps, at the beginning, the single work will completely absorb the attention; but, as we linger in appreciation and reflect upon it, our memory is sure to work. And the process of memory and comparison cannot be excluded on the ground that it is an external, irrelevant context to appreciation; for it actually functions to determine the degree of pleasure and absorption in a work of art. Moreover, this process of memory and comparison is not confined to the individual observer; it is social and historical as well. All art movements are inspired by the desire to improve on, or to create something different from, the conserved tradition. The process of creation itself involves comparison and the recognition of a standard. And for our civilization at any rate these movements are international. They are not the products of isolated discrete groups, impenetrable to each other, but of a relatively universal, continuous experience.

As for the uniqueness of aesthetic value, that, to be sure, is a fact; yet uniqueness is never the whole of any object. Those aspects which ally it with other things are just as genuinely its own as those which differentiate it from them; they equally are a part of its beauty. The attempt to separate any part of a work of art from the rest as "the real part" is an unwarranted and arbitrary dismemberment. The work is whole, and beauty belongs to it as whole. Hence, when, through comparison, you attend to the qualities that are shared with other works, you are still judging the reality and beauty of the object, quite as much as when you seek to taste its unique flavor. A competent judgment can neglect no aspect. The judgment that a work of art is better or worse than another in some general aspect touches it just as surely as the feeling for its distinctiveness. And if it be true that so far as things are unique they are all on a level, it is equally true that so far as they are not unique they are capable of being serialized, and our total judgment upon them must follow the lines of comparison.

It is impossible, therefore, not to compare works of art one with another. We will concede to the impressionist that anything which anybody finds beautiful is beautiful momentarily; but we must insist on the everyday fact that, because of the operation of the standard as a result of growing experience in art, what once seemed beautiful often ceases to seem so. And we must also insist that among the things surviving as beautiful we inevitably set up a hierarchy, a scale. A plurality of values, each unique and in its own way indispensable to a complete world of values, is not inconsistent with relations of higher and lower among them. The impressionist has taught us to love variety and to renounce the bigotry of the old refusal to accept anything short of the highest. But in aesthetics–and in ethics too, I believe–the standpoint of Spinoza rules: "God is revealed in the mouse as well as in the angel, although less in the mouse than in the angel;" and, I should add, the revelation through the humbler mouse is necessary to a complete revelation of God, that is, of the Good. Or, as Nietzsche said, "*Vieler Edlern naemlich bedarf es, dass es Adel gebe!*" Our appreciation of *Midsummer Night's Dream* does not prevent us from appreciating *Alice in Wonderland*, just as our esteem for the man does not hinder our feeling for the peculiar charm of the child.

What takes place through the process of comparison is this: we come increasingly to realize what we want of art. Every artist seeks to express something in terms of the material with which he works. But it is only by experimenting with his medium that he learns what he can and what he cannot do; and it is only by constant hospitable, yet discriminating appreciation by us spectators that we, in our turn, discover what to demand of him and commend. Consider, for example, the history of painting. That we want of a picture, sometimes the delineation of emotion and action, yes; but above all and always, the representation of visible nature, with space and atmosphere and light–this purpose has been developed slowly and as the result of many experiments and comparisons. But having won it, we are secure in it. We shall still appreciate the beauty of the primitives and academics, but we shall not be able again to prefer them to the *plein-airistes*. Or recall the development of English poetry. We still admit the contribution of Dryden and Pope, but we shall never have to fight over again the battle won by Wordsworth and his contemporaries for imagination and emotion. Our conception of the purpose of poetry has been enriched by an insight that we cannot permanently lose. There are, to be sure, retrograde movements in the arts–like the Pre-Raphaelite movement in painting–but they are soon recognized as such.

Now with reference to the purpose of art to express in a given material, there are, I think, a few general principles of judgment applying to all the arts, implicitly or explicitly recognized in criticism, and capable of formulation. First, the complete use of the medium. We prefer, other things being equal, the work of art that has fully exploited the expressive possibilities of its medium to one that has failed to do so. As an illustration, I would cite the almost universal condemnation, at the present time, of neo-classical sculpture, in which the touch values of the surfaces of statues were destroyed. Of course some compensating gain may be claimed–a greater visual purity; yet, as we shall see, from the point of view of expression, the gain was negligible compared with the loss. So likewise, unless the *vers-libristes* can show some positive gain in expression,–a power to do something that normal verse cannot do, their work must rank lower than normal verse, which makes fuller use of the rhythmic possibilities of language.

Second, the unique use of the material. What we want of art depends, not only on comparison between works of art belonging to the same genre, but on comparison of the purposes of different genres, indeed of the different arts themselves. What we want of painting depends upon what we want of sculpture; what we want of poetry depends upon what we want of painting and music. We compare picture with picture; but equally we compare picture with statue and poem. We do not want the sculptor to try to do what the painter can do better, and vice-versa; or the poet to encroach on the domains proper to the musician and painter. We do not want poetry to be merely imagistic or merely musical when we have another art that can give us much better pictures and still another that can give us much better music than any word-painting or word-music. When we read a poem, we do not want to be made to think how much better the same thing could be done in a different medium. There is nothing so salutary in keeping an art to its proper task as a flourishing condition of the other arts. Here the great example is France, where the limitations of the different arts have been best recognized all the while the highest level of perfection has been reached in many arts contemporaneously.

Third, the perfect use of the medium in the effort to fulfill the artistic purpose of sympathetic representation–the power to delight the senses and create sympathy for the object expressed, on the one hand, and the range of the vision of the object, on the other; the depth and the breadth of the aesthetic experience. With reference to the former we ask: how vividly does the work of art force us to see; how completely does it make us enter into the world it has created; and, in doing this, how poignantly has it charmed us, how close has it united us to itself? The measure of this is partly subjective and irreducible to rules; yet experience in the arts establishes a norm or schema of appreciation through the process of comparison, largely unconscious, by which what we call good taste is acquired. There are certain works of art that seem to have fulfilled this requirement in the highest possible degree, thus attaining to perfection within their compass. Such, for example, are some of Sappho's or Goethe's lyrics, or the Fifth Canto of the *Inferno.* Nothing more perfect, more beautiful of their kind can be conceived. And to see how works of art may differ in degree of perfection of sympathetic vision, one has only to recall lesser works expressing the same themes. Yet we recognize greater works even than those cited–works in which, although the sympathetic vision is no more penetrating and compelling, it is broader, more inclusive. Goethe's *Faust* is greater than any of his lyrics because the range of experience which it expresses is vaster. A Velasquez is greater than a Peter De Hooch because, in addition to an equal beauty of expression through color and line and composition, an equal dominion over light and space, it contains a marvelous revelation of the inner life, which is absent from the latter. According to Berenson, no one has yet painted the perfect landscape because thus far only a certain few aspects have been expressed, but not all.

There are, I think, certain qualities which are generally recognized as necessary to the perfect fulfillment of the artistic purpose of a work; which follow, indeed, from the very meaning of art. Thus, without uniqueness and freshness there can be no perfection in artistic expression. A well-worn or even an identical expression may have value in the solution of a practical problem, or in bringing men into good-natured relationships with one another in social life; as when, for example, the officer cries "Halt!" repeatedly, or we say "Good morning" at breakfast; because, in such cases, the expression gets its significance from the context in which it belongs. But in art, where expression is freed from the particular setting within which it arises, thus attaining universality, the repetitious and imitative, having no environment from which they may derive new meaning, are purposeless. They are, indeed, worse than negligible, because having grown into the habit of expecting originality, we are disappointed and bored when we fail to find it. Originality is, of course, relative; it is not incompatible with the reminiscence of old works–what works of art are not reminiscent?–but it does prohibit saying the old things over again in the same medium; the artist must have a new message to put into the medium; or else, if the old themes are still near to his heart, he must invent a new form in which to express them, from which they will derive a new music. Closely allied to freshness are spontaneity and inner necessity, the signs of a genuine, as opposed to a factitious, expression. If we get the impression from a work of art that no part could be otherwise–not a single line or note or stroke of the brush–then we have the same sort of feeling towards it that we have towards the living thing that was not made by hands capriciously, but grew in its inevitable way in accordance with the laws of its own nature. Of course, works of art are products of thought, of plan, and conscious purpose; they are seldom composed all at one flash, but grow tentatively into their final form; nevertheless, in the words of Kant, "A work of art must look like nature, albeit we know that it is art." Sense charm and order are also necessary; for they are the conditions of a perfect sympathy and vision. We are indulgent towards the vigorous, impatient passion that bubbles over into rough and careless music or poetry, but are not satisfied with it. For art's task is not merely to express, but to dominate through expression, to create out of expression, beauty; and without order and charm of sense, there is no beauty. Compose your passion, we say to the musician; pattern it forth, we say to the poet; it will not lose its vigor; rather it will acquire a new power; for thus it will achieve restraint, the sign of art's dominion.

The recognition of the principles indicated presupposes, of course, that art really has a purpose with reference to which it can be judged as successful or unsuccessful. But I do not see how this can very well be denied. Art is one of the oldest of human activities, one might almost say institutions, and it is inconceivable that it should not have been directed by some intention, conscious or unconscious. To be sure, men have expressed this intention in varying, often in inconsistent ways, but the same is true of all other human activities and institutions. Few would deny, I suppose, that science and the state have purposes; yet how various have been the definitions of them. These variations have corresponded, without doubt, to adaptations to new conditions, yet throughout some unique purpose in human life has been subserved. So with art. Art has been identified now with one interest and now with another; what people want of art differs from one age to another, and each must define that for itself; yet throughout there has been a core of identity in the purposes it has served. In our own age we witness the attempt to distinguish the purpose of art from the purposes of other elements of civilization, with which it has often been fused and confused,– science, religion, morality. Correspondingly we witness the effort to limit the functions of political control; to take from its jurisdiction religion, culture, love. And this effort is for the sake of a fuller and freer realization of values.

Furthermore, not only has art a general function, but this function is differentiated among the different art forms and genres. No work of art can be judged without reference to its function. Its beauty consists in the fulfillment of this function. Now this function is, of course, largely unique for each art form and for each particular work of art, and every work has to be judged with reference to its individual purpose, yet a knowledge of other works of the same artist and the same genre, and of the general history of art, helps to divine this purpose and to judge of its relative success. There is a large measure of continuity in the intentions of a given artist and school of art. The development of painting in the last century is a striking illustration of such continuity. The painters sought to develop a definite tradition, thinking of themselves as carrying further the work of their predecessors. Of course these developments were largely technical in character, but beauty itself is the fruition of technique.

The people who base a skeptical opinion upon the historical changes in taste forget that taste is necessarily a growth; that it is developed by trial and error, through and despite the following of many false paths. Only if the standard were something delivered to men by divine revelation–as indeed the old dogmatists came very close to believing–would it be strange and inconsistent for changes to occur. But if, as is the fact, the standard is experimental and representative of actual artistic purposes, then change is normal. Moreover, the standard is not single and absolute, but plural and relative. Growth in taste means not only development along a given line, within a given form, but enlargement through the origination of new forms and beauties. It is not like the straight line growth of an animal, but rather radial, like the growth of a plant, sending out branches in every direction. An art may attain to perfection in a certain genre, and then continue only through the creation of new types. Thus sculpture and architecture reached a kind of perfection in the classic, beyond which it was impossible to go–the only possible development lay in the creation of new types.

If it is true, then, that the existence of standards has a sound basis in the aesthetic experience, how can their apparent failure to work and secure unanimity of judgment be explained? How account for the actual chaos of judgment? Partly, at least, because many judgments passed on works of art are not aesthetic judgments at all. These must be eliminated if any consensus is to be won. We may call these judgments "pseudo- sthetic" judgments. They fall naturally into several classes, which it will be worth while to describe.

First, there is the very large class of partisan judgments–judgments based, not upon a free appreciation, but upon some personal predilection or transient appeal. To this class belong the special preferences of boyhood and youth–the liking for Cooper and Jules Verne, for example– and those due to nationality, like the Englishman's choice of Thackeray and the Frenchman's of Balzac, or, what is a more flagrant case, the long resistance of the French public to the beauty of Wagner's music. The former type of judgment is corrected by the simple process of maturing, when the beauties appreciated in youth are not lost, but only given their due place in the hierarchy of aesthetic values; the latter type, on the other hand, being more deeply based, is more difficult to remedy. But that even this prejudice can be largely overcome is shown by the example of critics who, through prolonged sympathetic study, come to prefer the art of a foreign land. A notable example of this is Meier-Graeffe, who condemns almost all of modern German painting and exalts the French. [Footnote: See his *Modern Art*, and his special studies of Manet, Renoir, and Degas.] Patriotic preferences are so difficult to overcome because they spring from limitations of sympathy. Sympathy depends upon acquaintance, and few of us can acquire the same expertness in an alien language or artistic form that we possess in our own. Yet, understanding the reason for these deficiencies of judgment, we can go to work to improve them, through increasing our knowledge of foreign art.

No less inevitable psychologically is the preference for works of art that treat of the problems and conditions of contemporary life. Part of this, to be sure, is expressive merely of some transient mood of the popular mind. The enthusiasm, happily passing, for the plays of Brieux or the craze for Algerian landscapes in France after the acquirement of the colony, are examples. Such preferences, being superficially motivated, correct themselves with ease, giving way to some new fashion in taste. The preference for works of art that reflect the more serious and permanent problems of contemporary society is more firmly rooted. Men inevitably seek the artistic expression of the things that deeply concern them. The problems of the reconstruction of the family, of the working classes, and of government must continue to inspire art and to determine our interest in it, until new difficulties occupy our minds. The mere passage of time, however, brings a remedy for critical injustices flowing from this source; for, when present problems are solved, the difference between living art, which expresses them, and historical art, vanishes. Then, only those works which reflect the eternal enigmas have any advantage over the others. The same process tends to eliminate the prejudice, rooted in temperament, in favor of the old and familiar in art; or, following a different bent, in favor of the new and startling. In such cases, a just estimate can be made only when the new becomes the old, and both are reduced to a common level.

Another type of pseudo-aesthetic judgment is the imitative. By this I mean the judgment which is made because somebody else has made it, particularly somebody in authority. The imitative judgment is the expression, in the field of aesthetics, of what Trotter has called "herd instinct," the tendency on the part of the gregarious animal to make his acts and habits conform to those of another member of the same group, particularly if that member is a leader or represents the majority. The dislike of loneliness and the love of companionship operate, as we have already had occasion to notice, even in the sphere of the spirit. Differences here separate people just as other differences do. In art, herd instinct tends to make the judgment of the authoritative or fashionable critic take the place of spontaneous and sincere judgment. I do not mean that such judgments are usually consciously insincere; although they often are so, since men seek to ingratiate themselves by flattering even the aesthetic opinions of those whose love or protection they desire. I do mean, however, that they tend to suppress opinions which would reflect an autonomous appreciation. Moreover, whatever may be said for herd-instinct in the realm of politics and morals, where the need for common action makes necessary some sort of consensus among the members of a group, very little can be said for it in aesthetics, where no practical issues are directly involved. There, herd instinct simply substitutes sham appreciation for a vital and healthy reaction. Of course, imitative judgments must be distinguished from those that agree because they are based on a genuine contagion or community of feeling. This distinction may be a difficult one for the outsider to make; but is not so for the individual concerned. I do not deny the value of authority in aesthetics; what I am inveighing against is the substitution of authority for sincerity. In art, the suasion of the norm should be absolutely free, with no penalty except isolation from the best. The only value of authority is to counteract laziness and superficiality of appreciation; to stimulate those who would rest content with first impressions to a more studious and attentive examination. Yet, however great be our natural desire to convince others of beauty, we want their conviction to be as sincere as our own: we do not want it to be factitious,– suggested or dragooned. It is often too easy, rather than too hard, to win agreement.

The question of the place of authority in aesthetics is raised again by a consideration of another class of pseudo-aesthetic judgments, which I shall call ignorant judgments. These judgments are perfectly sincere, but express an aesthetic experience that is imperfect, owing to defective understanding of art. So many people judge works of art as if they could assimilate them immediately, without any knowledge of their purpose and technique. They fail to recognize that a work of art has a language, with a vocabulary and grammar, which has to be mastered through study. A work of art is a possibility of a certain complex of values, not a given actuality that can be grasped by merely stretching out the hand. Very little of any work of art is given–just a few sense stimuli; the rest is an emotional and meaningful reaction, which has to be completed in a determinate fashion. A work of art is a question to which the right answer has to be found. And in order to find the answer, it is necessary to know both what to look for and what not to look for. For example, in judging Japanese prints, one must realize, from the limitation of the medium, that one cannot look for all the fullness of expression of shadow and atmosphere possible in an oil painting; or in judging decorative or post-impressionistic painting, one must realize that the purpose of the artist is chiefly to obtain musical effects from color and line, not to represent nature realistically.

Because works of art are ideals, possibilities of experience, and not given things which everybody can appreciate without knowledge and effort, I am skeptical of all results obtained in laboratories of experimental aesthetics, where college students are asked to judge works of painting, music, and sculpture. An uninstructed majority vote cannot decide any question in aesthetics. Such experiments, with the exception of those that concern the most elementary reactions, yield interesting statistical results about the groups employed as subjects, but are of no value in aesthetics. And what wonder that we should find people disagreeing in their judgments when, because of ignorance, they are not reporting about the same objects!

Finally, an aesthetic consensus is possible only if non-aesthetic standards and all judgments based on false conceptions of the purpose of art are eliminated. Some of these judgments I have already discussed–the scientific and the moralistic. The purpose of art is sympathetic vision, not scientific truth or edification. It is often necessary, in order to win a vision of actual life, for the artist to possess scientific knowledge; but only as a means, not as an end. And again, insight into the more enduring preferences of men and the conditions of their happiness, upon which rational moral standards are founded, is indispensable to a complete interpretation of life; but there is much of life that can be envisaged sympathetically, that is, artistically and beautifully, with small hold on ethical wisdom. No one, I suppose, would regard de Maupassant as a wise man in the Greek sense of possessing a philosophical grasp of the norms which make up the conscience of men, yet few would deny him the supreme gift of delineating the pathos and comedy of passion. I do not doubt that men will always judge works of art from abstract standpoints; that to-day they will judge them from the points of view of science and morals, since we are so dominated by their sway; but I do claim that these standards are not aesthetic, and that so long as they control our estimates of art, there can never be anything except chaos in taste; for they will always come into conflict with the genuinely aesthetic point of view. And, I ask, why not grant to art its autonomy? If art has a unique purpose, different from that of science or morals, why should we not judge it in terms of that purpose?

Of course, since man's nature is one, not many, it will always be impossible entirely to get rid of the non-aesthetic bases of judgment. Personal predilection for a certain kind of subject-matter, patriotic preference for one's own language and style, the influence of authority and the lure of the crowd, the intrusion of the moralistic and the scientific bias,–all these must, to a greater or less degree, divide and dispute the hegemony of taste. Nevertheless, although it is impossible to reach a pure aesthetic judgment, we ought to strive to approach it, and, by dint of training and clear thinking about art, we can approach it. We ought to do this, not because of any formalism or purism, but for the sake of preserving the unique value of art, which is covered up or destroyed by the intrusion of non-aesthetic standards of judgment. For judgment does influence feeling, especially such a delicate and subtle thing as aesthetic feeling. The patriotic and the partisan judgments narrow appreciation, the imitative substitute a judgment for a feeling, the moralistic and scientific prejudices often inhibit the possibility of the aesthetic reaction at the start, or, if they allow it to begin, prevent the full sympathy and abandon which are required for its consummation. We can get scientific truth from science, why then seek it in art? We can obtain moral wisdom from the philosopher and priest, why require it of the artist? Reformers and statesmen will enlighten us concerning reconstruction, why not turn to them? I do not mean, of course, that art may not express the mystery and the wonder of science, the voice of conscience, the cry of distress; but even this is not science, or sociology, or morals; and art must and should also express dark passion, hot hate or love, and joy–in the sea, in sunlight, in the shadow of leaves on the grass, in the bodies of men and women–and the other myriad forms of human life and nature that are neither right nor true, but simply are. And furthermore: the tyranny of the scientific and the moral is the death of art. Art can live only when free. So long as men are subject to the exclusive habit of condemning and praising and analyzing and classifying, they are incapable of a free envisagement and expression. Between sociology and Puritanism, the artistic novel and the drama have become all but impossible in this country. During the nineteenth century, the predilection, among the Pre-Raphaelites, for the scientific and moral nearly killed landscape painting in England, its birthplace. And only in France, where alone of modern nations the moral and hygienic attitude towards the human body has not completely driven out the artistic, has there been a vital and enduring sculpture.

If the aesthetic judgment is given autonomy, a sure foundation for aesthetic norms can be established, because then art will be judged with reference to a perfectly definite purpose. Feeling will always tell us whether a thing is beautiful or not; but feeling itself will depend upon whether the implicit purpose of art has been realized; and, when we reflectively consider a work in relation to other works, we shall have a solid basis for comparison. Judgment will have a foundation in reason as well as in feeling. We shall ask of the artist, not whether he has instructed us or edified us, but solely whether he has given us a new and sympathetic vision of some part of our experience. The kind of vision that he gives us will depend, of course, upon the materials of his art–it will be one thing in sound, another in color or line or patterned words. Even as we demand of art in general a unique value, as fulfilling a unique function, so we shall demand of the different arts that each provide us with the unique beauty which its materials can create. We shall therefore commend the separation of the arts and view with suspicion any attempt to fuse them. Whatever be his materials, we shall demand of the artist always the same result: that he make us see, and command our sympathy and delight for his vision. Any judgment that we make, or any standard that we set up, must proceed upon a knowledge of this master purpose and of the materials and technique of the particular art through which it is to be realized. And such standards, experimental and tentative, but nevertheless potent and directive, are capable of discovery and formulation. Some of the larger and more important of these we shall try to set forth in our chapters on the special arts. An artist who works within these standards is sure to produce something beautiful; one who breaks them will fail or, rarely, find some hitherto undiscovered, surprising beauty in the medium.

There still remains for consideration the fear lest the recognition of standards may discourage new experiments and so interfere with the creative impulse. It is true that tragedies have occurred when criticism has been unsympathetic and malicious–remember Keats and the struggles of the early French impressionistic painters–but even then I doubt if any real harm to art has resulted. For the situation in aesthetics differs from the situation in ethics and politics where the retarding effect of convention is undeniable. In art there can never be the same closeness of alliance between convention and vested interests that is so repressive a force in the "world." It is probably true indeed that, as Plato said, "when the modes of music change, so do constitutions change"; for example, there is doubtless to-day some connection between imagist poetry, post-impressionistic painting, Russian music, and revolutionary sentiment–witness, in our own country, *The Masses* and *The Seven Arts*–but the link is too delicate to alarm the powers that be. The upholding of a standard must be allied with material interests if it is to be repressive of creation and novelty. But, as a free force, operating solely by influence, the standard has the effect only of keeping alive the love of excellence, and, by providing some stability in the old, creating that contrast between the new and the old, so stimulating to the new itself. For the impulse to originate operates best alongside of and in opposition to the desire to conserve. France has been the great originator in the plastic arts during recent times; but it has also been the only country where a genuine traditional standard has existed. When tradition is based on experiments, as in art, it cannot be in essence hostile to them. And all valid aesthetic principles are sufficiently broad and abstract not to interfere with novelty and creation.

When such principles as we have tried to formulate are admitted, the world of aesthetic judgments can be organized and some consensus about the beautiful achieved. Without an approach to a consensus, the aesthetic impulse can never be content; for it is indefeasibly sociable. Agreement in judgments depends upon a common experience, and this also art can provide. For beauty is constituted of elementary reactions to sense stimuli which are well-nigh universal among men, and of symbols and meanings which can be learned like any language. The delight in harmony and balance, order and symmetry and rhythm, and again, the pleasure in the unique and well finished, are felt by every one. The entire form side of art, its structure or design, is based on fundamental and enduring elements of human nature. The symbolism of sensation, its musical expressiveness, as we have called it, is rooted likewise in reactions and interpretations that either are, or may become, through suggestion and training, common property. There are, of course, the people who have no feeling for tones, and through defective memory for tones, no appreciation of musical design; there are also those who are insensitive to color and line. In many cases, through the training of the attention, these defects can be overcome; yet, in others, they are permanent and incurable. This fact limits the universality of art; oftentimes, when two people are discussing a work, they are not talking about the same object; for a large part of its potentialities are lost to one of them. Nevertheless, the validity of empirical standards among those who are capable of appreciating the whole of a work of art is not touched by this fact. Those who can agree, ultimately will agree. As for art as representation, that is a language readily acquired. It is an easier and more natural language than ordinary speech. What is meant by the colors and lines of a painting or statue, or by the mimic of the drama, is immediately grasped by any intelligent person; for to make use of images of things in order to represent them is a universal habit among men. The painting and sculpture of the Chinese are intelligible to us; not so their speech. Of course, to some extent, the language of painting and sculpture is conventional; the limits of accuracy of imitation are not set by nature, except at the extremes, but by the tradition or practice of painters. Yet the convention is a simple one, easily understood and accepted.

Chapter VIII

The Aesthetics of Music

In this and the following chapters which treat of the arts, I plan to make a concrete application of the aesthetic theory thus far developed. I want to show how the general principles which we have tried to establish can be used to explain the facts of our artistic experience. In doing this I shall hope to achieve a double purpose: first, to verify anew our theory of art, and second, to deepen and enlighten appreciation.

I begin with music because, as we shall see, there is a musical factor in all the arts, an understanding of which at the beginning will enable us to proceed much more easily in our survey of them. I shall confine myself to an elementary analysis; for a more detailed study would take us beyond the bounds of general aesthetics and would require a knowledge of the special technique of the arts which we cannot presuppose. Moreover, we shall not concern ourselves with the origin or history of the arts further than is needful for an understanding of their general character. We are investigating the theory, not the history, of taste, and are more interested in the present developed aesthetic consciousness than in its rudimentary forms.

As we appreciate it to-day, music lends itself readily to our definition of art. It is a personal expression—who, when listening to music which he enjoys, does not feel himself poured forth in the tones? It is social and public—what brings us together under the sway of a common emotion more effectively than concert or opera? It is a fixed and permanent expression, for we can renew it so long as men preserve the score where it is written; and, finally, it is free–who can find any practical or moral or scientific purpose in an etude of Chopin or a symphony of Mozart? Music is the most signal example of a mode of expression that has attained to a complete and pure aesthetic character, an unmixed beauty. Yet this was not true of music in its earlier forms, and a long process of development was necessary before freedom was realized. For we must look for the beginning of music in any and all sounds through which primitive men sought to express and communicate themselves. These were, first of all, the cries of the human voice, expressive of fear and need and joy–at once direct outpourings of basic emotions and signals to one's fellows, to help, to satisfy, and to sympathize. In the voice nature provided man with a direct and immediate instrument for the expression and communication of himself through sound. Then, perhaps by accident, man discovered that he could make sounds in other ways, through materials separate from his body, and so he constructed drums and cymbals and gongs; and by means of these, too, he communicated his needs and stimulated himself to rage and excitement–and his enemy to fear–in war dance and battle rush. And in doing this he was imitating nature, whose noises, exciting and terrifying, he had long known: the clap of thunder, the whistle of the wind, the roar of the waves, the crackling of burning wood, the crash of fallen and breaking things.

Out of unbeautiful noise sprang beautiful music. Men discovered that through the voice they could make not only expressive noises, but also pleasant tones; they found, perhaps by accident, that they could do much the same thing with reeds and strings; they observed that when they beat their drums at regular intervals to mark the motion of the dance, they not only danced together more easily, but also experienced joy in the very sounds they made; or that when they threshed the corn with rhythmic strokes or rowed a boat in rhythmic unison, their task was lightened and their wearied attention distracted to the pleasure of their noise. Hence at their dances of love or war or religion, they sang instead of shouted; and their instruments of irregular and expressive noise became instruments of rhythmical and melodious tones. Eventually, having experienced the pleasure there is in tones and rhythmical sounds, they made them for their own sake, apart from any connection with tribal festivals, and the free art of music was born. And yet, as we shall see, the significance of music depends largely upon the fact that tones are akin to noises; music could not take such a hold of the emotions of men did they not overhear in the tones the meaningful and poignant noises of voice and nature; to understand music, we must think of it against its background of expressive noise. In music we still seem to hear a voice that breaks the silence and speaks, the thunder that terrifies.

The material of music consists of tones, the conscious counterparts of periodic, longitudinal vibrations of the air. Tones differ among themselves in many attributes, of which the following are of chief importance for music: pitch, determined by rate of vibration, through which tones differ as higher and lower; color, determined by the complexity of the vibration wave, the presence of overtones of different pitch along with the fundamental tone in the total sound; intensity, dependent upon the amplitude of the vibration, through which tones of the same pitch differ as soft or loud; and finally, quality, that specific character of a tone, by reason of which middle C, for example, is more like the C of the octave below or above than like its nearer neighbors, B or D, whence the series of tones, although in pitch linear and one-dimensional, is in quality periodic, returning again and again upon itself, as we go up or down the scale.

The number of qualities in use in music–twelve in our scale of equal temperament–is, of course, not all there are in the world of tones; they are a human and arbitrary selection, governed by technical and historical motives, into which we shall not enter. Peoples with a different culture have made a different selection. But we are not concerned with the music of angels or of orientals, but with our own. With these twelve, with their possible variations in pitch, loudness, and tone-color, the musician has a rich and adequate material.

All the elements of an aesthetic experience are present in striking simplicity even in the single musical tone. There is the sensuous medium, the sound; there is a life expressed, a feeling aroused in us, yet so completely objectified in the sound that it seems to belong to the latter on equal terms with color or quality or loudness; there is a unity and variety and orderly structure in the dominance of the fundamental among the overtones and the fusion of all in the total clang. Thus every note is a complete little aesthetic organism. Yet the beauty of single tones is very slight,–less, I think, than that of single colors; they need the contrast or the agreement in consonance with other tones in order to awaken much feeling; they must be members of a wider whole; observe how, when sounded after other tones, they become enriched through the contrasting or consonant memory of those tones. Nevertheless, the single tone has its feeling, however slight, and to understand this is to go a long way toward understanding the more complex structures of music.

In the first place, tones, unlike noises, are all pleasant. Although we cannot be sure why this is true, there can be little doubt, I think, that the regularity of the vibrations of the former, in contrast with the irregularity of the latter, is largely responsible. The clang, with its ordered complexity, is a stimulus that incites the sense organ and connected motor tracts to a unified and definite response, unlike noise, which creates confusion. The pleasure in the single tone is similar, in its causes, to the pleasure in the consonance of two tones. As we should expect from this analogy, the pleasure is greater in rich tones, which contain many partials, than in thin tones, which are relatively uninteresting. But the feeling of tones is something more than mere pleasantness; it is also a mood. Now this mood of tones is partly due to associations,–some superficial in character, like the pastoral quality of flute tones or the martial character of bugle tones, others more fundamental; but it has also a still deeper-lying root. For a sound stimulus awakens not only a sensory process in the ear, the correlative of which is a sensation, but also incipient motor reactions, which, if carried out, would be an emotion, but which, being too slight and diffuse, produce only what we call a mood. Every sensation has a meaning for the organism in an environment where it has constantly to be on its guard for danger or assistance; every sensation is therefore connected with the mechanism of reaction, with its attendant emotions. In ordinary experience, there are objects present to which the organism may actually respond, but in the aesthetic experience there are no real objects towards which a significant reaction can take place; in music, the source of the sound is obviously of no practical importance, while in such arts as painting and sculpture where interesting objects are represented, the objects themselves are absent; hence the reaction is never carried out, but remains incipient, a vague feeling which, finding no object upon which it may work itself off, is suffused upon the sensation. These sense feelings are the subtle, but basal, material of all beauty.

The variety of moods expressed in tones is almost endless. When we experience them, they come to us as the inner life of the total concrete tones, but they depend actually upon the working together of all the tonal attributes,–color, quality, pitch, and loudness. There is the subtle intimacy of violin tones compared with the clear arresting ring of the trumpet; the emotional differences between qualities like C and G, too delicate for expression in words; the piercing excitement of the high, bright tones, compared with the earnest depth of the low, dull tones; the almost terrifying effect of loud tones compared with the soothing influence of soft tones.

The precise psychophysical mechanism through which the different moods are aroused is for the most part hidden from us; yet in certain particulars we can form some idea of it. For example, the richness of feeling in the tones of certain instruments as compared with others is doubtless due to the fact that through the presence of more overtones and the admixture of noise, the reaction is more complex; the tense excitement of high and loud tones, as compared with the soft and low, is probably connected with the fact that their higher vibration rate and greater amplitude of vibration produce a more marked effect, a more pervasive disturbance,–the organism does not right itself and recover so rapidly and easily. These direct and native elements of feeling are then broadened out and intensified through other elements that come in by way of association. For example, in order to sing high tones, a greater tension and exertion of the vocal chords is needed than for low tones; loud tones suggest loud noises, which, as in breaking and crashing and thundering, are inevitably associated with fear; the loud is also the near and present and threatening, the low is distant and safe. Although each tone, as separate and individual, possesses its own feeling in its own right, the tonal effects are immensely accentuated by contrast with one another,–the high against the low, the poor against the rich, the loud against the soft–and through the summation, by means of repetition, of the influences of many tones of like character; the full meaning of music depends upon the relations of tones, especially the temporal relations.

This fact was fully recognized by Aristotle, who raised the question why tones are so much more expressive than colors. Music is almost the sole important art that relies on the expressiveness of the sense material alone, independent of any element of meaning. To be sure, the beauty of oriental rugs depends entirely on their color and line harmonies; for the meanings which the patterns have for their oriental makers is generally unknown to us of the western world; yet what we feel when we contemplate them cannot compare in volume and intensity with what we experience when we listen to music. And Aristotle correctly assigned one of the chief reasons for the superior significance of music–its temporal character. A color or line scheme may express a momentary mood, with perhaps just the most rudimentary movement as we go from the dark to the bright colors, or as we follow the motion of the lines as they curve or converge; yet it cannot express an action or process that begins, proceeds, continues, ends. When we look at the colors or lines of a painting or rug, we feel intensely, but there is no development or process of feeling; if the mind moves, it moves inevitably not with, but away from, what it sees. But tones are given to us in succession; we are forced to move with them; hence they come to express for us, in ways which we shall try to analyze, the changing and developing process of the inner life.

In its temporal aspect, music has two chief characteristics, rhythm and melody. In our music these are inseparable; yet they can be separated for the purposes of analysis; and a rhythmical roll of drumbeats or a careless succession of tones harmonically related proves that each may produce an aesthetic effect without the other. We shall consider melody first.

A mere succession of tones, however pleasing separately, does not make a melody; for melody depends on a definite scale and on certain relations between the tones of the scale. These relations illustrate the three modes of aesthetic unity. First, there is harmony. Tones are harmonically related when they belong to the leading chords of the key. The tones of such chords, when sounded together, are consonant. Now harmony, which is an aesthetic feeling, although not identical with consonance, which is a purely sensory relation between tones, depends nevertheless upon consonance. In order to understand harmony, we must therefore first understand consonance, and, in order to do this, we must begin by describing the experience and then look for its possible causes. As for the first, consonant tones, when sounded together, seem to fit one another, almost to fuse, despite the fact that the different tones are distinguishable in the whole. This fitting together, in turn, seems to depend on a resemblance or partial identity between them. For example, the most consonant tones are a note and its octave, which are, perhaps, actually identical in quality; but lesser intervals are also alike, as for example a note and its fifth, which are more readily mistaken for one another than two dissonant tones, say a note and its seventh. As for the explanation of consonance, we know that consonant tones have identical partial tones and are caused by vibration rates that stand to one another in simple ratios. Thus in a clang composed of a tone and its fifth, the first partial of the fifth is the second partial of the prime, and the vibration ratios are as two to three. The bearing of this second fact on the question of partial identity will become clear if we consider the concrete case of a tone produced by 24 vibrations per second, whose fifth would then be produced by 36 vibrations per second, and then consider the same tone and its dissonant second, the ratio of whose vibrations is 24 to 27; in the former case, there is a common part of 6 vibrations, a fourth of the total number of the first tone; in the latter, only 3, an eighth. That identity of partial tones is not a sufficient explanation of consonance--as Helmholtz thought it to be--is proved by the fact that simple tones, which have no partials, may still be consonant. Nevertheless, an identity of partials does undoubtedly contribute to the consonance of the complex tones used in our music; ultimately, however, the final reason for consonance must be sought in some underlying identity within the tones themselves, an identity that seems to be given psychologically in their resemblance, and with which physically the simplicity of their vibration ratios probably has something to do. And that in music the feeling of harmony should depend upon partial identity is what we should expect from our previous study of harmony in general.

The second of the tonal relations upon which melody depends is contrast. First, there is the contrast between the high and the low; even when notes are harmonically related, as a note and its fifth, they are in contrast, in so far as the one is measurably higher and more distant than the other. Of equal importance is the rivalry between the fundamental tones in the leading harmonic chords; for example, the rivalry between the tonic and the dominant. For each of these claims to be the center of the melodic progression, and draws to itself all the tones which belong to its chord. Dissonance is a cause of rivalry; for a dissonant tone is one that will not fit into a given harmony; yet since it is still a part of the melody, must have its home somewhere, and belongs therefore in another harmony, which, through this tone, is set up in rivalry with the prevailing one. A tone that did not belong to any harmony would not be a dissonance, but a discord,–a tone without meaning musically. Dissonances, like other contrasts, enrich the melody by establishing rival harmonies; discords destroy melodies. Just as the drama has little significance without conflict, so melodies are uninteresting without dissonances.

Were it not for the third of the tonal relations, melodies would lack unity and system and go to pieces under the stress of rival forces. This third relation may be call finality[1]; it belongs among relations we have called evolutionary. By it is meant the fact that certain tones demand and naturally lead into other tones, in which they seem to find their completion or fulfillment. For example, the tones of a chord demand the fundamental tone of the chord; dissonances must be "resolved,"–must be followed by other tones of their own harmony; the diatonic tones over and above the tonic–the "upleader" and "downleader"–naturally lead into the tonic; and all the tones demand, either immediately or through the mediation of other tones, the tonic of the scale to which they belong. This principle of finality, which, in the classic music, is the basis of what is called "tonality," by establishing the tonic as the center of reference and point of completion of all tones, gives to melody its dramatic unity. Through it, by creating the tonic chord as fundamental, the rivalry between the tonic, dominant, and subdominant is overcome, and all dissonances finally resolved into unity. Definite scales and tonal laws and schemes of composition are of the utmost importance for musical composition; there are, of course, many of these besides the classical, and they are all partly conventional; but that does not matter so long as, by being

1. The explanation of this is obscure; there is no unanimity among the specialists in musical theory.

well known, they enable the melody to move along definite lines, arousing and fulfilling definite expectations. Those forms of modernist music that dispense with scales altogether, in which therefore there are no fixed *points de repere* like the tonic or dominant of the older music, can express chance momentary moods by means of rich and strange colors, but not an orderly and purposeful experience.

Of course, in our modern harmonic music the melodic movement proceeds by means, not of single tones, but of chords. Yet no new principle is introduced by this fact. For the chords have in part merely the significance of highly enriched tones, the harmonized tones of the chords taking the place of the partials of the single notes and imparting a more voluminous color, which may have its own beauty as such; and, in addition, they simply confer upon the melody another dimension, as it were, the tonal relations of harmony and contrast operating between the tones of the chords simultaneously, as well as temporally between the successive elements of the melody.

The orderly beauty which the tonal relations confer upon music is further enriched and complicated by rhythm. Rhythm in music is of two sorts: a rhythm of time and a rhythm of accent, or increased loudness. Through the one, the duration of a musical composition is divided up into approximately equal parts filled by notes and rests of definite length, and through the other, the light notes are subordinated to the heavy notes. The two, however, are interrelated; for the bars are divided from each other by the accents, and the accents recur at approximately equal intervals.

The pleasure in rhythmical arrangement is derived from two sources: first, from the need for perspicuity which is fulfilled through the regular grouping of the tonal elements in the bars,–their length being adjusted to the average length of an attention wave, and the number of tones that fill them to the number of items which can be taken in at one act of attention,–and through the subordination of the light to the heavy within the bars, the bars to the measures, and the measures to the periods. The second source of satisfaction in rhythm is the combination of feelings of balance and harmony aroused–a rhythm is not only a pleasing perspicuous order, but an emotion. For every recurring accent and interval competes with its predecessor for the mind's attention, yet is in agreement with it since it, too, fulfills the law that pervades them all.

The full significance of both melody and rhythm depends, however, upon their interrelation, the concrete musical structure, the motive or melody in the complete sense, being an indissoluble unity of both. Now if we take the term will with a broad meaning, Schopenhauer's characterization of melody as an image of the will still remains the truest aesthetic interpretation of it. For, when we hear it, we not only hear, but attend to what we hear; we hear each tone in its relations of harmony or contrast or fulfillment to other tones, freighted with memories of its predecessors and carrying with it expectations, which the following tones fulfill or deny. The melody begins, let us suppose, with the tonic note. This note then becomes for us a plan or purpose; for as it goes, it leaves in the mind a memory of itself, no mere pale sensation–no image ever is–but a motor set, an expectation and desire to hear the note again. If the next note is harmonically related, this purpose is partially fulfilled and we get the satisfaction of a partial success. If, however, the tone does not belong to the tonic chord, but, let us suppose, to the subdominant, it comes as a hindrance, an obstacle, or perhaps as a new and rival purpose springing up in the course of the fulfillment of the old,–a purpose which can be satisfied only through the other tones of its chord. Hence the tension of conflicting expectations and the excitement as now the one and now the other is fulfilled in the succeeding notes. Yet, since all other harmonies are subordinated to the tonic harmony, and even through their very opposition increase our desire for it, they must give way to the fundamental purpose with which we started; and when the tonic does eventually triumph, it fulfills not only itself, but all lesser desires of the melody; in it we find what we have been seeking, we arrive where we set out to go. And in this success we not only obtain what we first wanted, but more–an experience enriched by every conflict, and harmonious ultimately through the inner adjustment and resolution of its elements; for in hearing the final note we hear the memories of all previous tones, also. When the departures from the keynote are many and distant and sudden, and the melody wanders into the bypaths of foreign harmonies, moving along broken and zigzag lines, it expresses an exciting, a dangerous and difficult adventure; when, however, the departures are gradual and confined for the most part within the limits of a single harmony, moving in a smooth and curving path, it expresses a life that is secure and happy, tending to repose as the line approaches the horizontal, and as repetitions of the same note predominate.

Rhythm enters into melody to differentiate and emphasize. By means of accent and time-value, the different tones are weighted and their relative value fixed. The heavy tones assert their will with a more insistent energy; the long tones upon which we linger make a deeper and more lasting impression; while the light and short tones in contrast become points of mere passing and transition. If, moreover, we include the element of tempo, then all the temporal feelings are introduced into melody–the excitement of rapid motion, the calmness of the slow; the agony of delay, of waiting and postponement, with the triumph and relief when the expected note arrives at last. Finally, the effects of shading must be added, the contrasts between piano and forte–loudness that brings the tones so near that they may seem threatening in their insistence; softness that makes them seem far away and dreamlike.

Following the large idea introduced by Schopenhauer, which was enriched by the minuter studies of Lotze, Wundt, and Lipps, we may sum the foregoing analysis in the statement that music expresses the abstract aspects of action, its ease or difficulty, its advance or retrocession, its home coming or its wandering, its hesitation or its surety, its conflicts and its contrasts, its force or its weakness, its swiftness or slowness, its abruptness or smoothness, its excitement or repose, its success or failure, its seriousness or play. Then, in addition, as we shall see, all modes of emotion that are congruous with this abstract form may by association be poured into its mold, so that the content of music becomes not a mere form of life, but life itself.

It is, of course, obvious that our analysis has confined itself to the barest elements of the musical experience. Our music to-day, with its many-voiced harmonies, with its procession of chords instead of single tones, with its modulation into related keys, has an infinite wealth and complexity defying description. A large part of the astonishing effect of music is derived from the fact that in a brief space we seem to hear and absorb so much: the careers of multitudinous lives compressed into an instant. Yet the meaning of the complex whole can be understood, I think, from such an analysis of the simple structure as has been given.

The methods by which the larger musical wholes are built up illustrate principles of aesthetic structure with which we are already familiar. There is the harmonious unification of parts through the simple repetition of motives, their inversion or imitation in higher or lower keys, either successively or simultaneously; the execution of the same theme in another time or tempo; and through the interweaving of themes. There is the balance of contrasted or competing themes; the subordination of the lesser to the more striking and insistent motives; the preparation for, emergence and triumph of, a final passage that resolves all dissonances and adjusts all conflicts. Because of music's abstractness, the connection between the parts of a musical composition may be loose or subtle, taxing the synthetic powers even of the educated listener; yet some contrast or analogy of feeling must always unite them. The structure of the whole may be either static or dramatic; in the former case the dramatic element is confined to the themes, the purpose of the whole being merely to work out all their significant variations,–to embroider and repeat them in new keys and rhythms and tempos, and to contrast them with other themes. Repetition is the great creative principle of musical development, the composer seeking to say over again in ever new forms what he has said before. And this, again because of the abstractness of music, is a significant process; to repeat the concrete is tiresome and trivial, but an abstract form is always enriched by appearing in a new shape.

The explanation of musical expression thus far given, although it suffices to account for the basis of all musical feeling, is, I think, inadequate to its full volume and intensity. There is a concreteness of emotional content in some musical compositions–an arousal of terror and longing and despair and joy–infinitely richer than any abstract forms of feeling.

To account for this, two sources of explanation suggest themselves. First, the arousing of emotions through deep-lying effects of rhythm. It is a well-known fact, cited in most discussions of this subject, that the motor mechanism of the body is somehow attuned to rhythm. When we hear rhythmical sounds, we not only follow them with the attention, we follow them also with our muscles, with hand and foot and head and heart and respiratory apparatus. Even when we do not visibly move in unison with the rhythm–as we usually do not–we tend to do so, which proves that in any case the motor mechanism of the body is stimulated and brought into play by the sounds. There is a direct psychophysical connection between the hearing of rhythmic sounds and the tendency to execute certain movements. But there is an equally direct relation between emotions and tendencies to movements, through which the former find expression and are given effect in the outer world. To every kind of emotion–love and hate and fear and sorrow and joy–there corresponds a specific mode of motor manifestation. The connection between rhythmic sound and emotion is therefore plain; the link is a common motor scheme. Rhythms arouse into direct and immediate activity the motor "sets" that are the physical basis of the emotions, and hence arouse the corresponding emotions themselves, without any ground for them outside of the organism. And these emotions, since they are aroused by the sounds and not by any object to which they might be directed and upon which they might work themselves off in a meaningful reaction, are interwoven into the sounds,–they and the sounds come to us as a single indissoluble whole of experience. The emotions become the content of the sounds. And hence the strangeness of the musical experience–the fact that we feel so deeply over nothing.

The second cause for the concreteness of the musical experience I take to be certain emotions and feelings which are aroused by association, not with the rhythmic elements of music alone, but with the tone-color, intensity, and melody also. There is a human quality, a poignancy and intimacy, about much music, which can be understood only through its analogy with the sounds of the human voice. For the human voice is emotionally expressive through its mere sound alone: one can know a large part of what is going on in the breasts of people who talk in a foreign tongue just by listening to the sound of their voices–their excitement or boredom, their anger, love, or resentment; and one becomes conscious of these emotions, as in hearing music, without knowing what they are all about. All human emotions betray themselves in speech through the rise and fall, range of intervals, loudness or softness, tempo and differences of duration of tone. Now, although it is far too much to say that music is actually an imitation of the voice, it is nevertheless true, as Diderot thought, that in certain musical passages we overhear the voice. There is never any exact similarity between music and vocal sounds, but there is enough resemblance to awaken by association the feelings that are the normal accompaniments of such sounds. Any tone analogies that there happen to be are felt as such. This is notably true of all music that has a peculiar lyrical and human quality,–the music that readily becomes popular because it seems to speak direct to the heart.

Originally, all music was song, and since speech and song employ the same organ, it would be surprising indeed if something of the same expression of the emotions that overflows into the one should not also overflow into the other, and that musicians should not, unconsciously or consciously, tend to choose their melodies because of such analogies. Instrumental music probably got its first melodies from song, and despite its vast present complexity and independence, has never completely lost touch with song. Since the first meaningful sounds that we hear are those of the voice, music must always have for us the significance of a glorified speech.

The fault of the original proposers of the speech theory was that they thought it a complete explanation of the facts of musical expression. Its explanatory value is, however, strictly limited, and supplemental to the more basic considerations adduced; yet it remains a necessary part of the complex theory of the complex fact we are studying. And the acceptance of it as such does not imply a belief in the speech theory of the origin of music. Song did not grow out of impassioned speech, but arose coeval with speech, when men found–perhaps by accident–that they could make with their voices pure and pleasing tones and intervals of tones, and express something of their inner selves in so doing. Yet, as I have suggested, it would be strange if speech did not react upon song–if the first vocal tones were not purified words, and the first intervals an approximation to those of speech. Thus in song, lyric poetry and music arose together as a single art for the expression of feeling, until the development of instrumental music freed the one and the invention of writing freed the other; while speech kept to its different and original purpose–the expression of ideas for practical ends, and produced an aesthetic form of its own only at a later period and under independent influences.

The complete understanding of musical expression involves, finally, as was suggested at the beginning of this chapter, the recognition of the analogy that exists between music and the noises produced by nature and human activities.

Through the imitation of their rhythm, force, and tempo, some of these can be directly suggested by musicians. Yet this direct suggestion, although employed by the greatest composers, plays a subordinate part in music, and, since it introduces an element of representation of the outer world–*tonmalerei*–is usually felt to involve a departure from the prime purpose of music: the expression of the inner world through the emotional effects of pure sound. In the best program music, therefore, the purpose of the composer is not the mere imitation of nature–which is never art at all, and in music is always recognized as an unsaesthetic *tour de force* of mere cleverness–but rather the arousal of the feelings caused by nature. And as an aid in the expression of such feelings, imitation, when delicately suggestive rather than blatant, will always play a part.

There are, however, subtler and remoter analogies between music and noise, which produce their effects whether the musician wills them or not. Such, for example, are loud bursts of tone suggesting falling or crashing, events which usually have a terrifying significance; crescendoes, suggesting the approach of things, so often full of expectancy and excitement; diminuendoes, suggesting a gradual departure or fading away, bearing relief or regret. And there are doubtless hundreds of other such associations, too minute or remote or long- forgotten to recover, which add their mite of feeling to swell and make vast the musical emotion. As Fechner pointed out, these associations may work quite unconsciously, giving evidence of their functioning only through the feeling tones which they release. So important is the part which sound plays in our lives that there must be an especially large number of such underground associations aroused by music. All of our experiences are connected together by subconscious filiation; but it is only in art that their residual feeling tones have a full opportunity to come into the mind; for in everyday life they are crowded out by the hurry of practical concerns. In the earlier stages of the development of music they must have contributed a still larger share to musical expression, when the different forms of music were connected by habit and convention with particular crises and occasions, religious, domestic, and social, in the life of individuals and groups. But even to-day, despite the new freedom of music, they are not absent.

Looking back over our analysis of music, we see that it is characterized by the expression of emotion without the representation of the causes or objects of emotion. This fact, which has now become a well-recognized part of aesthetic theory, distinguishes music from all the other arts. Music supplies us with no definite images of nature, as painting and sculpture do, and with no ideas, as poetry does. It contains feelings, but no meanings. Music offers us no background for emotion, no objects upon which it may be directed, no story, no *mise en scene.* It supplies us with the feeling tones of things and events, but not with the things or events themselves. It moves wholly in a world of its own, a world of pure feeling, with no embodiment save only sound. It may express terror, but not terror over this or that; joy, but whether the joy that comes from sight of the morning or of the beloved, it cannot tell. In one brief space of time, it may arouse despair, hope, triumph–but all over nothing.

Yet–and this is the central paradox of music–despite its abstractness, nay, because of this very quality, it remains the most personal and intimate of the arts. For, itself offering no images of things and events to which we may attach the feelings which it arouses, we supply our own. We fill in the impersonal form of musical feeling with the concrete emotions of our own lives; it is our strivings, our hopes and fears, which music expresses. By denying us access to the world about us, music compels us to turn in upon ourselves; it is we who live there in the sounds. For, as we have seen, the rhythmic tones seize hold not only of our attention, but of our bodies also–hand and foot and head and heart, resounding throughout the whole organism. And, where our bodies are, there are we. Moreover, our life there in the sounds need not remain without objects because the music does not describe them to us; for out of our own inner selves we may build up an imaginary world for our feelings. As we listen to the music, we shall see the things we hope for or fear or desire; or else transport ourselves among purely fanciful objects and events. Music is a language which we all understand because it expresses the basic mold of all emotion and striving; yet it is a language which no two people understand in the same way, because each pours into that mold his own unique experience. In itself abstract and objectless, it may thus become, in varying ways, concrete and alive.

The great variety in the interpretation of musical compositions has often been used as an argument against the existence of emotions in music, but is, as we have seen, the inevitable result of their abstractness. This abstractness may, indeed, be so great that apparently opposite concrete emotions, such as love and religious adoration, despair and joy, may be aroused in different people, according to different circumstances, by the same piece. The music of the opera can be used in the cathedral. Yet strikingly dissimilar emotions have common elements–worship is the love of God; joy may be a rage equally with disappointment; and at their highest intensity, all opposed emotions tend to pass over into each other: hope into fear, love into hate, exaltation into depression. The elementary feelings out of which our complex emotions are built are few and simple; hence each one of the latter is identical in some ingredients with the others. And even the elementary feelings may have common aspects of intensity and tempo, of strain and excitement. Some musical compositions, like the fugues of Bach, seem to express nothing more than such extremely abstract modes of feeling, without arousing any associations that would impel the mind to make a more concrete interpretation. To express feelings of this kind in language is, of course, impossible, for the reason that our emotional vocabularies have been constructed to communicate only the emotions of everyday life. Other types of music–like the romantic tone poetry of a later day–which are more abundant in their associations, and hence richer in their emotional content, are difficult of translation for another reason: the rapidity of succession and subtlety of intermixture of the expressed feelings are beyond the reach of words, even of a poet's, which inevitably stabilize and isolate what they denote.

But abstract and objectless emotions occur in other regions of experience beside the musical, even beyond the entire field of the aesthetic. All except the most healthy-minded and practical people are at times filled with vague fears, longings, and joys, the objects or causes of which they cannot formulate. Normally, feeling is directed towards definite objects and leads to action upon them, but may nevertheless become isolated from its proper connections, and function without issue. The extreme cases of this are the pathological states of mania and depression, where such feelings assume proportions dangerous to the existence of the individual. Intoxication and hysteria present analogous, though more transient phenomena. And one may observe the autonomous development of mere feeling even in the healthy life, as when one remains jolly after all occasion for it has ceased, or angry after the cause for anger has been removed. All feelings tend to acquire a strength beyond what is necessary for action and to endure after their proper objects and conditions have disappeared; hence the luxury of grief and revenge and sentimentality.

In their most general character, musical emotions stand on a level with other purposeless emotions, except that they are deliberately induced and elaborated to an extent and complexity unmatched elsewhere. But while these emotions are morbid and evil outside of music, within music they are innocent. For outside of music they spring from dislocations of the practical and striving core of the personality, where, if persistently indulged in, they exacerbate the disturbance of which they are the sign, interfering with action and eventually endangering the health and happiness of the individual; while in music, being induced from the outside by mere sounds, they have no ground within the personality itself where they can take root, and hence exert only a harmless and transient effect upon the mind; they belong to the surface, not to the substance of the self, to imagination, not to the will. Or when, as sometimes happens, the deeper and perhaps morbid strata of the self are reached by the sounds, the feelings which are awakened from their sleep there, where they might be productive of evil dreams, find an orderly and welcome release in the sounds–they are not only aroused, but carried off by the music. This the Greeks understood when they employed music as a healer of the soul and called this effect catharsis.

If, indeed, music were just a means for the arousal of feelings, it would not be a fine art, but an orgy. For, in order to be aesthetic, feelings must be not merely stimulated by, but objectified in, the sense medium, where they can be mastered and known. But the intimacy of music is not in contradiction with the freedom and objectivity characteristic of all art. For musical feelings, although they are experienced as our own, are nevertheless also experienced as the sounds; in music we live, not as we live ordinarily, within our bodies, but out there, in a rarer and unpractical medium–tone. And in this new region we gain dominion over our feelings, through the order which the form of the music imposes upon them, and also self-knowledge, because, in being externalized in the sounds, our feelings become an object for our reflection and understanding. In music the light of reflection is turned straight upon ourselves.

The poignancy of music depends upon just this fact that through it we get a revelation of ourselves to ourselves. In the other arts, this revelation is indirect, occurring through the representation of the lives of other, real or fictitious, personalities; but in music, it is direct; for there the object of expression is oneself. Even in the lyric poem, where the reader and the poet tend to become identical, the unity is less complete; for when embodied in words, feelings become more exterior than when put forth into tones; a tone is closer to the self, because like a cry or a laugh, it is less articulate.

Moreover, words are means of communication as well as expression; they therefore embody of any experience only as much as can be passed from speaker to hearer; the unique is for the most part lost on the way; but in music the full personal resonance of experience is retained. In music we get so close to ourselves that at times it is almost frightening.

And this is the reason why, on all the high or serious occasions of human life, music is alone adequate to express its inner meaning. At a marriage or a funeral, in church or at a festival, the ceremonial is traditional and social; it expresses the historical and group significance of the situation, but not that which is unique and just one's own; it always contains, moreover, much that is outgrown and unacceptable–a creed of life or love or death that belongs to the past, not to us. But the music embodies all that we really believe and feel about the fact, its intimate, emotional essence, clear of everything irrelevant and external.

But music does more than express the inexpressible in ourselves; it gives us entrance into a supernatural world of feeling. Except at the rare high moments of our lives, its joys and despairs are too exalted for us; they are not ours; they belong to gods and heroes. In music the superman is born into our feelings. Music does for the emotions what mythology and poetry do for the imagination and philosophy for the intellect–it brings us into touch with a more magnificent life, for which we have perhaps the potency, but not the opportunity here. And in doing this, music performs a great service; for, outside of love and war, life, which offers endless occasions for intense thought and action, provides few for passionate feeling.

Thus far our study of the art has been confined to so-called absolute music. We must now complete our survey by a rapid consideration of the union of music with the other arts. Because of its abstractness, music, of all the arts, lends itself most readily to combination with others; yet even in the case of music the possibility of union is limited by the existence of a clear identity between the arts combined. Thus, music goes well with the temporal arts, poetry, the dance, and the drama, and particularly well with the first two because they are rhythmical; it will also unite with architecture, because that is another abstract art; but with the static, concrete arts like painting and sculpture, it will not fuse. One might perhaps accompany a picture with a single chord whose emotional meaning was the same as that of the color scheme and the objects represented, but not with more; for the aesthetic experience of the picture is instantaneous and complete, while that of the music requires time for its development and fruition; hence the two would soon fall apart, and a person would either have to ignore the music or cease to look at the picture.

Originally, of course, music was always combined with some other art, and first of all, probably with the dance. In its earliest form, the dance was a communal religious expression, about which we shall have little to say, since it belongs to the past, not to living art. For to-day the dance is a free art like music. The beauty of the dance consists, first, in the free and rhythmical expression of impulses to movement. This expression, which is direct for the dancer who actually carries out her impulses in real motion, is for the spectator indirect and ideal, for he experiences only movement-images aroused by movements seen, and then, by feeling these into the limbs of the dancer, dances with her in the imagination. And to secure this free and large, even though vicarious, expression of pent-up impulses to movement is very grateful to us whose whole movement life is impoverished, because restricted by convention and occupation to a few narrow types. But the dance would have little interest for men were it not for another element in its beauty: the expression of the amorous feelings of the spectator. These, although really located in the breast of the spectator, are nevertheless embodied in the personality of the dancer, whose charm they constitute. Finally, the content of the dance may be further enriched through the use of symbolic costume and mimetic gestures, suggesting emotions like joy or love or grief, emotionally toned ideas like spring, or actions such as courtship. Now music, with its own rhythmical order and voluminous emotional content, has an obvious kinship with the rhythmic form and amorous substance of the dance, and so can well serve to accompany it.

The result of the union is to enforce the rhythmic experience through the medium of sound, the dance keeping time with the music, and, through the heightened emotional tone and increased suggestibility created by the music, to deepen the sympathetic rapport between dancer and spectator. Thus the music is given a concrete interpretation through the dance, and the dance gains in emotional power through the music. In the union, the gain to the dance is clear and absolute; but the music pays a price for the concreteness of content which it secures, by forfeiting its power to express chance inner moods–what it gains in definiteness it loses in scope and universality. And only music with a strong and evident rhythm is capable of union with the dance; the more complex and subtle music, aside from the impossibility of making its delicate rhythms fit into those of a dance, has a variety and sublimity of meaning so far transcending the personality of any human being, that to attempt to focus it in a dancer, no matter how charming, would be a travesty.

Of equal naturalness and almost equal antiquity with the union of music with the dance, is its union with poetry. In song this union is a real fusion; for the tones are the vocal word-sounds themselves, purified into music. Here, of course, unlike absolute music, the tones are expressive, not only as other tones are through their mere sound, but also through their meaning. And this can well be; for as Schopenhauer remarked, just as the universal may be illustrated by any object which embodies it, so the vague musical content of a tone may be fused with the concrete meaning of a word of like feeling. And for many hearers music doubtless gains by thus becoming articulate; for, being unable to supply out of their own imagination the concreteness which music lacks, they welcome having this done for them by the poet; yet the gain is not without a corresponding loss. For when the musical meaning is specialized through the emotions that are the burden of the song, it necessarily loses the power which it would otherwise have of expressing one's own inner life–once more, what it gains in definiteness it loses in scope. It no longer possesses the unique function of the musical. Hence, if we love the music, we shall not care whether or not we understand the meaning of the words, and what we shall value in the song will be only the peculiar intimacy which it derives from its instrument, the voice. Only rarely is it otherwise, as in some of the songs of Schumann, when the poetic interpretation is so beautiful and so completely at one with the musical feeling, that we prefer to accept it rather than substitute our own interpretation for the poet's. But even so, the music, if genuine, will have value without the words. At the opposite pole are those songs, often popular, where the music, having little worth in itself, is a mere accompaniment for the words. In all cases, however, the music can lend to the poetry some of the intimacy which is its own, so that its burden has a deeper echo in the soul.

Yet much of poetry is unfit for union with music. This is true, first, of all highly intellectual poetry, where the emotions are embodied in complex and abstract ideas. One could not, for example, readily set Browning to music. Music may be deep, mystic, even metaphysical in its meaning, but it cannot be dialectical. The emotions that accompany subtle thought, even when intense, are not of the voluminous, massive kind which music expresses; they lack the bodily resonance of the latter; they are, moreover, clean-cut and static, while in music everything flows in half-lights, like a river moving in moonlight. On the other hand, poems which express rapidly developing states of mind, which contain quick, subtle transitions, are equally unfit for union with music. For music, although always in motion, is always in slow motion; it needs time to get under way, and time for its development in embroidering, varying, and repeating its theme. And this difficulty applies in a general way to every union between poetry and music. For words are primarily practical and communicative, and therefore cut short the passion which they express; whereas tones, never having had any other purpose than expression, draw it out and let it have its way. Moreover, poetry, because of its definiteness, is compatible with only a limited range of variation, beyond which it becomes monotonous, while music, because of its abstractness, permits of variations almost endless, and is enriched by every new shape in which its meaning can appear. If, therefore, poetry is to keep time with the slow movement of the music and conform to its mode of development, the verses have to be repeated again and again; but this destroys the poetic form—as in the oratorio, with its senseless iterations.

Finally, the temporal and developmental character of the drama would seem to fit it for union with music. Yet the union of these two arts is confronted with the same difficulties that beset the connection between poetry and music. The movement of the acting drama is swift and straight, that of music is slow and circular; hence if the music is to have its way, the action of the drama must stand. In consequence of this, there is little real action in most operas, prolonged dialogues in song taking its place. Only rarely—as for example in Strauss' "Salome," perhaps—is the form of the drama preserved. As a rule the unity of the musical form is also destroyed, the thread of the story being substituted for it. Last, as in the song, the universality of the music is renounced in favor of the interpretation given to it by the program. In the *leit-motif*, indeed, as Wagner uses it, where a musical phrase is provided with a fixed connotation of ideas and acts which is understood by the hearer whenever it recurs, opera ceases to be music at all in the strict sense, and becomes a musical language. Yet in the opera, as in the song, the music, when genuine, possesses its own independent meaning, which can be appreciated without the *mise en scene* or the program. And then only rarely, as in the Toreador song in "Carmen," is the action so close to the inner meaning of the music, that the latter seems to gain by the interpretation.

It follows that Wagner's dream of making the opera a sum of all the values of poetry, drama, and music, and so an art more beautiful than any one of them, is fallacious. For, as we have repeatedly seen, in uniting the arts, there is gain as well as loss; something of the form or meaning of each has to be sacrificed. The work that results from the combination is really a new art-form, in which the elements are changed and their individuality partly destroyed; and its value is a new value, which may be equal to, but is certainly no greater than, that of any other art-form. To put the matter epigrammatically, when the arts are added together, one plus one does not equal two, but only one again.

Chapter IX

The Aesthetics of Poetry

Our study of music in the preceding chapter has prepared us for the study of poetry, for the two arts are akin. Both are arts of sound and both employ rhythm as a principle of order in sound. They had a twin birth in song, and although they have grown far apart, they come together again in song. In many ways, music is the standard for verse. Yet, despite these resemblances, the differences between the arts are striking. In place of music's disembodied feelings, poetry offers us concrete intuitions of life,–the rehearsal of emotions attached to real things and clean-cut ideas. Poetry is a music with a definite meaning, and that is no music at all. Much of poetry, gnomic and narrative, probably grew out of speech by regularizing its natural rhythm, independent of music. To-day poetry is written to be read, not to be sung; it is an art of speech, not of song.

All speech is communication, an utterance from a speaker to a hearer. In the case of ordinary speech, the aim is to effect some change of mind in the interlocutor that will lead to an action beneficial to one or both of the persons concerned. Ordinary speech is practical; its end is to influence conduct; it is command, exhortation, prayer, or threat. Poetry, on the other hand, is "the spontaneous overflow of powerful feelings"; its purpose is to express life for the sake of the values which expression itself may create, and to communicate them to others. The values are given *in the utterance itself*; they do not have to be waited for to come from something which may develop subsequently. They are the universal aesthetic values which may result from any free expression of life–the contemplative reliving of its joys, or the mastery of its pains through the courageous facing of them in reflection.

Since the appeal of poetry is to the sympathy and thoughtfulness which all men possess, there is no need that it be directed, as ordinary speech is, to particular men and women whose help or advantage is sought. The poet addresses himself to man in general, and only so to you and me. Even when ostensibly directed to some particular person, a poem has an audience which is really universal. Except in the first moment of creative fervor, the friend invoked is never intended to be the sole recipient of the poet's words. Oftentimes the poet appeals to the dead or to natural objects which cannot hear him. One might perhaps infer from this that there is no genuine impulse to communication in poetry; that it is pure expression, a dialogue with self. But this would be a false inference; for there is always some hint in every poem that a vague background of possible auditors is bespoken. No matter how intimate and spontaneous, no poem can escape being social, and hence, in varying degrees, self-conscious. Art is autonomous expression meant to be contagious.

The appeal of scientific expression is also to something universal in men–to their love of knowledge and understanding. But there is this difference between poetry and science: science seeks merely the intellectual mastery of things and ideas, and so is careless of their values; while poetry, even when descriptive or thoughtful, ever has *life* as its theme–the way man reacts to his environment and his thought. Poetry is never purely descriptive or dialectical. And this difference in the substance of the expression determines a difference in the direction of interest within the expression. In scientific expression, words lead us away to things–pure description, or to their meanings–mathematics and dialectic; but in poetry, since the values which we attach to things and ideas come from within out of ourselves and are embodied in the words, they keep us to themselves; we dwell in the expression itself, in the verbal experience–its total content of sounds which we hear, ideas which we understand, and feelings which we appreciate, is of worth to us.

Since poetry is an art of speech, we can understand it only through a study of words, which are its media. A single word is seldom an integral element of speech; yet it may fairly be called the atom, the ultimate constituent of speech. Now a word is a structure of a potentially fourfold complexity. First, it is a phenomenon of sound and movement–something heard and uttered. Its sound, and the movement-sensations from vocal cords and tongue and lips which accompany its production, are the sensuous shell of the word. Second, embodied in this as the speaker utters it, associated to it as the hearer understands it, is its meaning. The meaning is either an idea of a concrete thing or situation, or an abstraction. This is the irreducible minimum of a word, but is seldom all. For, in poetry, some emotional response to the object meant by the word impels to its utterance, and this is embodied in it when it is uttered, and a similar feeling is awakened in the auditor when it is heard or read. A word not only mirrors a situation through its meaning, but preserves something of the mind's response; it communicates the total experience,–the self as well as the object. Finally, the meaning of a word may not remain a mere idea, but may grow out into one or more of the concrete images of which it is the residuum. When, for example, I utter the word "ocean," I may not only know what I mean and re-experience my joy in the sea, but my meaning may be clothed in images of the sight and touch and odor of the sea–vicariously, through these images, all my sense experiences of the sea may be present in the mind. A word, therefore, sounds and is articulated, means, expresses feeling, and evokes images. All understanding of poetry depends upon the knowledge and proper evaluation of the functioning of these aspects of a word. Let us consider in a general way each one of them.

In ordinary speech, the sound and articulation of a word, although indispensable to utterance, and therefore a necessary part of it, are of little or no value in themselves; for our interest is centered upon the meaning or upon the action which is expected to result from its understanding. We do not attend to the quality and rhythm of the word- sounds which we utter or hear, and the articulatory sensations, although felt, have only a shadowy existence in "the fringe of inattention." But in poetry, which is speech made beautiful, the mere sound of the words has value. In hearing poetry, we not only understand, but listen; we appreciate not only the ideas and emotions conveyed, but the word-sounds and their rhythms as well. Even in silent reading, poetry is a voice which we delight to hear[1].

Yet, despite the importance which sound acquires in poetry, it never achieves first place; it never becomes independent, as in music; but shares hegemony with the other aspects of the word. In practical or scientific speech, the chief aspect is meaning; for it is the meaning which gives us knowledge and guides our acts. Indeed, for all practical purposes, the meaning of words consists in the actions which are to be performed on hearing them. If I ask a man the way and he tells me, the quality of his voice, the interest which he takes in telling me, and the images which float across his mind are of no importance to me, so long as I can follow his directions. But in poetry the situation alters once more. For there, since expression itself has become the end, and all action upon it is inhibited, the feeling which prompts it becomes a significant part of what I appreciate. In poetry the meanings are secondary to emotions. Yet the meanings are still indispensable; for they indicate the concrete objects or ideas

1. And for many this "inner speech" consists quite as much of articulation as of sound. The "sound" of a word is really a complex of actual sounds plus associated articulation impulses. Throughout the remainder of this chapter, when I refer to the sound of words, I shall have in mind this entire complex. We may therefore say that in silent reading poetry is a voice which we delight both to hear and to use.

towards which emotion is directed. In ordinary speech, meanings are guides to action; in aesthetic speech, they are formulations of feelings. And just in this power of a word to fixate emotion lies the chief difference between poetry and music, where feeling, being aroused by sound alone, is vague and objectless.

Ideally, every word in a poem should be charged with feeling; but actually this is not the case, for many words, taken by themselves, are too abstract or commonplace to possess any. Words all too familiar, or connectives, like "and" and "but" and "or," are examples of this; the former may be avoided by the poet, but the latter are indispensable. Originally, no doubt, every word had an emotional coloring, if only that of a child's curiosity; and some words have meanings too deeply rooted in feeling ever to lose it. No amount of familiarity can deprive such words as "death" and "love" and "God" of their emotional value. Words like these must forever recur in the vocabulary of poets. Yet, since in living discourse a meaning is seldom complete in a single word, but requires several words in a phrase or sentence, a word which by itself would be cold may participate in the general warmth of the whole of which it is a part. Consider, for example, the last line of the final stanza of Wordsworth's "The Lost Love":

She lived unknown, and few could know
When Lucy ceased to be;
But she is in her grave, and O!
The difference to me!

The first three words, by themselves, are completely bare of emotional coloring, yet, taken together with the last, and in connection with the whole stanza, and in the setting of the entire poem, they are aglow with the most poignant passion.

As for the image, the last of the aspects of a word, the judgment of Edmund Burke, in his "*Essay on the Sublime and Beautiful*" still remains true: in reading words or in listening to them, we get the sound and the meaning and their "impressions" (emotions), but the images which float across the mind, if there are any, are often too vague or too inconstant to be of much relevance to the experience. They are, moreover, highly individual in nature, differing in kind and clearness from person to person. The recent researches into imageless thinking are a striking confirmation of Burke's observation. It is now pretty clearly established that the meaning of words is something more than the images, visual or other, which they arouse. Probably the meaning is always carried by some sort of imagery, differing with the mental make-up of the reader, but the meaning cannot be equated to the imagery. For example, you and I both understand the word "ocean"; but when I read the word, I get a visual image of green water and sunlight, while you perhaps get an auditory image of the sound of the waves as they break upon the shore. Sound, meaning, feeling, these are the essential constituents of discourse; imagery is variable and accidental. It is impossible, therefore, to found the theory of poetry on the image-making power of words. And yet, imagery plays a primary role in poetic speech. For, as we have observed so often, feelings are more vital and permanent when embedded in concrete sensations and images than when attached to abstract meanings. Through the image, the poet confers upon his art some of the sensuousness which it would otherwise lack. It is not necessary that the image appear clear in the mind; for its emotional value can be conveyed even when it is obscure and marginal. When, for example, we read,

Freeze, freeze, thou bitter sky,
Thou dost not bite so nigh
As benefits forgot,

the word "bitter" may arouse no vivid gustatory image, the word "bite" no clear image of pain; yet even when these images are very dim, they serve none the less to establish the feeling of intense disagreeableness which the poet wishes to convey. Poetry, therefore, because it is more emotional than ordinary speech, is more abundantly imaginal.

Having distinguished in a general way the four elements of speech–sound, meaning, feeling, and imagery–we are prepared to study them singly in greater detail. We want to build out of a study of these elements a synthetic view of the nature and function of poetry, and apply our results to some of its newer and more clamant forms. Let us begin with sound. In our first chapter we observed that the medium of an art tends to become expressive in itself,–that in poetry the mere sound and articulation of words, quite apart from anything which they mean, may arouse and communicate feelings. What we have called the primary expressiveness of the medium is nowhere better illustrated than in poetry. But just what is expressed through sound, and how?

Every lover of poetry is aware of the large share which the mere sound of the words contributes to its beauty. This is true even when we abstract from rhythm, which we shall neglect for the time being, and think only of euphony, alliteration, assonance, and rime. There is a joy truly surprising in the mere repetition of vowels and consonants. For myself, I find a pleasure in the mere repetition of vowels and consonants all out of proportion to what, a priori, I should be led to expect from so slight a cause. And yet we have the familiar analogies by means of which we can understand this seemingly so strange delight, the repeat in a pattern, consonance in chord and melody. If the repetition of the same color or line in painting, the same tone in music, can delight us, why not the repetition of the same word-sound? In all cases a like feeling of harmony is produced. And the same general principle applies to explain it. All word-sounds as we utter or hear them leave memory traces in the mind, which are not pure images (no memory traces are), but also motor sets, tendencies or impulses to the remaking of the sounds. The doing of any deed–a word is also a deed–creates a will to its doing again; hence the satisfaction when that will is fulfilled in the repeated sound, when the image melts with the fact. And the same law that rules in music and design holds here also: there must not be too much of consonance, of repetition, else the will becomes satiated and fatigued; there must be difference as well as identity,–the novelty and surprise which accompany the arousal of a still fresh and unappeased impulse. This is well provided for in alternate rimes, where the will to one kind of sound is suspended by the emergence of a different sound with its will, and where the fulfillment of the one balances the fulfillment of the other. All these facts are illustrated in such a stanza as this:

Fear no more the heat o' the sun
Nor the furious winter's rages;
Thou thy worldly task hast done,
Home art gone and ta'en thy wages;
Golden lads and girls all must,
As chimney sweepers, come to dust.

Here, for example, the "f"-sound in "fear" finds harmonious fulfillment in "furious"; the "t"-sound in "task," its mate in "ta'en"; the "g"-sound in "golden," its match in "girls"; "sun" and "done," "rages" and "wages," illustrate a balance of harmonies; while in the consonance of "must" and "dust," the whole movement of the stanza comes to full and finished harmony.

Thus taken together, word-sounds, as mere sounds, are expressive of the general form-feelings of harmony and balance. But can they express anything singly? Is there anything in poetry comparable to the expressiveness of single tones or of colors like red and blue and yellow? To this, I think, the answer must be, little or nothing. Almost all the expressiveness of single words comes from their meaning. At all events, the sound and meaning of a word are so inextricably fused that, even when we suspect that it may have some expressiveness on its own account, we are nearly incapable of disentangling it. As William James has remarked, a word-sound, when taken by itself apart from its meaning, gives an impression of mere queerness. And when it does seem to have some distinctive quality, we do not know how much really belongs to the sound and how much to some lingering bit of meaning which we have failed to separate in our analysis. For example, because of its initial "s"-sound and its hard consonants, the word "struggle" seems to express, in the effort required to pronounce it, something of the emotional tone of struggle itself; but how do we know that this is not due to the association with its meaning, which we have been unable to abstract from? Even true onomatopoetic words like "bang" or "crack" derive, I suspect, most of their specific quality from their meaning. They do have, to be sure, a certain mimetic impressiveness as mere sounds; but that is very vague; the meaning makes it specific. The sheer length of the word "multitudinous" in Shakespeare's line, "the multitudinous seas incarnadine," seems to express something of the vastness and prolixity of the seas; but would it if it were not used as an adjective describing the seas, and if it did not have just the meaning that it has? Of course, in this case, the mere sound is effective, but it gets most of its effectiveness because it happens to have a certain meaning. Moreover, even the very sound quality of words depends much upon their meaning; we pronounce them in a certain way, with a certain slowness or swiftness, a certain emphasis upon particular syllables, with a high or low intonation, in accordance with the emotion which we feel into them. This is true of the word "struggle" just cited. Or consider another example. Take the word "blow." Who, in reading this word in "Blow, blow, thou winter wind," would not increase its explosiveness just in order to make its expressiveness correspond to its meaning?

There is, therefore, a fundamental difference in this respect between single word-sounds and single colors or tones; they are not sufficiently impressive in themselves, not sufficiently separable from their meanings, to have anything except the slightest value as mere sounds. In collocation, however, and quite apart from rhythm and alliteration, this minute expressiveness may add up to a considerable amount. In Matthew Arnold's lines,

Swept by confused alarms of struggle and flight
Where ignorant armies crash by night,

the hardness and difficulty of the consonants in their cumulative force become an independent element of expressiveness, strengthening that of the meaning of the words. Or in Tennyson's oft-quoted line, "the murmuring of innumerable bees," the sounds taken together have a genuine imitative effect, in which something of the drowsy feeling of the hive is present.

Following the general law of harmony between form and content, the beauty of sound should be functional; that is, it should never be developed for its own sake alone, but also to intensify, through re-expression, the mood of the thoughts. The sound-values are too lacking in independence to be purely ornamental. Poetry does indeed permit of embellishment–the pleasurable elaboration of sensation–yet should never degenerate into a mere tintinnabulation of sounds. The rimes in binding words should bind thoughts also; the tonalities or contrasts of vowel and consonant should echo harmonies or strains in pervasive moods.

It is by rhythm, however, that the chief expressiveness of the mere medium is imparted to verse. But here again we shall find sound and meaning intertwined–a rhythm in thought governing a rhythm in sound.

Only as a result of recent investigations can a satisfactory theory of modern verse be constructed. The making of this theory has been largely hampered, on the one hand, by the application of the quantitative principles of classical verse to our poetry; and, on the other hand, by forcing the analogy between music and verse. The insufficiency of the quantitative scheme for English verse is not difficult to perceive. Such a scheme presupposes that syllables have a fixed quantity of duration, as either long or short, and that rhythm consists in the regularity of their distribution. But, although there are differences in the duration of syllables, some being longer than others, there are no fixed rules to determine whether a syllable is short or long; and, what is a more serious objection, it is impossible to find any regularity in the occurrence of shorts and longs in normal English verse,–in all verse that has not been written with the explicit purpose of imitating the Greek or Latin. An examination of any line of verse will verify these statements. Take, for example, the first three lines of Shakespeare's song,

low, blow, thou winter wind,

Thou art not so unkind

As man's ingratitude.

Here the quantitative scansion is perhaps as follows:

- - - - *U* -

- - *U x U* -

U - *U* - *U* -

I have given the word "so" a double scansion because I conceive it impossible to determine whether it is really long or short. At any rate, there is certainly no regularity in the distribution of shorts and longs, except in the last of the three lines, and no correspondence, except in that line, between the quantitative scansion and the rhythmical movement of the verses. And whenever such a correspondence exists, it is due either to the fact that the incidence of stress tends to lengthen a syllable or to the fact that, oftentimes, in polysyllabic words, mere length will produce a stress. This is the modicum of truth in the quantitative view. But obviously stress governs, quantity obeys.

Although the quantitative theory of modern verse has been pretty generally abandoned, it cannot be said that the ordinary view which regards the foot as the unit of verse and its rhythm as determined by a regular distribution of accented and unaccented syllables, is in a much better case. For in the first place, by accent is usually meant word-accent; but monosyllabic words have no word-accent; hence, in a succession of such syllables, the accent must be determined by some other factor; and, granting this, there is the further fact to be reckoned with, that poetic accent is relative–the supposedly unaccented syllable is often very highly accented, more highly in fact than some of the so-called accented ones. Consider, for example, the line, "From sullen earth sings hymns at heaven's gate," where the word "sings," which in accordance with the conventional iambic scansion would be an unaccented syllable, is really strongly accented, more strongly, indeed, than "earth" which has an accent. As for the division of the line into feet, that is a pure artifice: who, in the actual reading of the above line, would divide the words "sullen" and "heaven" into two parts?

The basis of rhythm is, therefore, not word-accent. Value stress is the basis. Certain words, because of their logical or emotional importance, have a greater claim upon the attention, and this inner stress finds outward expression in an increased loudness, duration, and explosiveness of sound. Stress coincides with the word-accent of polysyllabic words because the accent is placed on those syllables, usually the root-syllables, which carry the essential meaning. And this stress is not simply present or absent in a syllable, but greater in some than in others; in iambic rhythm, usually greater in the even than in the preceding odd syllable; in trochaic, greater in the odd than in the immediately preceding even one. The rhythm is rather an undulation of stresses than an alternation of stress and lack of stress, something, therefore, far more complex and variegated than the old scheme would imply. And of this undulation, not the foot, but the line is the unit. The character of the undulation of the whole line determines the type of the rhythm, which may be very different in the case of lines of precisely the same kind of "feet." For example, the line quoted above, "From sullen earth sings hymns at heaven's gate," has a distinctly different rhythm from such another iambic line as "Shall I compare thee to a summer's day?" This difference is due, in part at least, to the fact that the highest peaks of the wave in the former are in the center of the line, in "sings" and "hymns," while in the latter they are at the end, in "summer's" and "day." This undulation of stress is present in prose and in ordinary speech; for there also there is a rise and fall of stress corresponding to the varying values of the words and syllables; but in prose, the undulation is irregular, while in poetry, it is regularized.

From the foregoing it is clear that rhythm does not exist in the mere sound of the words alone, but in the thought back of them as well. The sounds, as such, have no rhythm in themselves; they acquire rhythm through the subjective processes of significant utterance or listening. The rhythm is primarily in these activities, and from them is transferred to the sounds in which they are embodied. This comes out with additional force when we go farther into the analysis of the rhythm of verse. We have just seen that the line is one unit of the rhythm (this is true even when there are run-over lines, because we make a slight pause after the ends of such lines too); but within the line itself there are sub-units. These sub-units are units of thought. Every piece of written or spoken language is a continuous flow of thought. But the movement is not perfectly fluid; for it is broken up into elementary pulses of ideas, following discontinuously upon each other. In prose the succession of pulses is complex and irregular, without any obvious pattern; but in poetry the movement is simple and regular and the pattern is clear. Just as in poetry there is a rhythm of stress which represents a regularizing of the natural undulations in the stress of speech, so there is also a more deep-lying rhythm, which arises through a simplification and regularizing of the movement of thought-pulsations. The fundamental rhythm consists in an alternation of subject-group and predicate-group.

This duality, although always retained as basal, may, however, be broken up into a three- or four-part movement whenever the connecting links between the subject-idea and the predicate-idea acquire sufficient importance, or whenever the one or the other of the two becomes sufficiently complex to consist of lesser parts. For example, in Shakespeare's thirty-first sonnet, the thought-divisions are three for each of the following lines:

Thy bosom | is endeared | with all hearts
Which I by lacking | have supposed | dead;
And there | reigns love, | and all love's loving parts,
And all those friends | which I thought | buried.

These divisions are marked by pauses or casuras.

Here, then, in the regularizing of the number of thought-pulsations, we have another type of rhythm in poetry, and a rhythm which, coming from within, finds outward expression in sound. Cutting across the rhythm of stress, it breaks up the latter with its pauses, and imparts to the whole movement variety and richness.

But speech has not only its natural rhythm of stress-undulation and thought-pulsations; it has also, as we saw in the last chapter, a melody. The rise and fall of stress goes hand and hand with a rise and fall of pitch. The different forms of discourse, and the different emotions that accompany them, are each expressed with characteristic variations in pitch. Accepting Wundt's summary of the facts, we find that, generally speaking, in the declarative statement and the command, the pitch rises in the first thought-division, to fall in the second; while in the question and the condition, the pitch rises and falls in the first, and then rises again in the second. Doubt, expectation, tension, excitement–all the forward looking moods of incompleteness–tend to find expression in a rising melody; while assurance, repose, relaxation, fulfillment, are embodied in a falling melody. The high tones are dynamic and stimulating; the low tones, static and peaceful. Now in ordinary speech and prose, the change from one tone to another is constant and irregular, following the variation of mood in the substance of the discourse. How is it with verse? There is a simplification and tonality–identity in tone–which is absent from prose. The melody is more obvious and distinctive, because there is a greater simplicity in sentence structure and a higher unity of mood. Yet there is no absolute regularity; and the amount of it differs with the different kinds of poetry: there is more in the simple lyric than in the complex narrative; more, for example, in Shakespeare's sonnets than in his dramas. The inexpressible beauty of some lines of verse comes doubtless from a fugitive melody which we now grasp, now lose.

The existence of speech melody and the tonalities of rime, assonance, and alliteration suggest an analogy between verse and music. For some people, this analogy is decisive. Yet the fundamental difference between music and verse must be insisted on with equal force; the purity of tone and fixity of intervals between tones, which is distinctive of music, is absent from verse. In comparison with music, the melodiousness of verse is confused and chaotic; and this condemns to failure any attempt to identify the laws of the two arts. Still, we are not yet at the end of the analogy. Those who interpret verse in terms of music believe that, underlying or supplanting the rhythm of stress, there is another rhythm, similar to time in music, and capable of expression in musical language. There is, it is claimed, an equality of duration between one line and another, and between one foot in a line and another; these larger and lesser stretches of duration being divided up between syllables and pauses, each syllable and pause occupying a fixed quantity of time; just as in music each bar is divided up between notes and rests of definite value. Lanier, for example writes the first line of Poe's "Raven" as follows:

Once up | on a | mid-night | drear-y;

Fascinating as this procedure is, it is nevertheless a distortion of the facts. Poetry is meant to be read, not to be sung; when it is put to music and sung, it acquires a character which otherwise does not belong to it. We must not be misled by the historical connection between verse and song, nor by the frequency with which some verses are set to music. Our poetry must be understood as we experience it to-day, not as it was experienced in its origins. And there is surely much poetry which no one wants to sing. No one wants to sing a sonnet or Miltonic blank verse. The attempt to apply musical notation to verse is a *tour de force.* Careful observation and experience show that the syllables in verse have no fixed duration values, and that there is no constant ratio between them.

Nevertheless, musical time is not wholly absent from verse. You cannot set it to the metronome or express it in musical notation, yet it is there. When lines have the same number of syllables, the time required to read them is approximately the same, and we tend to make the duration of the thought-divisions equal. Our time-sense is so fallible, we do not notice the departures from exactness; and when the durations of processes are nearly equal and the values which we attach to them are equal, then we are conscious of them as equal. Attention-value and time-value are subjectively equivalent. Words which weigh with us give us pause, and we reckon in the time of the pause to make up for a deficiency in the time required to read or utter the syllables. And so time-rhythm enters as still another factor in the complex rhythm of verse.

The importance of this rhythm differs, however, with the different kinds of verse. In lyric poetry closely allied to song, it is clear and strong; while in the more reflective and dramatic poetry, it is only an undertone. In some cases, as in the nursery rime,

Hot cross buns, hot cross buns,
If your daughters don't like 'em,
Give 'em to your sons.
One a penny, two a penny,
Hot cross buns,

there is almost no rhythm of stress, but there is a rhythm of time; for despite the inequality in the number of syllables, each line has approximately the same duration, even the last line with its three monosyllabic words being lengthened out into equality with the others. The variety in the rhythm is secured through the unequal number of syllables in the same stretch of duration, the more rapid movement of many syllables being set off over against the slower movement of the few. Similarly, Tennyson's poem, which should be scanned as I shall indicate, has a rhythm which is chiefly musical.

Break, | break, | break,

On thy cold, | grey stones, | O sea!

And I would | that my tongue | might utter

The thoughts | That arise | in me.

The stresses are nearly even throughout; the meter cannot be accurately described as iambic, trochaic, or anapestic; yet there is a rhythm in the approximate temporal equality of the thought-moments. These verses are, however, rather songs than poems. The failure to distinguish between verses which are songs and those which are poems accounts, I believe, for the extremes to which the musical theory of verse has been carried.

Still another element of poetry which allies it to music is the repetition of the thought-content. Why repetition should be musical we already know: music is an art which seeks to draw out and elaborate pure emotion; repetition serves this end by constantly bringing the mind back to dwell upon the same theme. Moreover, repetition involves retardation; for a movement cannot progress rapidly if it has to return upon itself; and this slowness gives time for the full value of a feeling to be worked out. In all the more emotional and lyric poetry we find, therefore, recurrence of theme: the thought is repeated again and again; in new forms, perhaps, yet still the same in essence, successive lines or stanzas taking up the same burden; sometimes there is exact recurrence of thought, as in the refrain. And this repetition in the thought is embodied in a repetition of the elements of the sound-pattern; the wave type is repeated from verse to verse or recurs again and again; there is recurrence of melodic form or parallelism between contrasted melodies in different stanzas; there is tonality of vowel and consonant sounds in rime and assonance and alliteration; there may be an approach to identity in the time-duration of the various units. Parallelism or repetition is the fundamental scheme of such poetry. But between repetition with its retardation of movement and progress towards a goal there is a necessary antagonism; hence in the more dramatic and narrative forms of poetry, although recurrence is never entirely absent, there is less of it, and the movement approximates to that of prose. Emotion demands repetition, but action demands progression.

After our analysis of the rhythm of poetry, we are in a position to inquire into what can be expressed through it, and how psychologically this expression can be explained.

The expressiveness of rhythm is like that of music, vague and objectless, for which reason rhythm is properly called the music of verse. Almost everything in a general way which we have said about the expressiveness of music applies to poetic rhythm. This expressiveness cannot be translated into words with any exactness; the most that can be done is to find a set of words into which it will roughly fit, leaving much vacant space of meaning. That the emotional values of rhythms have character is, however, proved by the fact that some rhythms are better vehicles for certain kinds of thought than others are. Yet it often happens that, just as, in song or opera, the same melody is used to express joy or grief, love or religious emotion, so approximately the same rhythmic form is employed in the expression of apparently antagonistic emotions. Nevertheless, this fact is not fatal to expression; for, in the first place, there is much variety of rhythm within a given metrical form, so that what superficially may seem to be the same rhythm is really a different one; and, in the second place, as we have already observed in the case of music, there is much–in form and energy of movement–which contrasting emotions have in common, and this may be expressed in the rhythmic type. Think of the wide sweep of emotions which have been expressed in the sonnet form! Yet consider what varieties of rhythm and speech melodies are possible within this form, and how, nevertheless, there is an identity of character in all sonnets–how they are all thoughtful, all restrained, yet unfaltering in their movement!

Without going into details, which would lie beyond the scope of general sthetics, it is possible to state the following broad facts (compare the similar facts relating to melody) with reference to poetic rhythms: a rising rhythm expresses striving or restlessness; a falling rhythm, quiet, steadfastness. There is, however, no absolute contrast between the two kinds, because a falling rhythm is still a rhythm, and that means a movement which necessarily contains something of instability and unrest. The contrast is sharpest in the anapestic and dactylic, less sharp in the trochaic and iambic. Many a trochaic rhythm becomes in effect iambic when the division of the thought moments and the distribution of the pauses make the rhythm rise after the first few words; and conversely, many an iambic rhythm becomes trochaic through a similar shift in the attention. Within a single line, therefore, there may be both rising and falling pulsations. Much of the rare beauty of poetry comes from such subtle combinations of rhythmic qualities.

Through time and tempo also, poetic rhythm is expressive, much after the manner of music; by these means too, in addition to the mode of stress-undulation, it imitates the temporal and dynamic course of action and emotion, and so tends to arouse congruous types of feeling in the mind; it is swift or slow, gliding or abrupt, retarded or accelerated. Compare the slow and retarded rhythm of "When I have fears that I may cease to be," so well adapted to express the gravity of the thought, with the rapid and accelerated movement of "Hail to thee, blithe spirit!" so full of a quick joyousness. Or compare the light legato movement of "Bird of the wilderness, blithesome and cumberless," with the heavy staccato movement of "Waste endless and boundless and flowerless."

Yet, for all its expressiveness, the music of verse can never stand alone. It is too bare and tenuous by itself to win and keep the attention or to evoke much feeling. It does not possess the purity of color, the loudness, force, or volume of sound that belong to music and make music, almost alone of the arts, capable of existing as mere form. The rhythm of poetry, derived very largely from a rhythm of thought, has need of thought for significance. The thought and the music are one. For this reason poetry is better, I think, when read to oneself than when read aloud; for then the sound and the sense are more intimate; the attention is not drawn off to the former away from the latter. Moreover, try as he will, the poet can never make his word-sounds fully harmonious; some roughness and dissonance will remain; but in silent reading these qualities disappear. However, although by itself of small significance, the musical element in verse makes all the difference between poetry and prose. Through its own vague expressiveness it fortifies the emotional meaning of the poetic language, and, at the same time, sublimates it by scattering it in the medium. And finally it imparts an intimacy, a personal flavor, which also allies poetry with music; for the substance of rhythm is the movement of our own inner processes; the rhythm of thoughts and sounds is a rhythm in our own listening and attending, our own thinking and feeling; the emotional values spring from us as well as from the subject-matter. Hence even narrative and dramatic poetry have a lyrical tone; we ourselves are implicated in the actions and events portrayed.

The demands made by the form of poetry upon its substance are similar to those made by music upon the words in a song, only less stringent. The content must be emotional and significant; it cannot be trite and cold. The meaning of words would permit the poet to bring before the mind all possible objects, events, and ideas, but the music of words would be incongruous with most of them. Events narrated must be stirring, thoughts uttered must be emotionally toned, things described must be related to human life and action. Poetry may desert the royal themes of long ago—*arma virumque cano, maenin aeide thea*—and relate the lowly life of common folk, even the sordid life of the poor and miserable, but when doing so throws over it the musical glamour of verse and arouses the heat of sympathy and passion.

Although, since it makes use of words, poetry should always have a meaning, it need not have the definiteness of meaning of logical thought; it may suggest rather than explicate; its music is compatible with vagueness. But vagueness is not obscurity; the poet should always make us feel that we understand him; he should not seek to mystify us, or keep us guessing at his meaning. Yet, since the poet operates with words and not with mere sounds, great subtlety and precision of thought are possible in poetry, although not argument and dialectic. Poetry may express the results of reflection, so far as they are of high emotional value, but cannot well reproduce its processes; the steps of analysis and inference are too cold and hard for the muse to climb.

On the other hand, poetry does not permit of the development and iteration of pure feeling which we find in music; for poetic rhythms and melodies lack the variety and fluency of the musical. Yet poetry is capable, where music is not, of expressing brief, quick outbursts of feeling; for a few words, by referring to the causes and conditions of feeling, may adequately express what music needs time and many tones to convey. Poetry wins beauty by concentration, whereas music gains by expansion. There is also a similar relation between prose and poetry in this respect; the severity of the form imposes upon poetry a simplicity which contrasts with the breadth and complexity of prose. As Schopenhauer remarked, every good poem is short; long poems always contain stretches either of unmusical verse or unpoetic music. Yet, in comparison with prose, the tempo of music is slow; we have to linger in the medium in order that its rhythmic and tonal beauties may impress us, and this slowness of movement is imparted to the thought; even narrative and dramatic poetry suffer retardation; for which reason the poetic form must be abandoned if great rapidity of expression is sought.

From our study of the materials and forms of its expression, it becomes clear how the subject-matter of poetry is the inner life of mood and striving and passionate human action. Emotions may be poured forth in words, and, by means of words, actions may be described. But neither passion nor action appear in poetry as they are lived and enacted; for the poet, working in a medium of words, has to translate them into thoughts. Words cannot embody the real experiences which they express; experience is fleeting and falls away from the words, which retain only an echo of what they mean. Only what can be relived in memory can be contained in a word, and not even all of that; for a word is not a mere embodiment of an experience, but a communication also, and only its public and universal content can pass from a speaker to a hearer. Now, this socialized content of a word is a thought. Even passion the most spontaneous and lyrical has to be translated into thought,–not the abstract thought of scientific expression, but the emotionally toned thought of art, thought which, while condensing experience, still keeps its values. Emotional thought is the substance of poetry. However, albeit an image of the inner life, poetry does not volatilize it into pure feeling as music does, but distinguishes its objects and assigns its causes. Poetry is concrete and articulate where music is abstract and blind. Since words, through their meanings and associated images, can express things as well as man's reactions to them, poetry can also reflect the natural environment of life, its habitat and seat. And yet, because the poet has to translate things into ideas, nature never appears in poetry as it is in itself, but as it is implicated in mind. For the poet, sea and sky, the woods and plains and rivers, birds and flowers, are the symbols of human destiny or the loci of human action. Emotion overflows into nature, but this involves the taking up of nature into man. Not nature, but man's thoughtful life is the poet's theme.

If the foregoing statement is correct, emotional thought rather than imagery is the substance of poetry. For poetry, as music with a meaning, can be quite free of definite images. The thought formulates a mood and finds a sensuous embodiment in musical language, and that suffices for beauty. And yet in poetry, as has been observed, thought tends to descend into imagery. By being connected with a sensuous material, a thought acquires a firmer support for feeling than it could possess of itself as a mere concept. Especially effective is the descent to the lower senses; for they are closest to the roots of emotion. Let me recall again the Shakespearean lyric which I have quoted before in a similar connection, omitting the last lines of each stanza:

Blow, blow, thou winter wind,
Thou art not so unkind
As man's ingratitude;
Why tooth is not so keen
Because thou art not seen,
Although thy breath be rude.
Freeze, freeze, thou bitter sky,
Thou dost not bite so nigh
As benefits forgot;
Though thou the waters warp,
Thy sting is not so sharp
As friend remembered not.

Here are images of cold–winter, freeze; of touch–blow, breath; of pain–tooth, bite, sting, sharp; of taste–bitter. How vividly they convey the ache of desolation! Only in words which are imaginative as well as musical are the full resources of verbal expression employed.

All the various forms of metaphorical language have the same purpose: by substituting for a more abstract, conceptual mode of expression a more sensuous and imaginative one, to vivify the emotional quality of the situation. When Keats sings,

... on the shore Of the wide world I stand and think Till Love and Fame to nothingness do sink,

he has in mind to convey to us that renunciation of merely personal ambitions which comes to us when we "survey all time and all existence." And how does he do it?

By evoking the image of the wide stretch of the shore of the sea, which, making us feel our nothingness as we stand and look out upon it, has the same effect, only more poignant. Of the world we have no image–not so, of the shore of the world; and toward what we cannot imagine we cannot easily feel. Oftentimes the metaphor is latent, a mere adjective undeveloped in its implications, as in "bitter" sky; yet the purpose is the same. Incidentally the poet unifies our world for us through his metaphors; not as the scientist does by pointing out causal and class relations, but by exhibiting the emotional affinities of things. He increases the value of single things by giving them the values of other things. Every metaphor should serve this purpose of emotional expression and unification, should be part of an emotional thought; otherwise it is a mere *tour de force* of cleverness, unrelated to the poetic interest and intrinsically absurd,–the world has no shore and the wind is not bitter; feeling alone can justify such comparisons. Moreover, too many metaphors, or metaphors too elaborately developed, by scattering the attention, or by drawing it away from the meaning of which the image should be a part, have the effect of no image at all. The poetry of Francis Thompson, for example, loses rather than gains vitality through its imaginative exuberance. We object to decadent poets, not because they are sensuous, but because they lack feeling; with them sensation, instead of supporting emotion, supplants it. Such poets seek to atone for their want of vigorous feeling by stimulating our eyes and ears.

If, as I believe, emotional thought rather than imagery is the essence of poetry, then the modern school of imagists and their French forbears among the "Parnassiens" are mistaken. Their effort comes in the end to a revival of the old thesis *ut pictura poesis*, the attempt to make poetry a vision of nature rather than an expression of the inner life. They would lead poetry away from the subjectivity of emotion into the outer object world. Now, it is indeed possible for the poet to represent nature through the images which words evoke in the mind, and these images may have significance for feeling. Their very evocation in musical language is bound to lend them some warmth of mood. Yet–as Lessing showed in his *Laocoon*, despite all the crabbed narrowness of his treatment–it is hopeless for the poet to enter into rivalry with the painter or sculptor. The colors and forms of things which the poet paints for the eye of the mind are mere shadows in comparison with those which we really see.[Footnote: The best the poet-painter can do is to express his memories of the outer world; but apart from some vivid emotion, memories are unsatisfactory in comparison with realities.] We admire the marvelous workmanship of such verses as the following of Gautier, but they leave us cold; even the melody of the language is incapable of making them warm. How poor they are beside a painting!

Les femmes passent sous les arbres
En martre, hermine et menu-vair
Et les deesses, frileux marbres,
Ont pris aussi l'abit d'hiver.
La Venus Anadyomene
Est en pelisse a capuchon:
Flore, que la brise malmene,
Plonge ses mains dans son manchon.
Et pour la saison, les bergeres
De Coysevox et de Coustou,
Trouvant leures echarpes legeres
Ont des boas autour du cou.

Of course, poetic pictures can be painted–Gautier has painted them–but the standard for each art is set by what it can do uniquely well. If the poet works in the domain of the painter, we tend to judge him by the alien standards of another art, where he is bound to fall short; while if he works within his own province, we judge him by his own autonomous laws, under which he can achieve perfection.

Oftentimes, confessing the inability of the image to stand alone, these poets make it into a symbol of some mood or emotional thought. Yet the image remains the chief object of the poet's care; it was clearly the first thing in his mind; the interpretation is an afterthought. The poem therefore falls into two parts–a picture and an interpretation, with little organic relation between them.

Finally, the effort to detach poetry from the inner world and make it an expression of outer things, is incompatible with its musical character. For music is essentially subjective, an expression of pure mood unaffixed to objects. As rhythmical, poetry shares the inwardness of music; wherefore, unless its rhythm is to be a mere functionless, ornamental dress, whatever it expresses should have its source in the inner man. Of course, through their meanings, word-sounds indicate the causes and objects of emotion–and this differentiates music from poetry–but in poetry the emotion is still the primary thing, springing from inner strivings, and not from objects, as in painting and sculpture. It is therefore no accident that the contemporary imagists tend to abandon the forms of verse; their poetry has little or no regular rhythm; it approximates to prose. For in proportion as poetry becomes free, it ceases to be tied to musical expressiveness, and may become objective, without prejudice to its own nature. Prose poetry, and prose too, of course, may be highly emotional and subjective, for words can express emotions directly without any rhythmical ordering; yet prose need not be subjective, as poetry must be. There is no absolute difference between prose and poetry; for even prose has its rhythm and its euphony, its expressiveness of the medium; yet in prose the rhythm is irregular and accidental and the expressiveness of the medium incomplete, while in poetry the rhythm is regular and pervasive and ideally every sound-element, as mere sound, is musical. But this more complete musical expressiveness of the medium restricts poetry to a more inward world.

By abandoning the strict forms and restraints of regular rhythms, the writers of free verse think to gain spontaneity and something of the amplitude of prose; yet it is doubtful whether they gain as much as they lose. For, in the hands of the skillful poet, the form, having become second nature, ceases to be a bond; and the expression, by taking on regularity of rhythm, acquires a concentration and mnemonic value which free verse cannot achieve. In comparison with free verbal expressions, verse forms are, indeed, artifices; yet they are not artificial, in the bad sense of functionless, for they possess irreplaceable values. Nevertheless, it would be strange if they were not from time to time abandoned, the poet reverting to the freedom of ordinary speech; just as now and then, in civilized communities, we find vigorous and sincere men who tire of culture and take to the woods.

The triplicity of the word, as sound, image, meaning, provides a certain justification for the variety of tastes in poetry, and accounts for the difficulty of setting up a single universal standard. There is an unstable equilibrium between the three aspects of words; hence poetry tends to become predominantly music or painting or thought, yet can never succeed in becoming completely any one of these. And it is inevitable that some people should be more sensitive to one rather than to another of the aspects of words, preferring therefore the more musical, or the more thoughtful, or the more pictorial poetry. And so we have poems that would be music, and others that would be pictures, and still others that would be epigrams. And each kind has a certain right and beauty; but no kind has the unique beauty that is poetical. We do not ask their makers not to produce them, nor do we condemn the pleasures which they afford us, but we cannot commend them without reservation. For the best poems achieve a synthesis of the elements of words,–they are at once musical and imaginative and thoughtful. Yet with difficulty; for there is an antagonism among the elements: when the music is insistent, the thought is obscured; when the images are elaborate, their meaning is lost to sight; when the thought is subtle or profound, it rejects the image and is careless of sound. Swinburne's poetry is full of philosophy, but is so sensuous and musical that we miss its thoughts; Browning is too subtle a thinker to be a musician. The complexity of poetry is the source of its strength, lending it something of the inwardness of music and the plasticity of the pictorial arts; but is also the source of its weakness. Seldom does it achieve the technical purity and perfection of music and painting and sculpture. Music has a clear and simple medium, painting and sculpture work with colors and forms which almost are what they represent; but word-sounds are not what they mean, and what they mean is not precisely the same as the images which they evoke; too often the correspondence is factitious and artificial, rarely is there fusion. Yet, as I have tried to show, when meaning is made central, sound may fit it closely, and when the meaning is emotional, the music of sound may echo its cry, and the image, instead of rebelling, may serve. Emotional thought is the essence of poetry and the link between its music and its pictures.

Of the different modes of poetry, the lyric has rightly seemed the most typical. Being an expression of a single, simple mood, its subject-matter is most closely akin to the musical expressiveness of the rhythm and euphony of the medium. When, moreover, the mood is a common one, there occurs that identification of self with the passion expressed characteristic of music: the utterance becomes ours as well as the poet's; the "I" of the poem is the "I" who read. This is especially true when the setting and causes of the emotion are without name or place or date; the poem then shares the timelessness and universality of music. In such a lyric there is complete symmetry in the relation between speaker and hearer; the poet unburdens his heart to us, and we in receiving his message tell it back to him. When, on the other hand, in explaining his feelings, the poet relates them to events and persons which have been no part of our experience, this symmetry is lost; we no longer utter the poem ourselves, but merely hear the poet speak. Such poetry is already approaching the dramatic; for although still the expression of the poet's life, it is no longer an expression of the reader's life, and the poet also, as he lives past his experience, must come at length to view it as if it were another's.

And yet, paradoxical as it may sound, dramatic poetry is dramatic in proportion as it is lyrical–that is, according to the degree to which the poet has made the life of others his own. Dramatic poetry, when truly poetic, is a series of lyrics of the less universal type. In another respect, however, dramatic poetry is essentially different from the lyrical. For, in dramatic poetry, each utterance is a response or invitation to another utterance, while in lyric poetry, utterance is complete in itself. The one is social, the other personal: in the appreciation of the lyric, the reader is just himself; in the appreciation of dramatic poetry, he is a whole society, becoming now this man and now that. The unity of the one is the unity of a single mood; the unity of the other is the interaction of the dramatis person as it works itself out in the mind of the reader. And this difference, as we have seen, is imaged in the form. Being self-contained, the lyric is a harmonious whole, in which the parts may be repeated for emphasis; looking backward and forward, the dramatic utterance is a progressive and incomplete whole, which cannot stay for iteration. Lyric poetry is like a communication from friend to friend, intimate and meditative; dramatic poetry is like a passionate conversation which one overhears.

The life portrayed in the epic poem is even less direct than that which is portrayed in the drama; for there the poet does not impersonate the agents in the story, but describes them. His description is the first thing which we get; we get the action only indirectly through that. Hence the story-teller himself–his manner of telling, his reactions to what he tells, his sympathy, humor, and intelligence–are part of what he expresses. He himself is partly theme. No matter how hard he may try to do so, he cannot exclude himself; through his choice of words, through his illustrations, through his style, "which is the man," he will reveal himself. We inevitably apprehend, not merely his thoughts, but him thinking. In the epic form of poetry, the poet has, moreover, an opportunity for a more direct mode of self-revelation, an opportunity for comment and judgment upon the life which he portrays. And this we should accept, not in a spirit of controversy or criticism, but with sympathy, as a part of the total aesthetic expression, striving to get, not only the poet's story, but his point of view regarding it as well.

This duality in the life of the epic involves a two-foldness in its time. In both lyric and dramatic poetry, life moves before us as a single stream actual in the present; but in the epic there is the time of the story-teller, which is present, and the time of the events that he relates, which is past. And being past, these events appear as it were at a distance, at arms' length and remote; they lack the vivid reality of things present. Moreover, since the past is finished, unlike the present which is ever moving and creating itself anew, the epic, in comparison with the drama, comes to us with its parts as it were coexisting and complete, more after the manner of space than of time. And just as a spatial thing allows us to survey its parts by turn, since they are all there before we look; so, in reading an epic, we feel that we can proceed at our leisure and, despite the causal relation, take the incidents in any order. It is not so in the drama, where events move rapidly and make themselves in a determined sequence. This is what Goethe meant when he said that substantiality was the category of the epic, causality of the drama, although, of course, this distinction is not absolute.

Finally, the fact that the epic poet tells rather than impersonates his story, enables him to enlarge its scope; for by means of descriptions he can introduce nature as one of the persons of the action. He can show the molding influence of nature upon man, and how man, in turn, interacts not only with his fellows, but with his environment. Fate, in the sense of the non-human determinants of man's career, can show its hand. In the *Odyssey*, for example, shipwreck and the interference of the gods are factors as decisive as Odysseus' courage and cunning. By contrast, in lyric poetry, nature is merely a reflection of moods; in dramatic poetry, it is simply the passive, causally ineffective stage for a social experience wholly determined by human agents. This distinction is, however, not absolute. In *Brand*, for example, through the stage directions and the utterance of the persons, we are indirectly made aware of the control exerted by the physical background of the action; in the Greek drama we learn this from the Chorus and the Prologue.

Chapter X

Prose Literature

There is an almost universal feeling, expressed in many common phrases, that prose literature is not one of the fine arts. The reason is this: in prose literature there is a conspicuous absence of beauty of form and sensation, of the decorative, in comparison with the other arts. The vague expressiveness and charm of the medium, the musical aspect, is largely lacking. Not wholly lacking, of course, as a multitude of beautiful passages testify; yet, in general, it remains true that, in prose, the medium tends to be transparent, sacrificing itself in order that nothing may stand between what it reveals to thought and the imagination. It fulfills its function when the words are not unpleasant to the ear, and when their flow, adapting itself to the span and pulsation of the attention, is so smooth as to become unnoticeable, like the movement of a ship on a calm sea,—when it is a means to an end, not an end in itself.

Prose literature is, therefore, incompletely beautiful. The full meaning and value of the aesthetic are not to be found there, but rather in poetry, painting, sculpture, music, architecture. Yet prose literature remains art, if incomplete art—a free, personal expression of life, for the sake of contemplation. As free, it differs from verbal expression in the service of practical ends, and as personal, it cannot be classed with science. Throughout the long course of its history, it has tended to become now the one, now the other of these—and its lack of the decorative element has done much to make this possible–but its power to outlast the moral and political issues which it has so often sought to direct, and its well-merited rejection by sociologists and psychologists as anything more than material for their work, are sufficient evidence and warning of where it properly belongs,–among the arts. The sacrifice of the musical element in the medium does not have to be justified on practical grounds as making for efficiency, or on scientific grounds as favoring analysis, but may be understood from the artistic standpoint. For it was only through a method and medium that renounced the musical manner of poetry, with its vaguely expressive, yet rigid forms, that the fullness and minuteness of life could be represented.

Even the more fluently musical manner of poetical prose is unsuited as a medium for the expression of the kind of life which is represented in normal prose. Poetical prose is appropriate for the expression of deeds and sentiments of high and mystical import only, but not for the expression of the more commonplace or definitely and complexly articulated phases of life. For the latter, the broader and freer and more literal method of strict prose is the only appropriate medium of expression. The unmusical character of prose style is not determined by weakness, but by adaptation to function.

And, although the medium of prose is attenuated almost to the vanishing point, where it may seem to be lost, it may nevertheless borrow from its content a beauty of rhythm, imagery, and form that will seem to be its very own. For in language, as we observed in our discussion of poetry, the meaning and the symbol are so closely one, that it becomes impossible, except by analysis, to distinguish them. Prose rhythm is fundamentally a rhythmical movement of ideas, like poetic rhythm, only without regularization; yet, since the ideas are carried by the words, it belongs to them also; images blossom from ideas, yet they too seem to belong to the words in which they are incarnated; and the harmony and symmetry which thoughts and images may contain as we compose them synthetically in the memory, make an architecture of words.

The transparent medium of prose shares the beauty of its content, just as a perfect glass partakes of the color of the light which it transmits.

The psychologic roots of prose literature are the impulses to self- revelation and to acquaintance with life. Every thing that has once entered into our lives, no matter how intimate, craves to come out; the instinct of gregariousness extends, as we have noted, to the whole of the mind. The completely private and uncommunicated makes us as uncertain and afraid of ourselves as physical loneliness. But in addition to the dislike for any form of isolation, even when purely spiritual, there is another factor which determines self-revelation,–the desire for praise. We want a larger audience for our exploits than the people immediately involved in them, so we tell them to any listening ear. The friend whispering his confession illustrates the one motive; the hero bragging of his deeds illustrates the other.

The desire to hear another's story is the obverse of the desire to tell one about oneself, just as the impulse to welcome a friend is the complement of his impulse to seek our companionship; we receive from him exactly what he takes from us,–an enlargement of our social world, the creation of another social bond. If we cannot hear his story from his own lips, we want to hear it from some third person, who will surely be glad to relate it, since he, as bearer of the news, will bring to himself something of the glory of the hero. There is malice enough in gossip, but most of it is the purest kind of mental and emotional satisfaction. Our interest in it is of exactly the same kind as our interest in novels and romances. The stories which we tell about ourselves and our friends make up the ephemeral, yet real prose literature of daily life.

Most stories probably had their origin in more or less literal transcriptions from real life. History is the basis of literature. However, as stories are passed from one person to another, fiction encroaches upon fact. Details are forgotten and have to be filled out from the imagination; then a sheer delight in invention enters in; it is so interesting to see if you can make a world as good as the real one, or even outdo it in strangeness and wonder, provided, of course, you can still get yourself believed. Even in the relation of real events, creation inevitably plays a part; the whole of any story is not worth telling; there must be selection, emphasis upon the most striking particulars, and synthesis.

Besides the opportunity which it gives of unhampered control over the story, fiction has still other advantages. The interest which we take in tales of real life is bound up with personal appeals. This is most racy in gossip, but something of the kind lingers in all narratives of fact. Literature can become disinterested and universal in its appeal only when, keeping the semblance of life, it becomes a work of pure imagination. It is then, as Aristotle said, more philosophical, that is, more universal and typical, than history.

Another advantage of fiction as compared with history is its completeness. The knowledge which we possess of the lives of others is the veriest fragment. We know, of course, our own lives best; but even of these, unless we are at the end of our years, we do not know the outcome. We know next well the life of an intimate–wife, child, sweetheart, friend–yet not all of that; there is much he will not tell us and much else which we cannot observe; for even he dwells with us for a brief time only, and then is gone. Of other people, we can know still less; we can observe something, we can get more from hearsay; but that is a chaos of impressions; the larger part is inference and construction, a work of the imagination, which may or may not be true. Even the biography, carefully made from all available data in the way of personal recollections, letters, and diaries, although it may approach to wholeness, remains, nevertheless, very largely a construction, a work of literary fiction. The autobiography comes still closer; yet, since it is designed for a public which cannot be expected to view it in a solidly detached fashion, it suffers from the reticence which inevitably intrudes to suppress. In fiction alone, none except artistic motives need intervene to bid silence.

However, although fiction be a purely ideal world of imagined life, it is essentially the same as the real social world. For that world is also imaginary. We have direct experience of our own lives alone; the lives of others can exist for us only in our thought about them. To be sure, our daily contact with the bodies of our friends and associates gives to this thought something of the pungency of self-knowledge; yet in absence, they live for us, as the characters in a novel, only in our thought. And the majority of the people, personally unknown to us, who make up our larger social world–and for most of us this includes the great ones who are such potent factors in determining it–are real to us in the same way that Diana or Esmond are real. All historical figures belong to this world of imagination. Our friends too, as they pass out of our lives or die, and we ourselves eventually, will sink into it.

Our interest in the fictional world of the writer is, moreover, essentially the same as our interest in the real world. Its persons arouse in us the same emotions of admiration, love, or dislike. They satisfy the same need for social stimulation, the same curiosity about life. Just as we have certain instincts and habits of movement that make us restless when they are not satisfied, and afford us a wild joy in walking and running when we are released from confinement, so we have certain instincts and habits of feeling towards persons which demand objects and produce joy when companions are found. An unsatisfied or superabundant sociability lies back of our love of fiction. We read because we are lonely or because our fellow men have become trite and fail to stimulate us sufficiently. If our fellows were not so reticent, if they would talk to us and tell us their stories with the freedom and the brightness of a Stevenson, or if their lives were so fresh and vivid that we never found them dull, perhaps we should not read at all. But, as it is, we can satisfy our craving for knowledge of life only by extending our social world through fiction. Fiction may teach us, edify us, make us better men–it may serve all these purposes incidentally, but its prime purpose as art is to provide us with new objects for social feeling and knowledge.

The interest which we take in fictitious action is also like that which we take in real action. The same emotions of desire for the attainment of a goal, suspense, hope, fear, excitement, curiosity and its satisfaction, joy, despair, are aroused. And we have a need to experience these emotions at high pitch greater than our everyday lives can satisfy. Our lives are seldom adventurous all over; there are monotonous interludes with no melody, offering us little that is new to learn. Our love for war and sport shows that we were not built organically for humdrum. Now literature helps to make up for this deficiency in real life by providing us with adventures in which we can participate imaginatively, and from which we can derive new knowledge. If real life did supply us with all the intense living that we demand, we might not care to read, although the love of adventure grows by feeding, and many an active man revels in tales which simulate his own exploits.

It follows that the novelist should imitate life, yet at the same time raise its pitch. The realists imitate life deliberately, and we measure their worth by their truth, but they select the intense moments. The romancers and weavers of fairy tales, on the other hand, instead of choosing the vivid moments of real life, in order to stimulate the emotions, accomplish the same end by exciting wonder and amazement at the exaggerations and unheard-of novelties which they create. Yet even they give us truth, not truth in the sense of fact, but in the sense of a world which arouses the same elementary emotions, intensified though they be through amazement, as are aroused by fact. It matters not how outlandish their tales so long as they do this. Love stories are so widely interesting because love is the one very vivid emotion in most people's lives, although there are other experiences–warfare, the pursuit of great aims, the clash of purposes and beliefs, the growth of souls–equally intense. Dante's three themes, Venus,

Salus, Virtus, broadly interpreted, cover the range of literary subjects.

Of course, since we secure no personal triumphs in reading, and every one wishes to play his own part successfully in real life, literature cannot become a substitute for life, except with the artist who triumphs in making his story. Nevertheless, as Henry James says, fiction may and should compete with life, and this it can do by giving us the feelings aroused by action without imposing upon us the responsibilities and the fateful results of action itself; there we can learn new things about life without incurring the risks of participation in it. We can play the part of the adventurer without being involved in any blame; we can fall in love with the heroine without any subsequential entanglements; we can be a hero without suffering the penalties of heroism; we can travel into foreign lands without deserting our business or emptying our purses. Hence, although no one would exchange life for literature, one is better content, having literature, to forego much of life.

The elements of every story are these five: character, incident, nature, fate, and milieu–the social, historical, and intellectual background. Character and incident are capable of some degree of separation, so far as, in novels of adventure, the personalities necessary to carry on the action may be very abstract or elementary, and so far as, in so-called psychological novels, the number of events related may be very small and their interest dependent upon their effect on character; but one without the other is as inconceivable in a story as it is in life itself, and the development of fiction has been steadily in the direction of their interdependence. Aristotle's dictum regarding the superior importance of plot over character applies to the drama only, and because character cannot well be revealed there except through action. The construction of character depends upon the delineation of distinctive and recognizable physical traits, a surprisingly small number sufficing, a mere name being almost enough; upon the definition of the individual's position in a group–his relation to family, townspeople, and other associates–a matter of capital importance; and, finally, information about his more permanent interests and attitudes. This construction is best made piecemeal, the character disclosing itself gradually during the story, as it does in life, and growing under the stress of circumstances. The old idea of fixity of character does not suit our modern notions of growth; we demand that character be created by the story; it should not preexist, as Schopenhauer thought it should, with its nature as determinate and its reactions as predictable as those of a chemical substance. And although in their broad outlines the possibilities of human nature are perhaps fewer in number than the chemical substances, the variations of these types in their varying environments are infinite. To create a poignant uniqueness while preserving the type is the supreme achievement of the writer of fiction. We want as many of the details of character, and no more, as are necessary to this end.

By incident is meant action expressing character or action or event determining fate. There are a thousand actions, mechanical or habitual, performed by us all, which throw no light upon our individuality. Almost all of these the novelist may neglect, or if he wishes to describe them, a single example will serve to reveal whatever uniqueness they may hide. There are an equal number of actions and events like blind alleys leading nowhere; from these also the novelist abstracts; it is only when he can trace some effect upon fate or character that he is interested. The delineation of nature or the milieu is governed by the same reference: a social or intellectual environment, no matter how interesting in itself, without potent individualities which it molds, or scenery, no matter how romantic, unless it is a theater of action or a spiritual influence upon persons, has no place in a story. Each of these, however, may by itself become the subject-matter of a literary essay, provided the writer's own moods and appreciations are included; otherwise it is a topic for sociology, history, or topography, not for literature.

By fate in a story I mean the writer's feeling for causality. As the maker of an image of life, the writer must portray life as molded by its past and by all the circumstances surrounding it. He must present character as determined by personal influence, by nature and the milieu; he must have a vivid sense for the interrelation of incidents. The feeling for fate is independent of any special philosophical view of the world; it does not imply fatalism or the denial of the spontaneous and originative force of personality; it is simply recognition of the wholeness of life. Nor, again, does it imply the possibility of predicting the end of a story from the beginning, for the living sequence, forging its links as it proceeds, is not mechanical; but it does imply that after things have happened we must be able to perceive their relatedness—the beginning, middle, and end as one whole. In the story, there must be the same kind of combination of necessity and contingency that there is in life: we must be sure that every act and incident will have its effect, and we must be able to divine, in a general way, what that effect will be; but owing to the complexity of life, which prevents us from knowing all the data of its problems, and owing to the spontaneity of its agents and the creative syntheses within its processes, we must never be able to be certain just what the effect will be like; our every calculation must be subject to the correction of surprise. Suspense and excitement must go hand in hand with a feeling for a developing inner necessity. There is no story without both. Yet no formula for the amount of each can be devised. The dependence of man upon nature makes inevitable the occurrence of what we call accidents, violent breaks in the tissue of personal and social life, unaccountable from the point of view of our human purposes. By admitting the part played by the non-human background in determining fate, the naturalistic school of writers have enlarged the vision of the novelist beyond the range of the tender-minded sentimentalist. It is to be expected, moreover, that coincidences should occur,—the meeting of independent lines of causation with consequences fateful to each. A careful investigation would disclose that most interesting careers have been largely determined by coincidences. The only demand that we can make of the artist in this regard is that he do not give us so many of these that his work will seem unreal. We must not feel that he is making the story in order to surprise us and thrill us–the purpose of melodrama; the story should make itself. Hardy's *The Return of the Native* is an illustration of failure here; the coincidences are so many that it seems magical, the work of a capricious genius, not of nature.

By fate in a story we do not mean, of course, the mere causal concatenation of events, for some relation to a purposeful life is always implied. But since this relation is a general condition applying to all art, we shall consider it here only as it affects the unity of a story. No rule can be laid down for the compass of a story; it may cover a small incident, as in many short stories, or it may embrace the whole or the most significant part of a life. The requirement that there be a beginning, middle, and end holds, but does not enlighten us as to what constitutes an end. Death makes one natural end to a story, since it makes an end to life itself; but within the span of a life the parts are not so clearly defined. Yet despite the continuity and overlapping of the parts of life, there are certain natural breaks and divisions,–the working out of a plan to fulfillment or disaster, the termination or consummation of a love affair, the commission of a crime with its consequences, or more subtle things, such as the breaking up of an old attitude and the formation of a new one. In life itself there are incidents that are closed because they cease to affect us deeply any more, purposes which we abandon because we can get no farther with them or because they have found their natural fulfillment, points of view which we have to relinquish because life supplies us with new facts which they do not include. The unity of a story should mirror these natural unities. The search for the wholeness of life should not blind us to the relative isolation of its parts; and there is fate in the parts as well as in the whole.

The selection of incidents for their bearing upon fate, the selection of significant traits for the construction of character, with the resulting unity and simplicity of the parts and the whole, is responsible for most of the ideality of fiction as compared with real life. Real life is a confused medley of impressions of people and events, a mixture of the important and the unimportant, the consequential and the inconsequential, with no evident pattern. Of this, literary art is the *verklartes Bild.* It is not because, in literature, men are happier and nobler that life seems superior there; but because its outlines are sharper, its design more perspicuous, the motives that sway it better understood. It has the advantage over life that a landscape flooded with sunshine has over one shrouded in darkness.

The way the literary artist builds up the ideal social world of fiction follows closely the method which we all employ in constructing the real social world. In real life we start from certain perceived acts and utterances, to which we then attach purposive meanings, and between which we establish relations. The process of interpretation is so rapid that, although strictly inferential in character and having imagination as its seat, it seems, nevertheless, like direct perception. As we see people act and hear them talk, it is as if we had a vision, confused indeed, yet direct, of their inner lives. And yet, as we have insisted, the real social world is constructed, not perceived.

The literary artist, unless he calls dramatic art to his aid, cannot present the persons and acts of his story; he can only describe them and report their talk. Description must take the place of vision, a recorded conversation the place of a heard one. Yet, by these means, the artist can give us almost as direct an intuition as we get from life itself; he can make us seem to see and overhear. From the acts which he describes we can infer the motives of the characters, and from the reported conversations we can learn their opinions and dreams. Or the novelist may insert a letter which we can read as if it were real. The resulting image of life will be clearer than any we could construct for ourselves; for the artist can report life more carefully than we could observe it; and he can make his characters more articulate in the expression of themselves than ordinary men, giving them a gift of tongues like his own. This last is especially characteristic of the drama, where sometimes, as in Shakespeare, men speak more like gods than like men. And we can listen to the intimate conversation of friends and lovers, upon which, in real life, we would not intrude.

This direct method of exposition through the description of acts and events and the record of conversations is the basis of every vivid story. It leaves the necessary inferences to the reader, just as life leaves them to the observer. In the hands of a master like Fontane, this method is incomparable; nothing can supplant it. It is the only method available for the dramatist, who, however, can make it still more effective through histrionic portrayal. Yet it does not suffice to satisfy our craving for knowledge of life, for only the broader, more obvious feelings can be inferred from the acts of men; the subtler and more remote escape. Even in conversation these cannot all be revealed; for many of them are too intimate to be spoken, and many again are unknown even to those who hold them. To-day we ask of the novelist that he disclose the finest, most hidden tissues of the soul. To this end, the microscopy of analysis, the so-called psychological method, must be employed. The novelist must perform upon his characters the same sort of dissection that we perform when, introspecting, we seek out the obscurer grounds of our conduct. And in the pursuit of this knowledge the novelist can oftentimes do better with his characters than we can do with ourselves. For utter sincerity regarding ourselves is impossible; the desire to think well of ourselves prevents us from recognizing the truth about ourselves. The novelist, on the contrary, can be unprejudiced and can know fully what he himself is creating. In order to accomplish this same purpose, the dramatist has to introduce bits of self-analysis, unusually sincere and penetrating, spoken aloud,–in the old style, monologues. And yet, without sacrificing the truthfulness of his own art, he cannot go so deep here as the novelist.

Through his analysis of his characters, the novelist must, however, construct them; otherwise he is a psychologist, not an artist. A synthetic vision of personality must supervene upon the dissection, and the emotional interest in character and action must subsist alongside of the intellectual interest. He must not let us lose the vivid sense of a living presence. In order to keep this, he must continue to employ the direct method of description of person and action, and report of conversation. How far the analytic method may be carried and at the same time the sense of personality kept intact, may be inferred from the work of Henry James, who, nevertheless, seems at times to fail to bring the out-going threads of his thought back into the web which he is weaving.

Again, in order to reach the social, historical, and metaphysical background of life–the milieu, the method of thought is the only available one. For the milieu is not anything that can be seen or heard or touched; it does not manifest itself to perception, but has to be constructed by a process of inference and synthesis. Much of it, to be sure, can be divined from the acts and conversations, from the dress and manners of the characters, but there is always more that has to be directly expounded. The writer cannot rely upon the reader's perspicacity to make the right inferences, or upon his knowledge to supply sufficient data; nor can he make his characters tell all that he may want told about their past and the life of the world in which they live, and through the influence of which they have become what they are. The novelist must construct for the reader the *mise en scene* of his story. Yet this must be held in complete subordination to the story. The intellectual background must lie behind, not athwart the story; it must be created for the sake of the story, not the story for its sake.

A philosophy of life, even, is the inevitable presupposition of every story. For no writer, no matter how direct and empirical he may be in his methods, can escape from looking at life through the glass of certain political, social, and religious ideas. He may have none of his own construction, yet he will unconsciously share those of his age. The prose literature of our own age, aside from some minor differences of technique, differs from that of the past chiefly through its more democratic and naturalistic views of life. And just as we rightly ask of the novelist that he enlighten us regarding the subtler causation of human action, so with equal right we may ask him to exhibit the relations of the persons and incidents which he describes to social organization, spiritual movements, and nature; for only so can they be seen in their complete reality. Yet right here lurks a danger threatening the enduring beauty of every story thus made complete. For the social and cosmic background of life, as we have observed, can be constructed only through thought, and thought, particularly regarding such matters, is peculiarly liable to error. The artist who goes very deep into this is sure to make mistakes. Even when he tries to use the latest sociological, economic, and political theories, he runs great risks; for these theories are always one-sided and subject to correction; they never prove themselves to be what the artist thinks and wants them to be–concrete views which he can apply with utter faith. How many stories of the century past have been marred by the author's too ready application of Darwinism to social life! When we can separate the story from its intellectual background, the inadequacy of the latter matters little; for we can apply metaphysical and political criticism to the theory and enjoy the story aesthetically; but many of our writers come to life with preconceived ideas deeply affecting their delineation of it. The picture no longer seems true because we feel that a false theory has prevented the artist from viewing life concretely and clearly. We could, for example, accept as natural and inevitable the ending of *Tess of the D'Urbervilles*, if Hardy had not presented it as an illustration of the cruel sport of the gods. As it stands with the author's commentary, we suspect that the girl's fate might have been different,–that perhaps he gave it this turn in order to prove his theory of life.

This fault is especially flagrant in the theory-ridden fiction of to-day. Determination through the past is overemphasized as against the influence of present, novel factors in a growing experience; heredity is given undue weight as against the inborn originality of personality and the uniqueness acquired through unique experiences; the influence of sensual motives is stressed at the expense of the moral; and so on through all the other abstractions and insufficiencies of "scientific" novel writing. The writer may well profit by everything he can learn from science; but he should not let his knowledge prevent him from seeing life concretely and as a whole. The literary man's science and philosophy are bound to be condemned by the expert, but his concrete delineations of life based on direct observation and vivid sympathy and imagination are impeccable. His theories may be false, but these will always be true. Nothing can take their place in fiction. It is they which give enduring value to such tales as *Morte d'Arthur*, despite all the crudity of the intellectual background.

Reflections upon life may become matter for literature in the essay, quite apart from any story. But the essay, like the story, unless it is to compete at a disadvantage with science and philosophy, must rely upon first-hand personal acquaintance with life, and artistic expression. The more abstract and theoretical it becomes, the more precarious its worth. I do not mean that the essayist may not generalize, but his generalizations should be limited to the scope of his experience of life. I do not mean that he should not philosophize, but his philosophy should be, like Goethe's or Emerson's, an expression of intuition and faith. Properly, the literary essay is a distinct artistic genre–the expression of a concrete *thinking* personality, and its value consists in the living wisdom it contains. Such essays as those of a Montaigne or a La Rochefoucauld make excellent materials for the social sciences, and can never be displaced by them as sources of knowledge of life.

Considerations similar to those which we have adduced regarding the implied philosophy of a story apply to its moral purpose. We cannot demand of the writer that he have no moral purpose or that he leave morality out of his story. For, since the artist is also a man, he cannot rid himself of an ethical interest in human problems or with good conscience fail to use his art to help toward their solution. His observations of moral experience will inevitably result in beliefs about it, and these will reveal themselves in his work. Yet we should demand that his view of what life ought to be shall not falsify his representation of life as it is. Just as soon as the moral of a tale obtrudes, we begin to suspect that the tale is false. We have such suspicions about Bourget, for example, because, as in *Une Divorce*, we are never left in doubt from the beginning as to the conventions he is advocating. And along with the feeling for the reality of the story goes the feeling for the validity of the moral; they stand and fall together. A story's moral, like life's moral, is convincing in proportion as it is an inference from the facts. The novelist, fearing that we may not have the wits to discern it, is justified in drawing this inference himself; yet it must show itself to be strictly an inference from the story–the story must not seem to have been constructed to prove it. "*Die Weltgeschichte ist das Weltgericht,*" wrote Schiller; even so, the delineation of life is the criticism of life. To show the scope of disillusion, monotony, repression–life's generous impulses narrowed and made timid by the social, economic, and political machine–would be a criticism of our modern world; there would be no need of moralizing. This the Russian novelists seem to have understood; they judged Russian life by describing it.

The man who writes literature as a means for promulgating political or moral ideas is either a conservative who desires to return to the conventions of the past, or else a radical who seeks the establishment of a new mode of life. The method employed by the former usually consists in exposing the restlessness and unhappiness of people who live in accordance with "advanced" ideas in comparison with the contentment of those who follow the older traditions. Such stories are, however, inconclusive, because they imply the false sociological thesis that the remedy for present ills is a return to the customs of the past. Happiness can indeed exist only in a stable society; but each age must create its own order to suit its changing needs; it cannot, if it would, go back to the old. These stories, therefore, although they often contain truthful and valuable pictures of the ills of contemporary life, and are useful in helping to conserve what is good in the spirit of the past, are nevertheless bound to be futile in their main endeavor.

The method of the radical usually consists of two parts: one of criticism, designed to show the misery due to existing laws and institutions; another of construction, the disclosure of a new and better system. But here, too, the constructive part of the story is likely to be weak. For whether the writer sets forth his program by putting it into the mouth of one of his characters or appends it as a commentary to his story, the practicability of his scheme is always open to question. It is only through trial that any scheme can be shown to be workable. There is, however, a new method that deserves better the name of "experimental romance" than Zola's own works. It consists in portraying people living in accordance with new sentiments and ideals, or even under new institutions imaginatively constructed. Yet this method also has its weakness, for it is difficult to make people believe in the reality of a life that has not been actually lived. Still, this difficulty is not fatal; for experiments in living are constantly being made all around us, which the discerning novelist needs only to observe and report. He can show the success of these or how, if they fail, their failure is due, not to anything inherently vicious, but simply to adverse law and opinion. Life is full of such stories waiting for some novelist who is not too timid to tell them.

We are thus brought round again to the thesis that the enduringly valuable elements of every story are its concrete creations of life. In the end, the story teller's fame will rest upon his power to create and reveal character and upon his sense for fate. There is just one thing that should be added to this–a rich emotional attitude toward life. It is the greater wealth of this that makes a novelist like Thackeray or Anatole France superior to one like Balzac. The personality that tells the story is as much a part of the total work as the characters and events portrayed, and must be taken into account in any final judgment of the whole. Without the author's vivid and rich participation, we who read can never be fully engaged, and we shall find more of life in the story, the more there is of him in it.

Chapter XI

Dominion of Art Over Nature: Painting

In literature, as we observed in our last two chapters, nature does not find aesthetic expression on its own account. In the lyric, nature appears only as the reflection of personal moods and thoughts, in the drama and novel and epic only as the theater of human action or the determiner of human fate. In painting and sculpture, on the other hand, the expression of nature is the primary aim. Of course, in so far as this expression is aesthetic, it is an expression not of nature alone, but of our responses as well; but nature is the starting point, not emotion as in lyric poetry, nor the effect upon destiny as in the epic.

Because they are expressions of nature, and because the copying of the human body, of trees, clouds, and the like is an indispensable part of their practice, painting and sculpture have seemed to give support to the theory of art as imitation. Yet, although the activity of imitation is a means to the creation of picture and statue, the mere fact of being a copy is not the purpose of the completed work nor the ground of our pleasure in it. Not its relation to anything outside itself, no matter how important for its making, but its own intrinsic qualities constitute its aesthetic worth.

This was true of the earliest efforts in these arts. The primitive artist copied not for the sake of copying, but because he ascribed a magical power to images. In the image he believed he somehow possessed the object itself, and so could control it; to the image, therefore, was transferred all the value and potence of the object. The object represented was deeply significant; it was perhaps the animal upon which the tribe depended for its food, its totem or guardian divinity; or else, as among the Egyptians, it was the man himself, of whom the image was meant to be an enduring habitation for the soul. If primitive men had copied indifferent objects, then we might infer that the mere making of an image was the end in view; but this they did not do, and it has never been the practice of any vigorous group of artists. Only when the means are valued instead of the end–technique in place of beauty–does this occur. Through such a mistaking of aims, new instruments of expression may be discovered, useful for a future genius, but no genuine art is produced. The genuine artist copies, not for the sake of copying, but in order to create a work of independent beauty.

This same transference of value to the image, with the consequent freeing of the image from the model, can be observed even in commemorative art. A king desires, perhaps, to perpetuate his memory; how better than through some enduring likeness in stone or paint? While he is alive and after his death this image will remind his subjects of him and his valorous deeds. The relation to the model seems to be fundamental; but in proportion to the success of the artist in making a likeness, the stone or paint will be made to seem all alive, and for those who cannot come into direct relations with the monarch, he will be effectively present in the statue or picture, even when, through death, he is removed from all social and practical relations. Who does not feel that Philip the Fourth is present on the Velasquez canvas; where else could one find him so alive? If the work is artistic, the spectator's interest will center in feeling the life in the color and line or sculptured form; that it happens to be an imitation of something else will become of secondary importance. This is clearest when the name of the subject is not known; then surely it is the life before us that can alone concern us. Any feeble copy would serve as a reminder, but a living drawing or statue brings the man or woman into our presence. The aesthetic interest in the work as living supervenes upon the interest in it as a mere reminder of life.

This freedom from the model and attainment of intrinsic worth in the work of art itself is furthered through the realization of beauty in the medium of expression. The colors, lines, and shapes which the artist uses have a direct appeal to the eye and through the eye to feeling; hence arise preferences for the most agreeable and expressive. The artist discovered that he could express his emotion not only through representing its object, but through the very colors or lines or shapes used in the delineation. These effects, found by chance perhaps in the first instance, would later be striven for consciously. In this way, through some grace of line, or symmetry of form, or harmony of color, the statue or picture would acquire a power to please quite independent of any ulterior use or purpose; once more, it would become alive and of value on its own account.

We shall begin our study of the representative arts with drawing and painting–representation in two dimensions–not because they preceded sculpture historically, but because, being more complex arts, a solution of the problems which they raise makes a subsequent survey of the similar problems of the simpler art relatively easy.

The media of pictorial expression are color and line, and expression is attained through them in a twofold fashion. In a picture, every element of color or line is expressive directly, just as color and line, of some vague feeling or mood, and, in addition, chiefly through its resemblance, represents some action or object. The former kind of expression is indispensable. No matter how realistic the imitation, unless the picture thrill like music, through its mere colors or lines, it is aesthetically relatively ineffective. It is not sufficient that the picture move us through the vicarious presence on the canvas of a moving object; it must stir us in a more immediate fashion through the direct appeal of sense. For example, a picture which presents us with a semblance of the sea will hold us through the power which the sea has over us; but it will not hold us so fast as a picture of the same subject which, in addition, grips us through its greens and blues and wavy lines. The one sways us only through the imagination, the other through our senses as well.

Sensitiveness to color as such, so self-evident to one who possesses it, seems to be wanting, except in rudimentary fashion, in a great many people. They are probably few, however, who do not feel some stirrings when they look through the stained glass of a cathedral window or upon the red of Venetian glass, or who are entirely indifferent to the color of silk. The reason for emotional color-blindness is probably not a native incapacity to be affected, but rather a diversion of attention; color has come to be only a sign for the recognition and subsequent use of things, a signal for a practical or intellectual reaction. In our haste to recognize and use we fail to see, and give ourselves no time to be moved by mere seeing. But when, as in art, contemplation, the filling of the mind with the object, is the aim, the power to move of the sensuous surface of things may come again into its rights.

The emotional response to color, vague and abstract and objectless, is, like music, incapable of adequate expression in words, and for the same reason. Words are capable of expressing only the larger and fairly well-defined emotions; such subtle shadings and complex mixtures of feeling as are conveyed by color and sound are mostly beyond their ken. Colors make us feel and dream as music does in the same incommunicable fashion. Or rather the only possibility of communicating them is through the color schemes arousing them. And for one who appreciates color this is sufficient; he can point to the colors and say–that is what I feel. To render his feeling also in words would be a superfluous business, supposing they could be adequate to express it; or, if they were adequate, that would make expression through color superfluous. The value of any medium consists in its power to express what none other can. Nevertheless, it is possible to find rough verbal equivalents for the simpler colors. Thus every one would probably agree with Lipps and call a pure yellow happy, a deep blue quiet and earnest, red passionate, violet wistful; would perhaps feel that orange partakes at once of the happiness of yellow and the passion of red, while green partakes of the happiness of yellow and the quiet of blue; and in general that the brighter and warmer tones are joyful and exciting, the darker and colder, more inward and restful.

To explain the expressiveness of color sensations is as difficult as to account for the parallel phenomenon in sounds. Here as there resort is had to the principle of association. Colors get, it is thought, their value for feeling either through some connection with emotionally toned objects, like vegetation, light, the sky, blood, darkness, and fire, or else through some relation to emotional situations, like mourning or danger, which they have come to symbolize. And there is little doubt that such associations play a part in determining the emotional meaning of colors–the reticence and distance of blue, the happiness of yellow, for example, are partly explained through the fact that blue is the color of the sky, yellow the color of sunlight; the meaning of black is due, partly at any rate, to association with mourning. Yet neither of these types of association seems sufficient to explain the full emotional meaning of colors. The conventional meanings of colors seem rather themselves to need explanation than to serve as explanations–why is red the sign of danger, purple royal, white a symbol of purity, black a symbol of mourning? Is it not because these colors had some native, original expressiveness which fashion and habit have only made more definite and turned to special uses? And if we can explain the reticence of blue through association with the sky, can we thus explain its quietness? Can the warmth of fire and the excitement of blood explain quite all the depth of passionate feeling in red? The factors enumerated play a part in the complex effect, but there seem to be elements still unaccounted for.

In order to explain the total phenomenon we must admit, as in the case of tones, some direct effect of the sensory light stimulus upon the feelings. Rays of light affect not only the sensory apparatus, causing sensations of color; their influence is prolonged into the motor channels, causing a total attitude of the organism, the correlate of a feeling. It would be strange if any sensory stimulus were entirely cut off by itself and did not find its way into the motor stream. But these overflows are too diffuse to be noticed in ordinary experience; they are obscured through association or are not given time to rise to the level of clear consciousness, because we are preoccupied with the practical or cognitive significance of the colors; only in the quiet and isolation of contemplation can they come into the focus. Of course the student of the evolution of mind will want to go behind these color emotions and inquire why a given color is connected with a given reaction. He may even want to connect them with instinctive responses of primitive men. But here we can only speculate; we cannot know.

The problem is further complicated through the fact that private color- associations are formed obscuring the aesthetic meanings, which can be rediscovered only through the elimination of the former. Color preferences are often determined in this way; yet sometimes they spring from another and more radical source–an affinity between personal temperament and the feeling tone of the preferred color. A consistent choice of blues and grays indicates a specific kind of man or woman, very different from the chooser of yellows and reds.

Although single color tones are expressive, they seldom exist alone in works of art. Significant expression requires variety. The invention of original and expressive color combinations is a rare gift of genius. Rough rules of color combination have been devised from the practice of artists and from experiment, the following of which will enable one to produce faultless patterns, but without genius will never enable one to create a new expression. Color combinations are either harmonious or balanced, the former produced by colors or tones of colors very close to one another, the latter by the contrasting or widely sundered. In the one case, we get the quiet commingling of feelings akin to each other; in the other, the lively tension of feelings opposed. Compare, for example, the effect of a Whistler nocturne with a Monet landscape. The colors that do not go well together are such as are not close enough for union nor far enough apart for contrast. They are like personalities not sufficiently at one to lose themselves in each other, yet not sufficiently unlike to be mutually stimulating and enlarging, between whom there can be only a fruitless rivalry turning into hate. Such are certain purples and reds, certain greens and blues. Yet, through proper mediation, any two colors can be brought into a composition. All colors are brought together in nature through the sunlight, and in painting or weaving by giving to rival colors the same sheen or brightness. Or again, the union may be effected by combining the two with a third which is in a relation of balance or harmony with each, as in the favorite scheme of blue, red, and green.

Despite their ability to express, colors cannot stand alone; they must be the colors of something, they must make line or shape. Lines, on the other hand, seem to be independent of color, as in drawings and etchings; yet there is really some color even there–black and white and tones of gray. That color and line are independent of one another in beauty, is, however, shown by works, such as Millet's, which are good in line but poor in color. Lines have, as we have already seen, the same duality of function as colors: they express feeling directly through their character as mere lines and they represent objects by suggesting them through resemblance.

There is, in fact, for those who can feel it, a life in lines of the same abstract and objectless sort as exists in colors and tones. Lines give rise to motor impulses and make one feel and dream, as music does. There are many who are cold to this effect; yet few can fail to get something of the vibration or mood of the lines of a Greek vase painting, a Botticelli canvas, or a Rembrandt etching. The life of lines is more allied to that of tones than of colors because it possesses a dynamic movement quality which is absent from the latter. This life is, in fact, twofold: on the one hand it is a career, with a beginning, middle, and end, something to be willed or enacted; on the other hand it is a temperament or character, a property of the line as a whole, to be felt. These two aspects of aesthetic lines are closely related; they stand to one another much as the temperament or character of a man stands to his life history, of which it is at once the cause and the result. Just as we get a total impression of a man's nature by following the story of his life, so we get the temperamental quality of lines by following them with the eye; and just as all of our knowledge of a man's acts enters into our intuition of his nature, so we discover the character of the total line by a synthesis of its successive elements.

It is as difficult, more difficult, perhaps, to put into words the temperamental quality of lines as to do the parallel thing with colors. Lines are infinite in their possible variations, and the fine shades of feeling which they may express exceed the number of words in the emotional vocabulary of any language. Moreover, in any drawing, the character of each line is partly determined through the context of other lines; you cannot take it abstractly with entire truth. It is, however, possible to find verbal equivalents for the character of the main types of lines. Horizontal lines convey a feeling of repose, of quiet, as in the wall-paintings of Puvis de Chavannes; vertical lines, of solemnity, dignity, aspiration, as in so much of the work of Boecklin; crooked lines of conflict and activity, as in the woodcuts of Durer; while curved lines have always been recognized as soft and voluptuous and tender, as in Correggio and Renoir. The supposition that the curved line is the sole "line of beauty" is the result of a narrow and effeminate idea of the aesthetic; yet it must be admitted that this form, since it permits of the greatest amount of variation, has the highest power of expression; but in many of its more complex varieties it loses much of its soft feminine quality, and takes on some of the strength of the other forms.

The expressiveness of lines is determined by several–at least three– factors. In the first place, the perception of lines is an active process. In order to get a line we have to follow it with the eye; and if we do not now follow it with our fingers, we at least followed similar lines thus in the past. Now this process of the perception of a line requires of us an energy of attention to the successive elements of the line as we pass over them and a further expenditure of energy in remembering and synthesizing them into a whole. This energy, since it is evoked by the line and is not connected with any definite inner striving of the self, is felt by us to belong to the line, to be an element in its life, as clearly its own as its shape. For example, a line with many sudden turns or changes of direction is an energetic and exciting line because it demands in perception a constant and difficult and shifting attention; a straight line, on the contrary, because simple and unvarying in its demands upon the attention, is monotonous and reposeful; while the curved line, with its lawful and continuous changes, at once stimulating yet never distracting attention, possesses the character of progressive and happy action. This, the primary source of the vital interpretation of lines is supplemented by elements derived from association. Lines suggest to us the movements of our bodies along paths of similar form, and we interpret them according to the feeling of these movements; in the imagination, we may seem to move along the very lines themselves as paths. Every skater or runner knows the difficulty of moving along a path full of sudden turns and angles, a difficulty which, if he is in good trim, may nevertheless afford him pleasure in the overcoming; the delightful and various ease of moving along curved lines; the monotony of a long, straight path, but the quick triumph of going right to the end along a short and terminal line of this character. But lines suggest to us not only the movements, but also the attitudes of our bodies. They may be straight and rising,–rigid or dignified or joyously expanding; they may be horizontal and lie down and rest; they may be falling and sorrowful; or the shapes whose outlines they form may be heavy or light, delicate or ungainly or graceful, as bodies are. Finally, the interpretation of lines may be further enriched as follows: The sight of a line suggests the drawing of it, the sweep of the brush that made it; we ourselves, in the imagination once more, may re-create the line after the artist, and feel, just as he must have felt, the mastery, ease, vigor, or delicacy of the execution into the line itself. Few can fail to get this effect from the paintings of Franz Hals, for example, where the abounding energy of the artist is apparent in each stroke of the brush. Artists feel this life in execution most strongly; yet, since almost every one has had some practice in drawing lines, it is potentially a universal quality in a painting.

Lines may be unified according to the three modes of harmony, balance, and evolution. The repetition of the same kind of line confers a harmonious unification upon a drawing, as in Tintoretto's "Bacchus and Ariadne," where the circle is to be found repeated in the crown and ring, in the heads of the three figures, in the breasts of Ariadne. Similar to this sameness of form is sameness of direction or parallelism of lines. Another kind of harmonious unification of lines is continuity, where out of different lines or shapes a single line is made. The classical geometrical forms of composition, as the circular or pyramidal, are good examples of this. The "Odalisque" of Ingres, where all the lines of the body constitute a single line, is a notable case. What Ruskin has called "the approach, intersection, interweaving of lines, like the sea waves on the shore,"–the conspiracy of all the lines in a drawing to form one single network, of which illustrations could be found in the work of every draftsman, is a kind of harmony of line. Symmetrically disposed shapes, and lines whose directions are opposed, have the balanced form of unity. Here, from a given point as center, the attention is drawn in contrary yet equal ways. Examples of this type of composition are abundant among the Old Masters; as a rigid form it is, however, disappearing. That the dramatic type of unity is to be found in lines will be confirmed by every one who has observed the movement, the career of lines. Whenever shapes are so disposed that they form a line leading up to a given shape, wherever, again, lines converge to a single point, there is a clear case of evolution; we begin by attending to the line at a certain point, proceed in a certain direction, then reach a terminal point, the goal of the process. In Leonardo's "Last Supper," the convergence of the perspective lines and the lines formed by the groups of Apostles is a case of evolution. The different types of unification are, of course, not exclusive. In the painting just referred to, all three are present: Christ and the Apostles are arranged along a single line, the two ends of which, despite their symmetrical and balanced disposition, converge to one central point, the Christ. Every pyramidal form of composition is a combination of balance between the elements at the bases of the triangle, convergence towards the apex, and harmony through the participation of the three elements in a single form. One of the most interesting and complex types of organization of lines is rhythm–the balanced, harmonious movement of lines. A line is rhythmical when there is a balanced alternation of direction in its movement, a turning now to the right and now to the left, or vice versa; proportion in the length of the segments made by the turns; and general direction–a tending somewhere.

As is assumed in the preceding paragraph, the elements of lines may be shapes or masses, as well as points. That is, not only do lines made up of points form shapes, but shapes in their turn, when arranged on a surface, necessarily make lines. Such lines are, as a rule, not continuous; yet since the eye takes the shapes successively and in a given direction, they are nevertheless true lines and possess the qualities of ordinary simple lines. The arrangement of masses in an undulating line, say in a landscape painting, has essentially the same value for feeling as a similar continuous line; compare this with a horizontal arrangement of masses, which has all the quiet and repose of a simple horizontal line.

Colors and lines, relying on the direct expressiveness which we have been studying, may stand by themselves, as in an oriental rug; yet in painting they have another function: to represent. And even in the purely ornamental use of color and line, the tendency towards representation is apparent everywhere; either the lines are derivatives of schematized pictures of men and plants and animals, or else such objects are introduced as motives without disguise. In painting, therefore, the color red has value not only as so much red, but as standing for the red of a girl's lips or cheeks; and that curved line is of significance, not as mere line alone, but as the curve of her limbs. In this way the native value of the sense symbols becomes suffused and enriched with the values of the things they represent. The two functions of color and of line should never be indifferent to each other; representation should not become a mere excuse for decoration, the objects represented having no value in themselves; nor should color and line be used as mere signs of interesting objects, without reference to their intrinsic value. On the contrary, the two functions should play into each other's hands. If, for example, the human body is represented, the colors and lines employed should be so disposed that they decorate the surface of the picture and hold us there through their sheer rhythm and quality; yet, at the same time, and through their very ornamental power, they should make us feel the more keenly the values of the object they represent. Between the immediate values of the colors and lines there should exist unity: stimulating colors should go with stimulating lines, quiet colors with quiet lines; and the resulting feeling tone of the medium should be in harmony with the feeling of the objects represented; the one should give the other over again, and so each enforce the other.

Since it is not the purpose of any art to represent mere things, but to express concrete "states of the soul," the center of which is always some feeling, exact fidelity in the representation of objects is not necessary for good painting or drawing. Only so much of things needs to be represented as is necessary to give back the life of them. Necessary above all is the object as a whole, for to this our feelings are attached; now this can usually be far better represented through an impressionistic sketch, which gives only the significant features, than by a painstaking and detailed drawing. Since, furthermore, the life of things can be conveyed through color and line as such, a certain departure from realism is legitimate for this end. Without some freedom from the exact truth of the colors and lines of things, the artist is unable to choose and compose them for expressive purposes; when exactly like the objects which they represent, they tend to lose all expressive power of their own, becoming mere signs or equivalents of things. A certain amount of variation from the normal may be necessary in order that the sense symbols shall call attention to themselves, in order that we be prevented, as we are not in the ordinary observation of nature, from looking through them to the things which they mean. Whenever, moreover, the artist wishes to render a unique reaction to a scene, he can do so only through a courageous use of the subtle language of color and line, which may require a distortion of the "real" local qualities of things; for, if he makes a plain, realistic copy of the scene itself, he can evoke, and so express, only the normal emotional responses to it.

When such departures from the truth of things are properly motivated, no one can be offended by them, any more than when the brilliant hues of nature appear black and white in a charcoal drawing. The amount of realism in any work of art is largely a matter of tacit convention. An artist may, if he wishes, use color with no pretense at giving back the real colors of objects, but for purely expressive purposes alone, relying on line for purposes of representation. This is often done in Japanese prints. All that is necessary is that we should understand what the artist is doing and find what he presents to us real and alive. On the other hand, an expressive use of color and line leading to a distortion of objects out of all possibility of recognition, or even a use which makes them seem unreal and awry, is without excuse. For since colors and lines are employed to bring things before the imagination, they should be made to serve this purpose successfully; the value which belongs to the things should have a chance to appear; but this can happen only if they seem to be actually present before us. Painting is not a mere music of color and line expressive of abstract and objectless emotions alone, but a poetry, which, through the picturing of objects to which emotions are attached, renders the latter concrete and definite. Not mere feeling, such as a color or a line by itself can convey, but feeling in the presence of nature, which can be expressed only when color and line are made into a recognizable image of nature, is the substance of painting. One cannot express the feeling of the weight and bulk of objects, of their distribution in three dimensions, or the value of their shadows or atmospheric enveloping, without the representation of weight and bulk and shadow and atmosphere and perspective. Every increase in the power to represent nature, every advance in the mastery of the object, adds a new power over the expression of feeling, which varies with the object. The realist is, therefore, right in his demand that nature itself be painted; only he should remember that the nature which presents itself in art is never the naked object, but veiled in feeling; and, as so veiled, may sometimes be seen pretty much as it really is; then again with parts concealed, and sometimes even transformed. Both a realism that tries to unite fidelity to the full qualities of the object with musical expression in the medium, and so to render the more typical responses to nature, which depend, for the most part, on the object itself, and a symbolism or expressionism that sacrifices fidelity for the expression, through the mere medium, of more personal responses, are in their rights. Only the limits of both tendencies are illegitimate–the use of color and line to produce mere images of things on the one hand, or purely musical effects on the other.

The subject matter or content of painting is determined by its language, color, and line. These, as we have seen, by an imitation more or less exact, represent nature, the world of concrete things as directly presented to us in vision, colored and shapely. The inner world is expressed only so far as it is revealed in the gestures and attitudes of the bodies of men or so far as it is a mood attached to things and their colors and shapes. Now space is the universal container in which all elements of the visible world are disposed. Every painting, therefore, should include a representation of space; it should never represent things as if they stood alone without environment or relation. Even in the portrait of a single individual some relation to space should be indicated; this is accomplished by the background, in which the figures should be made to lie, and to which they should seem to belong. In front, the space of a picture is limited by the plane of the surface on which it is painted; everything should appear to belong in the space back of this; nothing should seem to come forward out towards the spectator. But behind this, backwards, the space represented is unlimited, and its infinite depths may well be indicated by the convergence of perspective lines and the gradual fading of the outlines and colors of objects.

The represented space of the picture is not, of course, the real space of the canvas or of the room in which the picture hangs. The former is infinite, while the latter is only so many square feet in area. The frame serves the purpose of cutting off the represented space from all relation to the real space, of which the frame itself is a part. A confusion of these two spaces is sometimes found in crude work and in the comments of people upon genuine works of art. I have, for example, seen a picture of a lion with iron bars riveted to the frame and extending over it,–a represented lion in a real cage! And I once heard a man criticise one of Degas' paintings on the ground that "if the dancing girl were to straighten her bent body she would bump her head on the frame!" The rule that the color of the frame should harmonize with the main tones of the picture is no proof that they belong together; its purpose is merely to protect the colors of the painting from being changed through their neighborhood with those of the frame.

Although painting is essentially a spatial art, it includes a temporal element, the "specious present," the single moment of action or of motion. The lines are not dead and static, but alive; they progress and vibrate; by their means a smile, the rippling of a stream, the gesture of surprise, the movement of a dance, may be depicted. Successive moments, the different phases of an action or movement, cannot, however, be represented. Strict unities of space and time should be observed in painting. Only contiguous parts of space and only one moment of time should be represented inside a single frame. Both these unities were violated in old religious paintings where sometimes the Nativity, Flight into Egypt, Crucifixion, and Resurrection were all portrayed on one canvas.

The space of painting is no abstract aspect of things such as the geometer elaborates. To be in a common space with other things, implies, for the pictorial intuition of the world, to be played upon by the same light and to be enveloped in the same atmosphere. Space, light, and air constitute the milieu in which everything lives and moves and has its being in painting. To every difference in the arrangement and foreshortening of objects, to every variation in their lights and shadows and aerial quality, the sensitive soul responds. The close proximity of objects in a tiny room has an effect upon feeling very different from their wide distribution over a broad space. An equal difference depends upon whether light is concentrated upon objects or evenly distributed over them; upon whether it is bright or dim; upon whether they are near and clear in a thin air or far and hazy in a thick and heavy cloud. The masters of light and air, Rembrandt, Claude, Turner, evoke myriad moods through these subtle influences. A long development and the following of many false paths was necessary before painting discovered its true function as an expression of the elements, the once hard outlines of things softening in their enveloping embrace.

The representation of space, which painting alone of all the arts can achieve, does not imply, however, a representation of the full plastic quality of individual objects, which is the function of sculpture. This, to be sure, can be done in painting, as the great sculptor-painters of the Renaissance have shown; but it cannot be done so well as in sculpture; and when done tends to interfere with other things. It makes objects stand out too much by themselves, destroying their felt unity with other elements on the canvas, so that when provided with all the colors of life, they seem rather real than painted, and look as if they wished to leave the world of representation, where they belong, and touch hands with the spectator. The depth and the extent of space, the distance and the distribution of objects, light and shade and air, are all independent of the plasticity of individual things, which tends to disappear in proportion as they are emphasized. Only when attention is directed to the individual object does its full plasticity appear; see it as an element of the environing whole, and it flattens out to view.

There are, in fact, two ways of seeing, to each of which corresponds a mode of painting. On the one hand, we may see distributively, holding objects as individuals each in our attention, neglecting light and space and air. Or else we may see synthetically, first the whole which light and space and air compose, and then individual things as bearers of these. The one is the more practical way of seeing; because, for practical purposes, the separate thing that can be grasped and used is all important, and the film of light and air and the neighborhood of other things are of no account. The other is more theoretical and sthetic; for to a pure vision which does not think of handling, there are no separate things, but only differences of shape and color and location in a single object, the visible whole.

In the type of painting corresponding to the first way of seeing, objects are represented more as we think them to be, or as we should find them on further exploration, than as they actually appear to sight at any given moment; the outlines are clear and sharp and detail is emphasized. This mode of painting is most in place for interiors where there is an even distribution and no striking effects of light and shade, as in so many genre pictures of the Dutch school; but above all when the human significance of objects or their dramatic relations, which depend upon their being taken as separate things, is to be expressed. For example, to get the expression of the action of a woman pouring water into a jug, it is necessary that we feel the shape and color of the latter as aspects of a tangible reality having a distinct purpose, that of holding water; and this purposefulness makes of the object a separate, individual thing. Yet a too great distinction of objects and a too great elaboration of detail, as in Meissonier and the English Pre-Raphaelites, is inartistic; the picture breaks up into separate parts and all feeling of unity is lost. In the work of the Flemish and Dutch, on the contrary, we take delight in the perspicuity of things without losing the sense of wholeness; for there is a sameness and simplicity of color tone which unites them. A genuine and unique sthetic value is possessed by such work,–that of clear intuition of the visual detail and human significance of things.

Very often the unification in painting of this type is dramatic chiefly–some link of action or of symbolism which the elements of the picture have as meanings, a unity of content, therefore, and not a coloristic or a linear unity. The colors are essentially local colors, serving first to characterize and distinguish the objects properly, and then to lend to them severally high value through brightness and temperament; although harmonizing as mere colors, they are held together more through some connection in what they mean than through a unity of pure expression. The dominance of any one mass, too, depends more upon its superior significance as meaning than upon its claim upon the attention through any intrinsic quality of color. Nevertheless, even if secondary, the unity and dominance through color and line must be present, and should be consonant with the unity and subordination in the meanings. The painting of the great Italian masters was of this character. In a Madonna picture, for example, the elements representing the Holy Family are united through the spiritual oneness of the objects which they represent, and the Madonna is dominant through her superior significance for the religious life. The colors serve to characterize and distinguish the figures; yet between the former there is a harmony corresponding to the inner harmony of the latter; the spiritual dominance of the Madonna is expressed in a purely formal fashion through her larger size, central position, and more brightly gleaming garments.

In painting which corresponds to the synthetic way of seeing, all particular objects are subordinated to space and light and air; their outlines are melting, suggested rather than seen, and there is little emphasis on detail. Turner's painting of light and the more recent examples of impressionism afford abundant examples of this. In this style, unification is effected almost wholly through color and line as such, and through the light and space and air which they represent. Just to live in the same atmosphere or in the path of the same light, to be enveloped in the same darkness or shadow, or merely to participate in a single composition of colors or rhythm of lines serves to unite objects. The relative importance of elements, too, is determined rather by some intrinsic quality which arrests attention than by any supremacy as meanings.

Through such materials and methods as we have described, the possibilities and limits of expression in painting are determined. First of all, painting has the power, through color and line as such, to express the purely musical emotions; this we demand of painting just as we demand music of verse: without word-music, there is no poetry, no matter how high the theme; so without color and line music, no matter how skillful the representation or how noble the subject, there is no picture. Painting may give little more than this. In much of still-life painting, for example, the values attached to the objects represented are borrowed from the music of the medium. And even when the objects represented have a value in themselves, the superiority of their representation over the mere perception of them in nature comes from this source. Why, for example, does the painting of flowers by a real master afford a richer aesthetic experience than real flowers? Painted flowers have no perfume, rightly called the soul of flowers. It is because in painting the expressiveness of the purer and more subtly harmonious colors more than compensates for the lack of odor. Through the music of color and line we are made responsive to common things which otherwise would leave us cold, or if we are responsive to them, our sensitiveness becomes finer and keener. It is largely because he is so accomplished a musician in color and composition that Jan Vermeer can make the inside of a room or some commonplace act by a commonplace person the object of an intense and sympathetic contemplation.

For the beauty of landscape also, which the art of painting has created and which during the last century has become its favorite theme, the music of color is equally essential. In its highest form, that beauty requires emotional responsiveness combined with the power accurately to observe and reproduce the qualities of things; without observation and reproduction, the feeling is incommunicable; without feeling, the imitation is lifeless. Love of the object, which at once reveals and makes responsive, mediates the highest achievements of the art. By translating the object into the language of abstract color and line, it is purified for feeling; for those qualities toward which feeling is indifferent are eliminated; only so much as can enter into an expressive color or line composition survives. The artist gives us the illusion that he is reproducing our familiar world all the while that he is glorifying it through the beauty of the colors in which he paints it. The painting of the human body, especially the nude human body, belongs to the same class of subjects as the painting of landscapes. For the human body unclothed, and as unclothed severed from the conventional social world, is a part of nature and speaks to us as nature does through form and color. To bring that object before us with all its expressive detail; to make us, in the imagination, move with it and touch it; to caress it with our eyes; to awaken that passionate interest which makes us see and feel it more vividly than anything else in the world, yet to subdue passion wholly to a glowing contemplation, this is one of the highest achievements of pictorial art. And the artistic right to represent it in the woods by lake or stream, or in the meadow among other natural things, must be accorded to the artist despite all protests of convention and habit; we never actually find it there, to be sure, yet there it belongs for imaginative feelings. The maidens in Corot's paintings, for example, seem to belong as naturally to the landscape as the very trees themselves.

But the painter can depict the human body not merely as something sensuously beautiful, but as expressive, through gesture and pose and countenance, of character and thought. The complex psychic life of man is thus open to him for delineation. In the portrait, through the attentive study of the many varying expressions of the inner life, leading to the selection of some characteristic pose or action, the artist concentrates into a single image what seems to him to be the distinctive nature of the man. And he can express this nature over again, and so more effectively reveal it, in the mere colors and lines which he uses. Thus Franz Hals has embodied the abundance and good cheer of his burghers in the boldness and brightness of the lines and colors with which he paints them; and Hogarth, in the "Shrimp Girl," through the mere singularity of line and color, has created the eerie impression which we attach to the girl herself. The best portraits subordinate everything else, such as costume and background, to the painting of the inner life. Thus Velasquez brings before us the souls of his little Infantas despite the queer head-dresses and frocks which must have threatened to smother them. The background should serve the same end; if elaborate, it should represent a fitting environment; and if plain it should throw the figure into relief. Alongside of the portrait as a painting of the soul should be placed pictures of ideal characters; ideal, not in the sense of good, but in the sense of more highly complex and unified than actually existing persons. Such pictures symbolize for us the quintessence and highest level of definite types of life. Manet's "Olympia" and Goya's "Maja" belong here equally with Leonardo's "Christ" or "Mona Lisa," with Raphael's Madonnas and Michelangelo's gods and angels. In them is attained the most intense concentration of psychic life possible.

It is now pretty generally recognized that the unities of time and space exclude from the sphere of painting story telling and history, which require for effective representation more than the single moment included in painting. In order to tell a story in painting, one has to supplement what is seen with ideas which can be obtained only from a catalogue or other source external to the picture; one has to add in thought to the moment given on the canvas the missing moments of the action. But a work of art should be complete in itself and so far as possible self-explanatory; it should not lead us away from itself, but keep us always to itself. If the scene represented be a part of a story, the story should be so well known that its connection with the picture can be immediately recognized without external aid, and should admit of a certain completeness in its various parts. The life of Christ is such a story; everybody knows it and can interpret a picture portraying it forthwith; its various incidents and situations have each a unique and complete significance in themselves. Historical paintings are not necessarily bad, of course, but the good ones are good despite the history, and a proof of their excellence consists in the fact that when we see them they make us forget for the moment our historical erudition.

This norm does not exclude from the sphere of painting the expression of the relation of man to his fellows; it simply confines painting to the delineation of momentary and self-sufficient glimpses of social life. Pictures representing a mother and child, a pair of lovers, a family group, festival, tavern scene, or battle charge are illustrations. In Dutch painting the social life of Holland in the seventeenth century found its record; yet there is little or no anecdote. The genre, the representation of a group of people united by some common interest and with an appropriate background, has the same legitimacy, if not the same eminence, as the portrait. It does not possess the rank of the portrait because, since the interest is rather in the action or the situation portrayed, the figures are more merely typical, being developed only so far as is necessary to carry the action; seldom is a subtle and individualized inner life portrayed.

Objections are rightly raised, however, against pathetic, sentimental, and moralistic painting. Here color and line, the whole picture in fact, counts for little or nothing except to stir an emotion, usually of grief or pity or love, or to preach a sermon; the unity of form and content is sacrificed, the one becoming a mere means to the other. But, as we know, it is never the purpose of art merely to stir feeling; its purpose is to objectify feeling; if the art be painting, to put feeling into color and line, and only when feeling is experienced as *there* is it aesthetic feeling at all. And what shall we think of a picture like the "Doctor" of Luke Fildes', which is so pathetic that one cannot bear to look at it? Surely a picture should make one want to see it! Of course I do not mean that an artist cannot paint pathetic and sentimental subjects. The great painters of the Passion would disprove that with reference to the former and Watteau with reference to the latter. But a power to achieve beauty of color and line and to objectify pathos and sentiment through them was possessed by these painters to a degree to which few others have attained. For moralistic painting, however, there can be no excuse. You can paint visible things and as much of the soul as can appear through them; you cannot paint abstract ethical maxims. Of course a painter may intend his picture to be an illustration of some moral maxim, or may even, as Hogarth did, paint it to expose the sins of his age and create a beautiful work notwithstanding; but only if, in the result, this purpose is irrelevant and the concrete delineation everything.

Chapter XII

Dominion of Art Over Nature: Sculpture

The sculptor has this advantage over all other artists, that his chief subject is the most beautiful thing in the world–the human body. In two ways the body is supremely beautiful: as an expression of mind and as an embodiment of sensuous charm. In the body mind has become actually incarnate; there purpose, emotion, and thought have taken shape and manifestation. And this shape, through its appeal to the amorous, parental, and gregarious feelings, and through the complete organization of its parts, has no rival in loveliness. What wonder, therefore, that sculptors have always thought of their work as simply one of mere imitation of nature, the divine. Yet in sculpture, as in the other arts, the imitative process is never slavish, but selective and inventive. For the body is interesting to the artist only in so far as it is beautiful, that is, so far as it has charm and exhibits the control of mind; some of its details and many of its attitudes, having no relation to either, are unfit for imitation; and, although inspired by his model, the sculptor seeks to create out of his impressions a still more harmonious object.

To give to his material the semblance of the body beautiful is the technical problem of the sculptor. Although this semblance is primarily for sight, it is not exclusively so. For in sculpture shape is not two-dimensional, but plastic; and for the full appreciation of plasticity, the cooperation of touch is required. Moreover, not only the perception of the form, but also a large part of the appreciation of the charm of the body depends upon touch. Of course we do not ordinarily touch statues, but they should make us want to touch them, and we should touch them–in the imagination. The surfaces of the statue should therefore be so modeled as to give us, in the imagination, the pleasures that we get when we touch the living body. It is well known that these touch values were destroyed by the neo-classicists when they polished the surfaces of their statues. Such sculpture for the eye only is almost as good when reproduced in an engraving that preserves its visual quality, and is therefore lacking in complete sculptural beauty. But no plane reproduction can replace the best Greek, Italian, or French work.

The life of the statue should, however, be more than skin deep. We should appreciate it through sensations of motion and strain as well as through sight and touch, feeling the tenseness or relaxation of the muscles and tendons beneath. We should move with its motion or rest with its repose. And this does not mean that we should merely know that an attitude of quiet or of motion is represented; we should actually experience quiet or motion. In our own bodies sensations corresponding to these should be awakened by the visual image of the statue, yet should be fused with the latter, becoming for our perception its, not ours, in accordance with the mechanism of *einfuhlung* described in our fourth chapter. The light rhythmic motion of the figures in Carpeaux's "Dance" should thrill in our own limbs, yet seem to thrill in theirs.

Because it preserves the full three-dimensional presence of the body, sculpture is, next to the drama, the most realistic of the arts. This realism is not, however, an unmixed advantage for general appreciation. For, finding the shape of the body, men sometimes demand its color and life, complaining that the statue is cold and dead; or else, giving life to the form, they react to it practically and socially, as they would toward the real body. Yet, for the one attitude, the art itself cannot be held responsible, but rather some want of genius in the artist or lack of imagination in the spectator; and as for the other, although only a bloodless dogma would demand the elimination of passion and interest from the appreciation of sculpture–for unless the marble arouse the natural feelings toward the body it is no successful expression–nevertheless, good taste does demand that, through attention to form and a sense of the unreality of the object, these feelings be subdued to contemplation.

In order to keep the statue on the ideal plane, it should not be too realistically fashioned. If it looks too much like a man, we shall first treat it as a man, as we do one of Jarley's or Mme. Tissaud's waxworks, and then after we have been undeceived, we shall have toward it an uncanny feeling, totally unaesthetic, as towards a corpse. The statue, therefore, if life-sized, should not be given the colors or clothing of life. Tinting is not excluded, provided no attempt is made at exact imitation; and when the statue is of heroic, or less than the normal size, as in porcelain, both coloring and clothing may be more realistic. No hard and fast rules can be formulated; yet the principle is plain–there should be realism in one aspect, above all in shape, in order that there may be an aesthetic semblance of life, but not in all, in order that the statue may not be a mere substitute for life, awakening the reactions appropriate to life. Moreover, appreciating the beauty of his material, the sculptor may not wish to cover it up, as he would if he tinted it. As in painting, the attainment of beauty in the medium may interfere with full realism in execution. For the sake of beauty of color, the worker in bronze will be content to see the white man black, and for the sake of beauty of line he may even sacrifice something of exactness in the rendering of shape.

For there is a beauty in the media of sculpture, apart from what they may represent, quite as real, if not as obvious, as in the other arts. And without this beauty, there is no artistic sculpture. Its subtlety does not diminish its importance or its effect upon our feeling, for it makes all the difference between a mere imitation of nature and a work of art charming and compelling. We do not need to recognize its existence explicitly in order to appreciate it; yet, as soon as our attention is called to it, we admit it and accord to it that rare influence which before was felt but nameless.

In the first place, the color of the material is expressive. The black and gold of bronze have a depth and intensity, the whiteness of marble a coldness, clarity, and, serenity, inescapable. The weight and hardness, or lightness and softness, of the material, also count. If people do not feel the expressiveness of these qualities directly, they nevertheless do feel it indirectly, whenever they appreciate the superior fitness of marble and bronze for the embodiment of the heroic and supernatural, and of the light and fragile porcelain for the more fleeting and trivial phases of life. Size, too, is expressive. There is a daintiness and tenderness about a little statue, contrasting strongly with the grandeur and majesty of one of heroic size. The usual small size of the terra cotta figurines among the Greeks was appropriate for the genre subjects which they so frequently represented, and an Aphrodite in this material is rather the Earthly than the Heavenly Love.

There is also an evident beauty of line in sculpture, similar to the beauty of line in painting. The curved line is expressive of movement and grace; the horizontal, of repose; the crooked line, of energy and conflict. Compare, from this point of view, Rodin's "The Aged Helmet- Maker's Wife" with his "Danaid,"–how expressive of struggle and suffering are the uneven lines of the former, how voluptuous the curves of the latter! Michelangelo is the great example of the use of tortuous lines for the expression of conflict. Undulating vertical lines are largely responsible for the "grace and dignity" of the classic sculpture.

There is an organic unity of line in sculpture, similar again to that in painting. And by line I mean not only surface lines, but the lines made by the planes in which the body lies, the lines of pose and attitude. The predominance of a single type of line, the union of many lines to form a single continuous line, balance and symmetry of line, proportion of length and parallelism, are all to be found in sculpture. Especially important is rhythm–the harmonious, balanced movement of lines. In the "Venus de Milo," for example, the plane of the lower limbs from the feet to the knees moves to the left; there is an opposite and balancing movement from the right knee to the waist; the first movement is repeated in the parallel line from the right hip to the top of the head; this, in turn, is balanced by a line in the opposite direction running from the left hip to the right shoulder, parallel to the second line; but the equilibrium of line is not a rigid one, for the body as a whole moves in an undulating line to the left, imparting grace and a total unity.

The beauty of line in sculpture is, of course, no invention of the artist; for nature has created it in the body itself. The sculptor takes this beauty as the basis of his work, remodeling only by the elimination of details, through which purer effects of line are obtained, or by the selection and emphasis of pose, through which these effects are rendered more intensely expressive. All conventionalization is in the interest of increased beauty of line. But too great a sacrifice of the natural contours of the body, as in some of the work of the Cubists, results in a lifelessness that cannot be atoned for by any formal beauty.

The unification of line in sculpture is a matter not only of lines within the whole and of single contours, but of the total visual form of the whole, of silhouette. Although three-dimensional, every statue casts a two-dimensional image on the retina. It makes as many of these plane pictures as there are points of view from which it can be seen. One can easily convince oneself of this by viewing a statue from a distance, when it will flatten out to a mere outline or silhouette. As such, it should be clear and simple and pleasing, capable of being grasped as a whole irrespective of detail. Michelangelo demanded that every statue be capable of being put inside of some simple geometrical figure, like a pyramid or a cube; that there be no wayward arms or legs, but close attachment to the body, so close that the statue might be rolled down hill without any part being broken off. This last is perhaps too rigorous a requirement, but the best work of all periods exhibits visual clarity and concentration[1].

Within its contours the statue stands alone. This is the essential difference between painting and sculpture; the painted thing is always a part of a larger spatial whole within which it exists in relation to other things, while the sculptured thing exists by itself; the space of the statue is the space which it fills; there is no further space to which it belongs, no background in which it lies. The space of sculpture, like the space of painting, is of course a represented or imaginary space, to be carefully distinguished from the real space of the room in which it is placed and the floor upon which it stands. The pedestal serves the same purpose in sculpture as the frame in the sister art; it cuts off the ideal space which the statue fills from the real space where it is housed, raising it above the common ground of real life, with its practical and social attitudes, into the realm of contemplation. The pedestal should be of a different material from the statue, else it belongs with the latter, and fails to perform its separating junction. The plate, on the other hand, should be of the same material, otherwise the statue would be made to stand on our earth, and in the same space with us.

However, just as in painting every object should be represented as belonging to a wider whole of space, so in sculpture, every part of the body should be represented as belonging to the whole body. If, therefore, only a part of the body is sculptured, it should be evident that it is a part and not the whole. In the portrait statue, for example, if the head alone is represented, there should appear, along with the head, as much of the bust as will suggest attachment to the body,

---

1. Compare Adolf Hildebrand, The Problem of Form in Painting and Sculpture.

in order that it may not seem decapitated! It is because the torso is so obviously a fragment of an ideal whole that we do not feel it to be an uncanny mutilation of a man or woman. In its present condition, the "Venus de Milo" is not the statue of an armless woman, but a statue of part of a whole woman.

A statue is not sufficiently unified by representing a single individual or several individuals united by some common interest or by participation in some common action; the unity in the object should be expressed through a unity in the material of representation. The finest taste requires that every statue should be made of only one kind of material. One part, say the body, should not be of marble, and another part, say the girdle, of gold or bronze. Such a combination of materials gives the impression of two things juxtaposed, not of a single whole. If in defense of this one were to say that through the difference of materials real differences in the object are portrayed, consistency would require that the principle be carried out, that the hair be of another material, and the eyes of still a third, with the result of making the statue a sheer agglomerate. And when more than one individual is represented, even a unity of material is not sufficient; it is necessary, in addition, that the several figures in the group be in contact with each Other. It is not enough that they stand on the same plate; for the real empty space that we see between them will keep them apart. The ideal space to which they belong, and the spiritual or dramatic oneness, should be mediated by a material touch of hands or other parts of the body. Compare, in this connection, Rodin's "Citizens of Calais" where this principle is violated, with the three figures from the summit of his "Hell Gate," where it is observed. In the former we simply know that the figures belong together, but we do not feel them as together.

In the normal type of sculpture only one figure is represented. For this, there is, perhaps, a chief point of regard, in front, the same as that which we ordinarily occupy with reference to our fellow men. Yet, since the body is beautiful from every point of view, the statue, unless designed to fit into a niche, should be so made that we shall want to move around it and survey it from every angle. Here is another difference between painting and sculpture. In the group, however, where several figures are represented united by some common interest or by participating in some common action, this difference is already beginning to disappear. For, in order to appreciate the dramatic significance of the group, the point of regard from in front is essential. The other aspects remain important for their corporeal beauty, but, since that is not ordinarily paired with an equal inner significance, they come to acquire a secondary place.

Impressionistic sculpture represents a further departure from the normal and in the direction of the pictorial. Here part of the block from which the statue has been hewn is left an integral member of the piece; and out of it the figure seems to grow, as it were. It performs in the whole a function corresponding to the background of a portrait–the representation of the environment. Thus, in Meunier's "The Miner," the block represents the mine; in Rodin's "Orpheus and Eurydice," it represents the mouth of Hades; in his "Mystery of the Spring," a basin. Through the possibility of thus representing the relation of man to his environment a notable extension in the scope of sculpture is obtained.

When a background is introduced, the figure or figures, being members of a larger whole, require less detailed treatment, less clearness of outline. Their parts may even be left in large measure unfinished, the contours melting together with the block. A special point of regard, from which alone the figures are modeled, is obviously essential. Striking is the contrast of this type with the classic, where the utmost precision in modeling is necessary. Along with the diminished emphasis on clearness of form goes an increased effort at the portrayal of the inner, more spiritual life; sentiment and mystery find an unwonted place in the art. Rodin's "Psyche" is a good illustration. Yet, despite these differences, the classic demand for living surfaces, for rhythmical lines, for perspicuity and totality of silhouette, for singleness and unity of material, abides.

However, when the block attains prominence, the unification of the different figures through contact is no longer of equal necessity. The background serves the purpose of bringing the figures together, of providing a material bond between them. This is especially true in the various kinds of relief, between which and sculpture in the round, impressionistic sculpture is a sort of compromise. In relief there may even be a representation of perspective, the figures seeming to lie behind each other, flatter and smaller to indicate distance. But we shall not enter into the technique of this, which obviously approaches that of painting.

When the charm of the body is the prime object of expression, those actions and poses which exhibit grace and vigor are the ones naturally chosen. This beauty is best revealed in the single figure, because in the group there is usually some dramatic interest which diverts attention from it. The figure is preferably wholly or partially undraped, or when drapery is used, it should reveal the body underneath and possess beauty of line of its own. Elaboration of drapery for its own sake, or in order to display virtuosity in modeling, shows lack of true sculptural vision, which always has its eye on the naked form. Aside from lack of charm, the old and crippled are avoided because their inharmonious lines would appear again in a statue which reproduced them; it is not possible, as in painting, to make a harmony out of them through relation to other lines in the total work, for no other lines exist; nor can their natural ugliness be so easily made acceptable through beauty of color and light. Nevertheless, no one can dogmatically assert that the artist must confine himself in his choice of subjects. If by harmonizing the distorted lines of an ugly body with each other, and by enhancing the given purity and expressiveness of his material, the artist can create a beauty of form overlying the repellence of the subject, and if he can make us feel the tragedy or pathos of age and disease, no one can gainsay his work. In his "Aged Helmet-Maker's Wife," Rodin has perhaps accomplished this.

In the classic sculpture the expression of the inner life is subordinate to the expression of corporeal beauty. Or, so far as mind is revealed, the revelation occurs through the body as a whole,–through attitude and pose and act. In this way complete unity between the inner and the outer beauty is preserved. For when through subtle modeling of the face the expression of the intense and individualized life of thought is attempted, the beauties of soul and body tend to fall apart and become rivals for attention. In classic sculpture, therefore, the face is rightly somewhat inexpressive, or better, is expressive of only the broad and typical human emotions. Fine or deep qualities may, however, be expressed; for dignity, poise, intelligence, sorrow, and active joy make themselves manifest in the total *habitus* of the body no less than in the face.

The work of Michelangelo is a further proof that sculpture can express the spiritual life, not only in the face, but in the body also. The expression there is no different in essential kind from that found in the heroic classic sculpture. It is universal, typical, not individual, personal; of the gods, not of men. Its quality alone differs; it is monstrous, pathological, grandiose, instead of serene and happily balanced.

But sculpture can also portray the individualized psychic life. For this, the portrait bust is the most appropriate medium of expression. By separating the head, the natural seat of mind, from the rest of the body, the rivalry between the beauty of soul and form is obviated. How much sculpture can do in this way is shown by the work of the Greeks and Romans in ancient times, and by such men as Houdon and Rodin among the moderns. Think of the intense and concentrated expression of thought and emotion in the "Voltaire" of Houdon and the "Dalou" of Rodin! Success depends largely upon the modeling of the subtle lines of the face, where the more highly specialized workings of the mind leave their impress.

Whatever of character the face may express can be expressed over again in its image. Of course the unique responses of mind to definite situations, such as, for example, the conversation of a man with his fellows, cannot be portrayed in sculpture, which isolates the individual. But the characteristic mood and attitude, the permanent residuum and condition of these responses, can be portrayed; and this constitutes personality or character. As Schopenhauer declared, the character of a man is better revealed in the face when he is in repose than when he is responding to other men, for there is always a certain amount of dissimulation or insincerity in social intercourse. The impossibility of rendering the color and animation of the eye constitutes a real deficiency, but, as has often been pointed out, this is partly minimized through the fact that the expression of the eye depends largely upon the brows; by itself, the eye is inexpressive. The portrait statue has much the same purpose as the bust, and hence should be draped. The heroic, equestrian statue, however, expresses rather the imposing, socially perceptible side of the man, than the inner life of thought and sentiment revealed in the bust.

The development of sculpture has produced nothing more beautiful than the solitaire statues which the Greeks have left us; and when we think of Greek sculpture we usually have in mind these marble or bronze images of gods and heroes. But we should not forget the figurines of terra cotta, a genre sculpture, representing men and women in the acts and attitudes of daily life, at work and at play. The ideal of sculpture should not be pitched too high. There is no reason why, with the example set by the Greeks, sculpture should not portray the lighter and more usual phases of human life. If sculpture is to strike new paths, and be something more than a repetition of classical models, it must become more realistic. And, as we have already noted, by making use of the block as a sort of background, even some relation of man to his environment can be represented. Through the group the simpler relations of man with his fellows–comradeship, love, conflict, or common action–can be expressed; although the power of sculpture is greatly limited in this direction. Sculpture is often taxed by people who emphasize the importance of the political and industrial mechanism with inability to portray large groups of men and the more complex relations arising out of the dependence of man upon nature and society. But one may well urge the compensating worth which sculpture will always possess of recalling men to a sense of the value and beauty of the individual as such, especially in an age like our own where they tend to be forgotten.

The principles that apply to the use of historical, literary, and symbolic themes in painting hold with increased force in sculpture. We must admit the right of the sculptor to illustrate simple and well-known historical or fictitious situations. At the same time, however, we must remember that a work of this kind is subject to a twofold standard: first and indispensable, the sculptural, is the form animate and beautiful; then, are the life and action appropriate to the idea? The first is alone absolutely unequivocal. The second, on the other hand, is largely relative; for unless the sculptor has carried out the idea in so masterly a fashion that we can think of no other possibility–as Phidias is said to have done with his statue of Zeus–there must always be something arbitrary about any particular representation. This arbitrary element is increased in symbolic sculpture. You can perhaps depict an actual or fictitious human situation by means of sculptured bodies and make your image seem inevitable; but how can you make bodies the vehicles of abstractions? Moreover, sculpture is a realistic art; it presents us with the semblance of living forms, and if these forms are monstrous or are shown accomplishing impossible things, they cannot escape a certain aspect of the ridiculous. I have in mind Rodin's "Man and His Thought." If the man were only represented fashioning the figure with his hands, his hands guided by his thought; but the hands are inactive, and the figure grows by thought alone! Or consider "The Hand of God" by the same artist. To say that we are in the hands of God is a good metaphorical way of expressing our dependence upon the Destiny that shapes our ends; but it is another thing to exhibit us as actually enfolded by a hand.

The more sensitive we are to the beauty of the body and of the mind, so far as manifest through the body, the better content we shall be with normal sculpture and the less urgently we shall demand symbolism. Of course all statues may become symbolic, as all works of art may, in the sense of possessing a universal meaning won by generalizing their individual significance. Symbolic in this legitimate way were the statues of the Greek gods; thus Aphrodite, who was lovely, became Love, and Athena, who was wise, became Wisdom. But there is nothing arbitrary in such symbolism.

Chapter XIII

Beauty in the Industrial Arts: Architecture

In the arts which we have studied so far, beauty has been the sole or chief end; in the industrial arts, beauty can be only a part of their total meaning. No matter how much of an artist a builder or a potter may be, he is necessarily controlled by the practical needs which houses and pots subserve. This was the original condition of all artists; for "in the beginning," before life's various aims were distinguished and pursued in isolation, the beautiful was always married to some other interest. Our method of study has, therefore, reversed the temporal order; but with intent, for we believe that the nature of a thing is better revealed in its final than in its rudimentary form. To complete our survey of the arts, we must, however, give some consideration to those works in which the unity of the useful and the beautiful is still preserved; and as an example we have chosen architecture, the most magnificent of them all.

First, we must clear up what might seem to be an inconsistency in our thinking. In our definition of art we insisted upon the freedom of beauty and the contrast between the aesthetic and the practical attitudes, yet now we are admitting that some things may be at once useful and beautiful. It would seem as if we must either modify our definition of art or else deny beauty to such objects as bridges and buildings. But we cannot do the latter, for the beauty of Brooklyn bridge or Notre Dame in Paris is a matter of direct feeling, which no theory can disestablish. And it is impossible to solve the problem by supposing that in the industrial arts beauty and utility are extraneous to each other, two separable aspects, which have no intimate connection. For the fact that a bridge spans a river or that a church is a place of worship is an element in its beauty. The aesthetic meaning of the object depends upon the practical meaning. You cannot reduce the beauty of a bridge or a cathedral to such factors as mere size and fine proportions, without relation to function. No preconceived idea of the purity of beauty can undermine our intuition of the beauty of utility.

Yet the dependence of beauty upon utility in the industrial arts is not at variance with the freedom from practical attitudes which we have claimed for it. For the beauty is still in the realm of perception, of contemplation, not of use. It is a pleasure in seeing how the purpose is expressed in the form and material of the object, not a pleasure in the possession of the object or an enjoyment of its benefits. I may take pleasure in the vision of purpose well embodied in an object which another man possesses, and my admiration will be as disinterested as my appreciation of a statue. And even if I do make use of the object, I may still get an aesthetic experience out of it, whenever I pause and survey it, delighting in it as an adequate expression of its purpose and my own joy in using it. Then beauty supervenes upon mere utility, and a value for contemplation grows out of and, for the moment, supplants a value in use. I now take delight in the perception of an object when formerly I took delight only in its use; I now enjoy the expression of purpose for its present perceived perfection, when once I enjoyed it only for its ulterior results. Such intervals of restful contemplation interrupt the activity of every thoughtful maker or user of tools. Thus the practical life may enter into the aesthetic, and that which grows out of exigence may develop into freedom.

There is one more objection which may be urged against the aesthetic character of the expression of practical purpose, namely, that the appreciation of it is an affair of intellect, not of feeling. This would indeed be fatal if it were necessarily true; but all men who love their work know that they put into admiration for their tools as much of warm emotion as of mind. There remains, however, the genuine difficulty of communicating this emotional perception of useful objects, of making it universal. It must be admitted that the attitude of the average beholder towards a useful object is usually practical, not contemplative, or else purely intellectual, an effort to understand its structure, with the idea of eventual use. Most works of industrial art produce no aesthetic experience whatever. But to be a genuine and complete work of fine art, an object must be so made that it will immediately impel the spectator to regard it aesthetically.

From what we have already established, we know how this requirement can be met: by elaborating the outer aspects of the object in the direction of pleasure and expression. By this means the beauty of mere appearance will strike and occupy the mind, inducing the aesthetic attitude towards the outside, from which it may then spread and embrace the inner, purposive meaning. The obviously disinterested and warmly emotional admiration of the shape will prevent the admiration for the purposive adaptation from being cold and abstract. Hence, although from the point of view of utility the beauty of mere appearance may seem to be a superfluity, it is almost indispensable from an aesthetic point of view, since it raises the appreciation of the purpose to the aesthetic plane. And we can understand how enthusiastic workmen, whose admiration for their work is already aesthetic, must necessarily desire to consecrate and communicate this feeling by beautifying the appearance of their products; how inevitably, through the ages, they have made things not only as perfect as they could, but as charming.

When developed for the ends of the aesthetic life, the useful object exhibits, therefore, two levels of beauty: first, that of appearance, of form and sensation, line and shape and color; and second, that of purpose spoken in the form. The first is of the vague and immediate character so well known to us; the second is more definite and less direct, since it depends upon the interpretation of the object in terms of its function. The relation between the two is like that which obtains, in a painting, between color and line, on the one hand, and representation, on the other. When the first level of beauty is richly developed on its own account, it becomes ornament. In a Greek vase, for example, there is a beauty of symmetrical, well-proportioned shape, delicate coloring of surface, and decorative painting, which might be felt by people who knew nothing of its use; and, in addition, foı those who have this knowledge, a beauty in the fine balance of parts in the adjustment of clay to its final cause. These factors, which we have distinguished by analysis, should, however, be felt as one in the aesthetic intuition of the object; the form, although beautiful in itself, should reveal the function, and the decoration, no matter how charming, should be appropriate and subordinate. Otherwise, as indeed so often happens, the beauty of one aspect may completely dominate the others; when the object either remains a pretty ornament perhaps, but is functionally dead; or else, if it keep this life, loses its unity in a rivalry of beautiful aspects.

All these points are strikingly illustrated in architecture. The architects claim that their art is a liberal one aiming at beauty, yet most buildings to-day are objects of practical interest alone. Their doors are merely for entrance, their windows for admission of light, their walls for inclosure. Few people, as they hurry in or out of an office building or a railway station, stay to contemplate the majesty of the height or the elegance of the facade; they transact their business, buy their tickets, check their luggage, and go. Even when the building has some claim to beauty, the mood of commercial life stifles observation; or, if the building is observed, there is no strong emotion or vivid play of imagination, no permanent impression of beauty lingering in the memory, no enrichment of the inner life, such as a musical air or a poem affords, but only a transient and fruitless recognition. For this reason many have thought that buildings must become useless, as castles and ruined temples are, in order to be beautiful. Yet, in proportion as this is true, it involves a failure on the part of architecture, a failure to make the useful a part of the beautiful. A building, which was designed to be a habitation of man, when taken apart from the life which it was meant to shelter and sustain, is an abstraction or a vain ornament at best. If the company which peopled it are gone, it can win significance only if we re-create them in the imagination, moving in the halls or worshiping at the altars. We cannot get rid of the practical for the sake of the aesthetic, but must take up the practical into the aesthetic. For this reason architecture has achieved its greatest successes where its uses have been most largely and freely emotional, most closely akin to the brooding spirit of beauty–in religious buildings.

Most buildings, it must be admitted, are not beautiful at all. In order to be beautiful, they should be alive, and alive all over, as a piece of sculpture is alive; there should be no unresponsive surfaces or details; but most of our buildings are dead–dead walls, dead lines, oblong boxes, neat and commodious, but dead. The practical problems which the architect has to solve are so complex and difficult, and the materials which he uses are so refractory, that there is inevitably a sacrifice of the beauty of appearance to utility. The very size of a building makes it aesthetically unmanageable all over. Here the lesser industrial arts, like the goldsmith's, have an advantage in the superior control which the workman can exert over his materials; his work is that of a single mind and hand; it does not require, as architecture does, the cooperation of a crowd of unfeeling artisans. In architecture, mechanical necessities and forms threaten to supplant aesthetic principles and shapes. The heavy square blocks, the rectangular lines, seem the antithesis of life and beauty. "All warmth, all movement, all love is round, or at least oval.... Only the cold, immovable, indifferent, and hateful is straight and square.... Life is round, and death is angular[1]." What

1. Ellen Key, *The Few and the Many*, translated from a quotation in Max Dessoir, *Aesthetik und Allgemeine Kunstwissenschaft*, page 396.

vividness of imagination or sentiment can transmute these dead and hollow masses into a life universally felt?

And yet, in a series of works of art among the most magnificent that man possesses, this miracle was achieved. The Greek temples and Gothic cathedrals are so much alive that they seem not to have been made with hands, but to have grown. The straight lines have been modified into delicate curves, the angles have given place to arches, the stiff and mathematical have been molten into movement and surprise, the heaviness has been so nicely balanced or overcome that it has been changed into lightness, with the help of human and animal sculpture and floral carving the inorganic has been transformed into the organic, by means of painting and stained glass even the dull surfaces of walls and windows have been made to glow into life. Artists wrought each portion and detail, and built the whole for the glory of God and the city, a monument for quiet contemplation, not a mere article to be used. With few exceptions, any architectural beauty that we create is but a feeble echo of theirs. Some day we may be able to produce something worthy to be placed by its side, but only when we have sanctified our life with communal aims. The aesthetic effect of a building depends upon many factors, of which only a few can be analyzed by us in this short chapter. If we abstract from its relation to purpose, architecture is fundamentally an art of spatial form. Working freely with it, under the sole limitation of function, the architect can make of this form a complex, various, and beautiful language intelligible to all men, and possessed of a systematic, yet fluent logic. Of this language the simplest element is line. At first view, as we approach a building from the outside, its beauty, as in the case of sculpture, is essentially pictorial. For, although a building is a three-dimensional solid in reality, each view of it is a two-dimensional surface, bounded by lines and divided and diversified within by other lines. Now these lines have their life and beauty like the lines of a picture. How they get this life and what its specific quality is in the case of particular lines, we need not explain again; but no one can fail to feel the upward movement of the vertical lines of the Gothic style, the repose of the horizontal lines of the Renaissance style, the playful grace of the Rococo. Naturally, since the front of a building, where one enters, is the most important and the most constantly in view, its pictorial beauty is elaborated with especial care by the architect. This is the justification of the overshadowing preeminence of the facade in Renaissance palaces, which indeed was oftentimes the only visible part of the outside of the building. When, however, the building is perspicuous all round, it should, like a statue, present a beautiful view from every standpoint.

In architecture, as in painting, the visual elements are adapted to one or the other of the two chief ways of seeing. Either the surfaces are seen as wholes primarily and the details in subordination; or else the parts stand out clear and distinct, and the whole is their summation. The former is always the case when the surfaces are left plain with few divisions, or, if the surfaces are divided, when the lines intersect and intermingle, as is exemplified in late Renaissance or Baroque work, where the walls are covered with lavish ornament, the enframement of windows is broken by moldings and sculpture which carry into the surrounding spaces, and where, instead of embracing one story, the "orders" comprise the entire height of the building. The second possibility is well illustrated by the early classical Renaissance, where the surface of each story, sharply separated from the others by the line of the frieze, is divided regularly by arches or columns, each window clearly enframed, and every sculptured ornament provided with a niche.

There is, however, this fundamental difference between architectural and pictorial lines: the latter are usually pure kinematical lines, lines of free and un-resisted movement, while the former are usually dynamical, lines of force which move against the resistance of mass. In a picture objects are volatilized into light and have lost all weight; but in architecture, since they are present in reality and not in mere semblance, their weight is retained. A Greek column, for example, not only moves upward, but also against the superincumbent load of the entablature which it carries. The difference between the two arts can be appreciated by comparing the picture of a building with the building itself; in the former, despite the fact that we know how heavy the dome or pediment is, and how strong therefore the piers or columns that support it, we hardly feel them as heavy or strong at all–the forces and masses have been transformed into abstract lines and shapes. Sometimes, however, architectural lines and surfaces remain purely kinematical; on the inside of our rooms, for example, when the surfaces are smooth, and especially when they are decorated, we often feel no tension of conflicting forces, but only a quiet play of movements; it is as if the walls had been changed into the paper or paint that covers them. The vividness of the expression of mechanical forces in architecture depends, moreover, upon the kind of materials employed; it is greater in marble than in wood, and less in our modern constructions of steel and glass, where the piers move in single vertical lines from the bottom to the top of the building, than in the old forms, where the upper part of the building is frankly carried by the lower.

The mere expression of mechanical forces in a building would not, however, be aesthetic by itself, no matter how obvious to the mind. We must not only know these forces to be there, we must also feel them as there; we must appreciate them in terms of our own experiences in supporting weights and overcoming resistances. We must transform the mechanical into the vital, the material into the human. Art is an expression of life, not of mathematics. And this translation is not the result of an unusual, artificial attitude assumed for the sake of aesthetic appreciation; it is the natural mode of apperceiving force and mass. We cannot see a column supporting an entablature without feeling that it stands firm to bear the weight, much as we should stand if we were in its place. If this is a "pathetic fallacy," it is one which we all inevitably commit. Even the skeptic, if he were to examine carefully into his own mind, would find that he commits it, whenever he gives to the column, not a casual or merely calculating regard, but a free and earnest attention. If he gives his mind to the column and lets the column take hold of his mind, allowing his psychological mechanism to work unhampered, he will commit it. The aesthetic intuition of force–the human way of appreciating it–is, in fact, primary; the purely mechanical and mathematical is an abstraction, superimposed for practical and scientific purposes.

The interplay of humanized mechanical energies, of which architecture is the expression, may be conceived as the resultant of four chief forces, acting each in a definite direction: upward, downward, outward, and inward. The downward force is associated with the weight of the materials of which the building is constructed. To all physical objects we ascribe a tendency toward the earth. An unsupported weight will fall, and even when supported will exert a pressure downward. And this tendency is no mere directed force in the physical sense, but an impulse, in the personal sense. For when with hand or shoulder we support a weight, we inevitably interpret it in terms of our own voluntary muscular exertion in resisting it; even as we strive to resist it, so it seems to strive to fall. Although this force is exerted downward, it shows itself in the horizontal lines of a building, in string courses, parapets, cornices, friezes; for the horizontal is the line parallel to the earth, toward which the force is directed, and along which we lie when we rest.

Opposed to the downward force is the upward force. If an object does not fall, it must be supported by a force in the upward direction; the hand must exert a force perpendicular to the mass which it carries; the body must hold itself erect in order to bear its own weight. Just so, an architectural member, if it is not to collapse, must raise itself upward. Upward forces are revealed by the vertical lines of a building–the prevailing lines of columns, piers, shafts, pinnacles, towers, spires. We interpret vertical lines as moving upward, partly because the eye moves upward in scanning them, partly because we ourselves move in lines of this general direction in going from the bottom to the top of a building. Even when we are at the top of a building we apprehend its vertical lines as rising rather than as descending, because we ourselves had to rise in order to get there. Converging lines, as of towers and spires, we also interpret in the same way as going to the point of meeting above.

Acting in conjunction with the downward force is an outward one. The lower parts of a construction tend to spread out as they give way under the weight of the superincumbent masses; if they are very much broader than the latter, they give the impression of great weight carried. As a result, a horizontal line is introduced, and the longer it is in comparison with the vertical line of height, the heavier the effect. Compare, for example, the impression made by a tall and thin triangular shape, with a low and broad one; and compare also the relative lengths of the horizontal and the vertical lines. The former shape seems simply to rise, while the latter lifts. We seem to observe the working of this outward force, as Lipps has remarked, in the spreading out of the trunks of trees at the base and in the feet of animals; and we feel it in ourselves whenever we spread our limbs apart to brace ourselves to withstand a load.

Whenever the outward force is resisted, it gives evidence of the existence of a force operating in the opposed direction–inward. Without this force, the lower parts of a construction would lack all solidity and spread like a molten mass on the ground. This is especially striking where the material, instead of spreading outward and downward, seems to press itself inward and upward. Compare, for example, a shape whose base-line is smaller than the line of its top with one in which the reverse holds true. The former gives the impression of lightness and agility, with a prevailing upward trend, the other an impression of weight and heaviness, with a prevailing trend towards the ground. Obviously, the outward and the inward forces are correlative and complementary: we have already observed that a construction would collapse without the inward; we can now see that it would disappear entirely without the outward. Obviously, also, the inward and upward go together, and the downward and outward.

Even a plain rectangular wall manifests the interplay of these forces. The horizontal dimension represents the downward and outward force of the weight; the vertical dimension, the upward forces, which prevent the wall from collapsing in itself and hold it upright; while the lateral boundaries give evidence of the inward tension that keeps the mass together. But the most beautiful expressions of architectural forces are to be found in the historical styles. In each style there is a characteristic relationship between the forces, imparting a distinctive feeling. I shall offer a brief analysis of some of these.

Many have recognized that the classical Greek construction, as illustrated in the Doric temple, expresses a fine equilibrium between the upward and the downward forces, embodied in the vertical and horizontal lines respectively. The upward force is manifest primarily in the vertical columns, and is emphasized there by the flutings, the slight progressive narrowing toward the top, and the inward effort of the necking just below the echinus. The downward force is embodied in the horizontal lines of the lintel, architrave, cornice, and in the hanging mutules and gutta. The two forces come to rest in the abaci, which, as the crowning members of the columns, directly carry the weight of the entire entablature. The equilibrium between the horizontal and the vertical tendencies is, however, not a static but a moving one; for the two opposing forces are present in every part of the building from the stylobate to the ridge of the triangular pediment. The downward force is already manifest in the widened base of the column, where it works in conjunction with the inward tendency, and shows its effect at the critical points at the top of the supporting column–in the spreading echinus with its horizontal bands beneath and in the horizontal lines of the abaci. The upward force, on the other hand, is continued right through the solid mass of the entablature, in the vertical lines of the triglyphs, in the antefixes, and even to the very apex of the building, where the ascending lines of the triangular pediment meet. The resulting total effect is that of a perfect, yet swaying balance.

The aesthetic effect derived from the interplay of forces in the Ionic form is similar to that in the Doric, only more delicate and elastic. The slender columns, being less rugged and resistant than the Doric, seem to transmit the weight supported, which shows itself, therefore, in the outward spreading molded base; but this apparent lack of strength in the column is compensated for by the elastic energy in the coiled spring of the volutes, upon which, with the slight mediation of a narrow band, the entablature rests. Here most of the upward energy of the Ionic form is concentrated; for although the dentils of the frieze perform the function of the triglyphs, they are too small to do it effectively; the style lacks, therefore, the gentle harmonizing of forces all over, characteristic of the Doric, and evinces instead a clean-cut elastic tension at a given point. This effect is, however, somewhat softened by the breaking up of the downward force of weight by means of the recessed divisions of the architrave. In the Corinthian capital, which has the same general feeling as the Ionic, the elastic tension is still further diminished through the renewed emphasis on the mediating abacus, the reduction of the size of the volutes, and the overhanging floral carvings. However, by reason of the strength given by the bell and the projecting outward and upward curving form of the abacus, the suggestion of weakness in the Corinthian form is overcome, but the gentleness remains.

If the Greek construction expresses a balance between the upward and downward forces, the arched forms that followed express the victory of the upward. In the arch the upward force, instead of being arrested where the support meets the mass to be carried, is continued throughout the mass itself. Of the two chief types of arches, the round and the pointed, each has a specific feeling. We shall study the round form first, where the vertical tendency is indeed victorious, but only through reconciliation and compromise.

In the round arch all four forces are beautifully expressed. The upward is manifest, first, in the vertical pier, which acts very much as the column does, and, in Roman work, was often replaced by the column. The opposing downward force is expressed in the horizontal upper bound of the arch and in the line of the impost, also horizontal, which breaks the vertical line and so marks the place where the two forces come into sharpest conflict. In this conflict, the vertical is victorious; for, instead of being stopped by the impost, it is carried up throughout the entire construction by means of the upward and inward curving of the arch. The very curve of the arch shows, however, that the victory is not absolute; for its circular form is obviously determined as a compromise between an inward centripetal force, moving upward and diminishing the breadth of the arch to a mere point at its apex, and an outward centrifugal force, gradually spreading the arch downward until it reaches its greatest breadth at the impost, where it is arrested by the opposing vertical force in the pier. To the historical imagination, the round arch seems, therefore, to express the genial classical idea of a control by the higher nature which nevertheless did no violence to the demands of the lower. In the spherical dome the effect is the same, only the interplay of forces operates in three dimensions instead of two.

When arches are superposed, the upward movement proceeds in stages, beginning anew at each horizontal division of the wall space. The use of entablatures applied to the wall and of engaged columns, common in Roman work, seems to involve an attempt at a fusion of two contradictory styles, and is usually condemned as such. This contradiction can be solved, however, by viewing the entablatures as mere weightless lines of division of the wall, usually marking off the different stories, and by viewing the columns in a similar fashion as having no supporting function–which is actually the case–and as simply serving the purpose of framing the arches. At most they merely indicate the direction of the chief contending forces,–the parallel lintels signalizing the force of weight, and the vertical columns, standing one upon the other, pointing the movement of the upward force. They have, therefore, a pictorial rather than a dynamic significance.

Differences of feeling in arched forms depend upon the relative height of arches and supporting piers and columns. The vertical effect is strongly emphasized when the latter are relatively high, while the effect of weight is increased in flattened arches, which for this reason are especially appropriate for crypts and prison entrances. Interesting complications are introduced in arcades or intersecting vaults, where a single column serves as a support for two or more arches; for there the vertical force is divided, flowing in different directions in the little triangular piece of wall between, or along the ribs of the vaults. Something similar occurs in the Byzantine dome on pendentives, only instead of supporting the horizontal weight of a gallery or a vault, the triangular pendentives meet the outward thrust of a superposed dome.

In Renaissance architecture and the modern classical revivals, where Greek and Roman styles are freely adapted to novel modes of life and purpose, no essentially new form was added to architectural speech. There were combinations of old forms into more complex structures, but no new important elements. The most outstanding novelty is perhaps the reversed relation between the whole and the parts. In the classic styles, whether arched or Greek, the whole is built up of the parts additively; each is a relatively independent center of energy complete in itself; first the columns, then the architrave, frieze, and cornice, then the pediment; or first one row of arches, then another row on top of this, and so on. Coordination is the governing principle. But in the modern adaptations, even where coordination rather than subordination rules in the pictorial sphere, the whole is first dynamically and the parts are secondary. In the typical Renaissance facade, for example, the arches of the windows are rather openings in the walls than supporting members. They are centers of little eddies of force, rather than independent parts of the main determining stream of energy. The wall rises as a whole to its heavy overhanging cornice, despite the horizontal divisions marking the stories. There are, however, important differences between the various modern types; the earlier Renaissance forms, for example, keeping closer to the antique than the later Baroque and Rococo.

The complete triumph of the vertical tendency, foreshadowed in the Roman, was proclaimed in Gothic architecture in the use of the pointed arch. For in the round arch the vertical has not conquered after all; the horizontal is still active there, even to the apex of the arch, where the tangential line is parallel to the earth, the line of weight. But in the pointed style the victory of the vertical is clearly decisive,–the upward and inward forces, by elongating and narrowing the curve of the arch to a point, have dominated the downward and outward. The great height of the piers, the gabled roofs, the ribs of the vaults the pointed form of the windows, the towers, spires, and pinnacles,–all proclaim it. Yet this victory does not occur without opposition; for the higher the vaulting, the greater the weight to be carried; the greater, therefore, the outward thrust, which had to find its expression and its stay in the buttress. But even the buttress, although it bears witness to the outward and horizontal force of weight, was nevertheless so fashioned with its gable and pinnacle, or its own arched form, as to aid the upward movement. The thinness of walls and partitions, and the piercing of these with arches and windows, by lightening the force of weight, also contributed to increase the vertical movement. At sight of a true Gothic cathedral, we feel ourselves fairly lifted off the ground and rushed upward.

In thinking of the beauty of architecture, we are all too apt to consider the exterior exclusively, forgetting that the inside of a building, where we live, is even more important practically, and is capable of at least as great an aesthetic effect.

The characteristic aesthetic effect of the interior is a function of the inclosed space, the volume, not of the inclosing walls taken singly. The walls are only the limits of this space, they are not the space itself. Of course, the walls within have their own beauty, of surface and pervading energy, but this does not differ markedly from that of the walls seen from the outside, and what we have established for the one holds for the other. But the beauty of the inclosed space is something entirely new.

In itself, however, mere volume of space is no more aesthetic than mere bounding line or surface; in order to become beautiful, it must become alive. But how can space–the most abstract thing in the world–become alive? By having the activities which it incloses felt into it. Just as our bodies are felt to be alive because our activities express themselves there, so our rooms, because we live and move within them. As we enter a cathedral and look down the long aisle, the movement of our eyes inevitably suggests the movement of our bodies; or, as we look up and our eyes follow the ribs of the vaulting, it is as if we ourselves were borne aloft; in the imagination we move through the open spaces; and since we do not actually move, we locate our impulses to movement, not in our bodies, but in the space through which we take our imagined flight. Every object suggests movement to it, and we fill the intervening space with this imagined movement, provided only we stay our activities and give time for the imagination to work its will. Thus all space may become alive with the possibilities of movement which it offers.

The aesthetic effects of volume vary chiefly according to size and shape. In order to be appreciated, these effects must in general be somewhat striking; otherwise they pass unnoticed, and we simply take the interiors of our buildings as matters of course.

It is a curious fact that an impression of vastness can be secured by inclosing a relatively small space. A square, like the Place de la Concorde, or even the inside of a cathedral, produces a feeling of size almost, if not quite, as great as an open prairie or sea. The reason, I suppose, is that an inclosed space offers definite points as stimuli and goals for suggested movements. As we imaginatively reach out and touch these points, we seem to encompass their distance; and the volume of our own bodies seems to be magnified accordingly. The boundaries of the space become a second and greater integument. This is of decisive importance; for the aesthetic appreciation of size is relative to an appreciation of the size of our own bodies; in nature itself there is nothing either large or small. Along with the sense of vastness goes a sense of freedom; the one is the aesthetic experience resulting from the imaginative reaching of the goal of a movement, the other is the feeling of the imagined movement itself.

When, on the other hand, an inclosure is small, as in the case of a cell, and especially when the ceiling or vault is low, as in a crypt, it feels cabined and confined, because our own possibilities of movement are restricted. In order to avoid this feeling, if a space is limited in one direction, it must be free in another; if narrow, it must be long; if small in plan, it must be high, as in a tower.

The form of an inclosed space is also expressive. There are two chief types, the longitudinal and the radial; but since these may exist either in plan or in elevation, four possibilities result: the longitudinal-horizontal, as in an aisle; the longitudinal-vertical, as in a tower; the radial-horizontal, illustrated by every equilateral plan–triangle, square, regular polygon, and above all, the most perfect form of this type, the circle; and finally, the radial-vertical, of which domed spaces, like the Pantheon or St. Paul's, are examples. The terms used to designate them, together with the examples, afford a good idea of what these space forms are, making further description unnecessary. It is interesting to observe how different the expression of the square and the triangle is when they determine the plan of an inclosed space from what it is when they are the shapes of walls. In the case of the latter, according to the analysis which we have given of them, the figures represent an interplay of antagonistic horizontal and vertical forces, about an axis drawn perpendicular to the midpoint of the base line; while as plans they express forces homogeneous in kind radiating from their centers. The feeling of longitudinal forms is one of continued movement, forward or upward as the case may be; when the distance is very great, the feeling is of infinity, either of vista, as in an aisle, or of height, as in a tower, for even when the point at the end is clearly seen and known, we continue it in the imagination. The radial forms, on the other hand, even when the axes are very long, express completeness and security, for no matter how far we go in any one direction, we have to proceed along a line which brings us back to our starting point; in following to the top the movement of the curved line of a dome or an apse, the continuation of the same line carries us down on the other side to a point corresponding to the one from which we set out; if we wander, we return home.

With reference to the division of interiors into parts, the same two types are exemplified which we found in studying the visual and the dynamic aspects of buildings. Either the parts of the interior space are clearly marked off from each other, and the perception of the whole which they constitute is reached by a process of summation; or else, to one standing within, the space is first perceived as a whole, and its parts, lacking clear definition, are perceived subsequently. In the former type, the parts are of pronounced individuality, and the whole is their free and joint work; in the latter, the parts are merged, and tend to be lost in the whole. These two possibilities exist whether the space be of radial or longitudinal form. In general, the classical styles lend themselves to the coordinate type of division of the interior, while the later styles favor the subordination of the parts to the whole.

The other factors in the beauty of architecture, besides the expression of the forces resident in its forms, can receive only scant notice from us. Among these is light–its admission, exclusion, and diffusion. A house with ample windows flooded with sunshine shares the feeling of an open day; a cathedral, dimly lighted, stimulates a mood of brooding mystery and meditation, like some dark forest. Another factor is color. Color plays a double part in architecture: first, to enliven the neutral tones of certain materials; and second, to impart specific moods. It was no barbaric taste, but a keen feeling for life and warmth that induced the Greeks to paint their temples; and without their rose windows, Gothic cathedrals are like faces from which the glow of life is departing. The different colors have the same feelings in architecture that they have in painting. The reds and purples of ecclesiastical stained glass stimulate the passion of adoration, the blues deepen it, and the yellows seem to offer a glimpse of heavenly bliss. Sound, its presence or its absence, is another factor in architectural expression: the quiet of the church in contrast with the noise of the busy street outside, the peal of the organ, or the chorus of young voices. Although architecture is a spatial art and music a temporal art, they nevertheless go well together because the emotions aroused by both are vague and voluminous, and the sounds, reverberating from the walls and filling the inclosed spaces, seem to fuse with them. Ornamental carving performs a diversifying and enlivening function similar to that of color. So long as its lines follow those of the architectural forms, it may well be rich and elaborate. It is fitting, moreover, that buildings designed to be houses of the gods should contain their images, and that the same spirit that expresses itself in playful lines should become embodied in griffin and gargoyle. Finally, erected in the open, with no shelter or enframement, a building is, in large measure, a part of nature and possesses something of the beauty of nature. Rooted to one place like a tree, it shares the beauty of its site, and responds to the ever varying effects of light and shadow, rain and mist and snow.

The abstract beauty of architecture can be understood without any knowledge of the purposes of buildings. A Hindu who knows nothing of our civilization cannot fail to be responsive to Notre Dame, any more than we can fail to admire the beauty of Taj Mahal. The very simplest architectural forms, like the pyramids or the Washington monument, provided they are of sufficient size and mass, speak an eloquent language which is immediately understood. And the content of their speech is not so abstract as might be judged from our previous studies of it; for in architecture, as in music, concrete emotions and sentiments flow into the channel cut by the form. Longing, aspiration, and mystery have universally been felt into a form pointing skyward; and the feeling of incompleteness has been lost, and security regained, in an overarching dome.

There is, however, this difference between architecture and music. In music, the emotional content is purely personal; while in architecture, it may become social and historical. Architectural purposes are all social: the purposes of a family, a nation, a cult. And the purposes of the greatest of buildings–of those which serve the nation and religion–are also historical; about them gather the traditions of a community. Centers of the life of a people, created by it and enduring with it, they become its symbols; or outlasting it, memorials and witnesses to it. The vague emotions aroused by the architectural forms are pointed and enriched by this spirit: the vastness, seclusion, magnificence, mystery, and aspiration of the Gothic cathedral become associated with the life of the medieval Catholic church; the fine balance, clarity, and simplicity of the Greek temple with the best in Greek culture. This interpretation of a building in terms of its purpose and history is necessary to a complete aesthetic appreciation. Without it, a building may have many beauties, all the beauties which we have analyzed; but they are all separate, and there is no beauty of the whole. It is the life which the many parts and aspects serve that makes them into one.

This chapter is being closed with a brief discussion of architectural composition. The unity of a building is constituted primarily by the necessary adjustment of part to part which makes possible the life that it incloses. How the parts serve this purpose is not immediately evident to intuition; nor can it be; yet it should be intelligible to a thoughtful study. The knowledge thus gained may then enter into an imaginative vision, for which the building will seem like an organism pulsing with life.

This purposive unity cannot well be secured without spatial contiguity; here, as in sculpture, a unified life demands a unified material. Yet sometimes detached structures belong together functionally, and may be felt as one aesthetically, provided they are similar in design and some one of them is dominant; otherwise, each claims to be a distinct individual, and aesthetic rivalry is the result.

Functional unity, although necessary, is not sufficient for aesthetic unity; in addition, there must be formal unity–design, composition. To study this adequately would require a separate treatise, which has not yet been written, so far as I know, with anything approaching philosophical depth and completeness; but for our plan it will be sufficient to show how the general principles of aesthetic form are illustrated in architecture; and because of the perspicuity of things spatial, these principles are nowhere else so lucidly manifest.

Since architecture is a spatial art, unity in variety is chiefly a matter of harmony and balance rather than of evolution, and of these harmony is perhaps the most conspicuous. Harmony is secured in many ways.

First, by giving the whole building or parts of the building a simple geometrical form readily perceived,–for example, the cruciform plan of many Gothic cathedrals, the oblong plan and oblong surmounted by a triangle in the facade of the Greek temple, the octagonal shape of a Renaissance chapel. A higher degree of harmony is obtained when the same shape is repeated throughout the various parts of the building,–the cylinder in the columns, the triangle or semicircle in the arches and gables. A step further is taken in the same direction when the different similar parts are all of the same size, as in the Greek temple, where the columns are all of one size, and similar parts of columns of equal size, and the metopes and triglyphs likewise.

A more complex type of harmony, since it admits of greater variety, is proportionality. Proportionality may be of various kinds. It may be merely the existence of a definite numerical relation between the dimensions of single parts, or the areas of various parts, of a building. This, in turn, may be either a simple arithmetical relation, such as exists between the parts of a Greek facade, each being some simple multiple of the unit or module; or a more complex relation like the Golden Section, where the smaller is to the larger dimension as the larger is to the sum of both; or like that which obtains when different parts form a geometrical series, where each is smaller or larger than the preceding by some fraction of the latter. The relation between the length and breadth of the facade of the Ducal Palace in Florence illustrates the Golden Section; the heights of the stories of the Peller House in Nuremberg form a geometrical series. This type of harmony is most complete when the proportion between the dimensions of the different parts is the same as that of the whole building,–by the ancients called *concinnitas* because it produces a feeling akin to that of musical harmony. Dominance of a particular kind of line, horizontal or vertical, also gives harmony. Finally, harmony is secured by sameness of direction of line: the alignment of windows or parallelism between moldings dividing the surfaces of walls, for example.

The relations, so seemingly mathematical, upon which architectural harmony is based, need not be exact, for two reasons: minor deviations are not perceptible, and even when perceptible, they give to the whole a feeling of life. Our experience with living things has taught us that, despite their orderliness, there is no exact mathematical regularity in their proportions; hence forms which cannot be precisely formulated are better fitted to symbolize life to us than the rigidly geometrical. The same experience has taught us that the curvilinear forms are closer to life than the angular; hence again the tendency, for aesthetic purposes, to introduce minute departures from the plumb-line and rule. There is, however, a type of life specifically human, the life of reason, which is best symbolized by mathematical relations; hence the Greeks, and all those who have followed the classical ideal, all who have had a passion for reason, have felt the circle and the square, and every other exact embodiment of clarity and intelligence, to be beautiful. In no other art has the passion for the intelligible been so perfectly expressed as in classical architecture.

Next in importance to harmony as a mode of unity in variety in architecture is balance. Balance implies emphatic variety, or contrast. One mode of balance, that between the upward and the downward tendencies, we have already discussed. There is another mode, similar to that which exists in painting and sculpture, the balance between the right and left members of a building. In order that this type of balance may be appreciated, there must be some axis or line of mediation between the parts, from which the opposing tendencies take their start; otherwise we view the parts together, instead of in opposition. For example, there is balance between two wings of a building which are separated by some central member or link; balance between the aisles of a church on either side of the nave; balance between the sets of three columns right and left of the door in the Greek hexastyle temple. Such cases of symmetry between equal right and left parts are the simplest examples of balance; but there are other, more complex types. For example, the parts may be unequal, yet balance nevertheless, provided their inequality is compensated for by some enrichment of design or ornament in the lesser part. Or again, there may be a balance between contrasting shapes, such as the square and the triangle, when they make an equal claim upon the attention.

Although, since architecture is a static art, evolution is not so important as harmony and balance, it exists nevertheless. In a colonnade, as you look down it, with the height of the columns diminishing in perspective, there is a rhythmical movement of eye and attention toward the last column as a goal. There is the same rhythmical movement in following the arches on either side of the nave of a church leading to the apse.

There is a rhythmical movement in the progressive diminution of the height of the stories of a building, going towards the top. In such spatio-temporal rhythms, the proportional equality between the members corresponds to the equal intervals in temporal rhythms, and the alternation between member and intervening space, or between member and line of division, corresponds to the alternation between heavy and light accents. Last, evolution is present in architecture, whenever, often without rhythmical divisions, the attention is impelled to move along lines that meet at a point which serves as a climax, as in all triangular forms where the lines lead up to the apex,–pointed windows or arches, towers ending in belfries or pinnacles.

Dominance, with its correlative, subordination, are everywhere present in architecture. In general, size and a central position, which usually go together, determine preeminence. The largest masses and those which occupy a central position inevitably rule the others. The towers and the facade dominate the exterior of a Gothic cathedral, the middle doorway is superior to those which flank it, and within, the central and larger nave dominates the smaller aisles on either side. When there are many dominant elements, as is necessarily the case in a large building, they must be unified by balance, if there are two, or by subordination to one of them, if three or more; otherwise, each claims to be the whole and the building falls apart into its members. There cannot well be three vertical dominant parts, because the central one makes a claim to preeminence which cannot be satisfied without superiority in size. A central member should, therefore, either be made larger than those flanking it, or else should be reduced to the status of a mere subordinate link between the others.

In the horizontal division of a building into stories–as, for example, in the Palazzo Farnese near Rome–it is easier for the prominent parts to be equal, because they are better united by the evident contiguity of their masses, by their inclosure in a simple geometrical shape, and enframement between base and overhanging cornice. Yet here also we observe the tendency to make the middle larger or otherwise dominant, exemplified even in the building cited, where the central part is distinguished by the ornamental shield, upon which the attention is focused. When there are four horizontal divisions, our tendency is to divide them into groups of two; but unless this grouping is clearly marked by a molding or other such device, our purpose is defeated because each of the two can itself be divided into two parts, whence we get the four parts again, among which there is not sufficient unity. When, however, there are more than four stories, they cease to function as individuals and become members of a series, the rhythm of which creates the necessary unity. Even in this case, however, the tendency toward grouping into three with the middle dominant persists; for, as a rule, the stories are divided by moldings into three parts, of which the central part is the largest. Four equal stories are difficult because they at once resist an arrangement into threes and yet fall short of being the series which they suggest. When a series of stories is divided into three parts, a superior aesthetic effect is gained if the height of each story diminishes in some regular ratio from the bottom to the top, thus expressing the gradual overcoming of the downward force by the upward,–the rhythm becomes dynamical as well as kinematical.

All good architectural styles illustrate the principle of impartiality, which demands the careful elaboration of parts. Yet, as we have indicated, there are two possibilities: some styles are founded on the idea of the subordination of the parts to the whole, and so permit of a less elaborate execution of details, while others are based on the idea of coordination among the parts within the whole, and so require that each part be vividly clear, distinct from the others, and possessed of a pronounced individual beauty. These two types are exemplified in each of the three aspects of a building—the visual, the dynamic, and the voluminal. For the Greek and Roman architecture and for that of the Renaissance, the former was the ideal; while the latter is clearly characteristic of the more modern forms; between these stand the Byzantine, Romanesque, and Gothic, in which a union of the two types, in what has well been called an organic type, was attempted, and perhaps achieved in the last. The former has the feeling of the mechanical, rational view of life, which is the classical; the latter has the feeling of the mystical and organic view, which is modern.

Chapter XIV

The Function of Art: Art and Morality

That an interest is innocent and pleasure giving is no longer considered sufficient to justify its existence; it must also, in order to be sanctioned in our jealous and economical world, prove itself a beneficent influence upon the total man and the group. For the time being at least, the day of *laissez-faire* is done; men can no longer appeal to their personal needs, their inner necessities, or even their consciences, in defense of their activities. Public opinion, and sometimes reason, are the only arbiters of right. It may well happen that, in a new age, men will be more generous and less exacting, once again recognizing inherent rights in spontaneous activities; but that age is not ours. Not even art can claim privilege; in vain will the artist boast of his genius or the art-lover of his delights, if he can exhibit no pervasive good. It is not enough, therefore, that we should have described the peculiar, inward value of art; we must further establish that it has a function in the general life.

Three classes of people, the puritans, the philistines, and the proletarians, question the value of art in this sense. These classes are, of course, not new to our civilization, but are rather perennial types of human nature, appearing under one or another name and guise in every age. To the puritan, art is immoral; to the philistine, it is useless; to the proletarian, it is a cruel waste.

One illustration of the complexity of human culture is the fact that art has now been regarded as the symbol and ally of goodness, and now as its enemy. This paradox can, I think, be partly explained by making a distinction between the ethical and the moral point of view regarding conduct. From the one point of view, the good belongs to all free, creative acts that look toward the growth and happiness of individuals; from the other point of view, it consists in conformity to law, convention, and custom. It is evident that these two attitudes must sometimes come into open or secret conflict. For law and convention represent either an effort to fix and stabilize modes of conduct that have proved themselves to be good under certain conditions; or else, as is more often true than is admitted, an attempt to generalize the good of some special class or type of men and impose it as a norm for all; and obviously these efforts will, from time to time, be opposed either to the freedom of individuals, or to their growth, under changing conditions.

Now in the sense defined, the spirit of art is fundamentally ethical and, at the same time, fundamentally non-moral. It is fundamentally ethical, for art is itself a freely creative and happy activity, and tends to propagate itself in spontaneity in other fields; it is an inspiration in every struggle for liberty and the remolding of the world. The artist and art lover, who value the expression of individuality in art, cannot fail to appreciate it outside of art. On the other hand, the spirit of art is fundamentally non-moral, for the sthetic attitude is one of sympathy–an attempt at once to express life and to feel at one with it; it demands of us that we take the point of view of the life expressed and, for the moment at any rate, refrain from a merely external judgment. Through art we are compelled to sympathize with the aspiration towards growth, towards happiness, even when it leads to rebellion against our own standards and towards what we call sin. The sympathy, realism, and imagination of art are antagonistic to conformist morality. By making us intimately acquainted with individuals, art leads to skepticism of all general rules.

The puritan, therefore, who is an exponent of the extremest and narrowest conformist morality, is more nearly right in his interpretation of the relation between art and morality than more liberal people who, because of their love of art, seek to ignore or palliate the facts. Hence, in order to defend art, one must reckon seriously with the puritan.

The puritan is fearful, above all, of works of art that represent moral evil. The method of artistic representation, which aims at awakening sympathy for the life portrayed, is bound, he thinks, to demoralize both the artist and the spectator. But art is something more than sympathy, and there are other aspects of the aesthetic experience which tend to render that sympathy innocuous, even from the standpoint of the puritan. In the first place, the sympathy is usually with an imagined life that has no direct relation to the will and gives the spectator no opportunity to enter into and share it–he participates through the imagination, not through the senses. Moreover, neither the mind nor the will is a *tabula rasa*; no mature person comes to a work of art without certain habits and preferences already predetermined, which no mere imagination can destroy, but only, if at all, some concrete opportunity and temptation. Hence men can lead a manifold life, partly in the imagination and partly in action, without any corruption of heart or paralysis of will. In real conduct, to lead a double life is demoralizing because there choices are exclusive and each of the two lives tends to interfere with and spoil the other; but imagination does not conflict with reality, for they have no point of contact and do not belong to the same world.

In the second place, a work of art is an appeal to mind as well as to sympathetic feeling. It is no mere stirring of emotion and passion, but a means to insight into them. The attitude of reflection which it engenders is unfavorable to impetuous action. Providing no immediate stimulus to action, it allows time for a better second thought to intervene. Even when it offers suggestions for unwonted acts, it furnishes the spirit and the knowledge requisite for determining whether they will fit into the scheme of life of the spectator. It is characteristic of the puritanic critics of art, in their eagerness to find motives for condemnation, to overlook this element of reflection.

It is forgotten, finally, that by providing an imaginative experience of passion and adventure, art often becomes rather a substitute for than an incentive to them. The perfection of form, the deep repose and circle-like completeness of the work of art, tend to prevent one from seeking a corresponding real experience, which would have none of these qualities, but perhaps only misery and wear and tear instead. Thus the work of art may propagate itself in a search for new aesthetic experiences rather than in analogous conduct.

To the artist who is living the evil life which he expresses, there can be even less danger in expression, than to the spectator. For the expression is not the cause of his life, but only its efflorescence. The roots of evil lie deep below in the subsoil of instinct. Without expression, life would be much the same, only secret instead of articulate. The puritan shows a shocking naivete in thinking that he can reform life by destroying its utterance. Moreover, to express life implies a certain mastery over it, a power of detachment and reflection, which are fundamentally ethical and may lead to a new way of living.

Every form of life has an inalienable right to expression. In order to be judged fairly, it must be allowed to plead for itself, and art is its best spokesman. And that we should know life sympathetically is of practical importance; for otherwise we shall not know how to change it or indeed that it ought to be changed at all. Only by knowing other ways of life can we be certain of the relative worth of our own way; knowledge alone gives certitude. Without knowledge we run the risk of becoming ruthless destroyers of things which an intelligent sympathy might well preserve and find a place for in the world.

To all these considerations the puritan will doubtless oppose a truth impossible to deny. Experience, he will say, is one, not many; imagination and action are not separated by an impassable wall; things merely imagined or dreamed, even when they do not directly issue in action, may nevertheless influence conduct through a slow and subtle transforming effect upon the sentiments and valuations which make up its background. Character can be maintained only by a vigilant and steady control over impulses which are always threatening rebellion; purity of mind only through the rigid exclusion of the sensual, luxurious, and ignoble; imaginative sympathy with evil, even when sublimated in art, must necessarily undermine the one and becloud the other. "If thine eye offend thee, cut it out and cast it from thee."

The truth which the puritan announces does not, I think, warrant the inference which he draws from it or alter the situation as I have described it. For morality, to be genuine, must be a choice; the good must know its alternative or it is not good. Only those who already have a penchant for sin will be corrupted by imaginative sympathy with passion; a character that cannot resist such an influence is already undermined. Life itself is the great temptation; how can one who cannot look with equanimity upon statues and pictures fail to be seduced by live men and women? If men can resist the suggestions that emanate from life they can surely withstand those that come from art. And mere purity of mind is not equal in value to that insight into the whole of life which a freely creative art provides. We wish to penetrate sympathetically all of our existence; nothing human shall remain foreign to us; we would enter into it all; there is no region of the grotesque, the infernal, or the sinful from which we would be shut out. In comparison with the sublimity of this demand for the complete appreciation of life, the warnings of a rigorous moralism seem timorous, and the sanctuary of purity in which it would have us take refuge, a prison.

Whatever conflict there may be between the spirit of art and conformist morality, there is none with a genuine and rational ethics. For the latter would formulate ways of living suited to the diversity of individuals and sympathetic with their every impulse and fancy. It would impose external constraint only where necessary for the existence and perpetuation of social life, leaving to personal tact, good will, and temperance the finer adjustments of strain. But apart from aesthetic culture, there can be no rational morality, for that alone engenders the imaginative sympathy with individual diversity upon which the latter rests. Without imaginative sympathy morality will always be coarse, ruthless, and expressive of the needs and sentiments of some special type which sets out to reform or govern the world. Under such a regimen, which is actual in every community devoid of imagination, virtue must always remain suspect and vice tolerable; the one a hypocrisy, the other a secret and venial indulgence, and nature will take its revenge upon the law in violent or perverse compensations. Hence, instead of being a hindrance, art ought to be a help to a rational morality: its realism should foster sincerity, its imagination, sympathy and justice. The moralist inspired by art would seek to impose upon men only that kind of form and order which is characteristic of art–one which respects the peculiarities of the material with which it works, and issues in a system in which all elements freely participate[1].

The philistine's objection to art is that it is useless. And if we only knew what was really useful, this would be a damning indictment. But, not being much given to abstract reflection, the philistine is usually at a loss to inform us. However, by talking with him, we can eventually divine what he thinks the useful to be. Useful is what contributes to the procurement of those things which he and his congeners value–material wealth, power, and sensual enjoyment. Art is useless because it will not prepare a banquet, build a bridge, or help to run a business corporation. The artist is a contemptible fellow because he cares more for his art than for the things of the world; for whatever the worldling values he thinks every one else should value.

1. Compare Schiller, *On the Aesthetic Education of Man*, Fourth Letter: "The civilized man makes nature his friend, and honors her freedom, while he merely fetters her caprice."

To the artist, criticism of this kind seems to betray the most shameless arrogance, and he meets contempt with contempt. Who is he that would be the judge between worldly goods and beauty? Surely the philistine is no competent judge; for he only can judge fairly between two values who appreciates both, and, by his own confession, the philistine does not appreciate art. Hence the claim of the philistine seems not to merit consideration. Through his lack of sympathy for art, he puts himself beyond the possibility of fruitful debate. In this he is unlike the puritan, who is often all too sensitive to beauty for his own good–hence his alarms.

If the objection of the philistine were the same as the proletarian's, that art is a luxury, a waste of the energies of the community, which might better be employed in feeding the hungry and saving sinners, it would be more worthy of a hearing; and so he often represents it. But in this he is hardly sincere; and the appropriate answer is a *tu quoque*, the fitting reply to every piece of insincere criticism. Does the philistine feed the poor and save the sinners? Who is commonly more careless of the workers' needs and more cruel to the fallen in his self-righteous probity? For the philistine is often a puritan. And who is more luxurious than he? Who consumes more in his own person of the energies of the toilers? It costs little to maintain an artist, but it taxes thousands to support the philistine and his wife. Of course, in return, the worldling performs a service to the community in the organization of industries, but many of these do not sustain the needs of the masses and are devoted to the manufacture of luxuries for the well-to-do.

The insincerity of the philistine's attitude is disclosed by his changed attitude towards the artist who acquires fame and wealth through his art. For now that the artist shows himself capable of getting the things the philistine values, the latter accords him esteem. Or let an interest in art become fashionable, and once again the philistine is won over.

The traditional hostility between the philistine and the artist is offensive to reason, which would discover points of contact and reconciliation between all attitudes. One apparent place of meeting might seem to be just the worldling's love of luxury itself. Luxury is a development of pleasure of sense beyond the necessary, paralleling the freedom and refinement of sensation in art. There is, moreover, a certain imaginative quality in reputation and glory, so well-prized by the worldling, which, as we shall see, is akin to the ideality of art. And yet both the imagination and the luxury of the worldling are usually lacking in one element essential to real kinship with the spirit of art–disinterestedness. The worldling's dreams of glory are projections of ambition, his luxuries subtle stimulations of appetite or instruments of display, her self-adornment a fine self-exhibition or coquetry. The love of insight, the free emotion, the enjoyment of sensuous harmonies for their own sake, are lacking or subordinate. Glory and luxury are too often mere masks of ambition and appetite, and at best counterfeits of beauty. Nevertheless, the luxurious developments of ambition and appetite are ever on the verge of tending toward the aesthetic. For when ambition has no longer to struggle against the world and is satisfied, the imagination that served it may become free; and when appetite is cloyed, the instrumentalities of sensuous pleasure can find a new meaning as beautiful. Then the worldling becomes the patron of the artist and the two are reconciled. And all along this result was preparing. For instinct seldom completely dominates imagination and sensation; there is always some aesthetic freedom in the self-adornment and display of the wealthy. The absence of anxiety may release aesthetic interests that would have died in the struggle for existence; prosperity is often the herald of beauty.

The proletarian's criticism of art is of unimpeachable sincerity, for when he talks of art as a luxury he speaks from the heart and in answer to bitter experience of want. There is a genuine element of moral indignation in his feeling that there must be something wrong with a public conscience that countenances, even glorifies extravagance, all the while that women slave and children die of underfeeding and neglect.

This feeling is intensified when he compares the thousands paid for a single hour of a prima donna's song or a playwright's wit with his own yearly wage laboriously earned. What supreme worth does art possess that it should be valued so disproportionately?

Yet, sincere as this complaint is, it is largely misdirected; for art is not the extravagance which it may superficially seem to be. Most of the best art has been produced by poor men who never dreamed of the prices that would be paid for their work when they were old or after they were dead. And these prices represent no consumption of the labor and capital of the community, but only a transference of wealth from one man to another. Even when the artist is paid large sums for his picture or opera or play, these sums do not represent their real cost, but only what they can command in a market controlled by rich consumers. The real cost of genuine art is very small–only enough to maintain the artist in freedom for his work; for he would still produce without the incentive of large rewards. The seeming extravagance of art cannot, therefore, be blamed upon art itself, but upon the price system of modern capitalist economy. And this, of course, is clearly perceived by the "intellectual proletarians," who are willing to accord to the artist a place of honor as fellow-worker and "comrade," and direct their attacks, not upon him, but upon capitalism.

There is, however, a deeper root to the proletarian's grievance against the artist–the feeling that the moral principle of mutuality is violated in their relationship. The workman plows for him, cooks for him, builds for him, spins for him, but what does he do in return? He paints pictures, makes statues, writes novels or poems or plays or sonatas which the workman has neither the leisure nor the education to enjoy. The money paid by the artist to the artisan represents nothing which the former rightfully owns or can give, but only a claim to the labor of other men, enforced by the system of wage-economy. Of course, not only art but all speculation, all pure science and disinterested historical knowledge, is subject to this criticism. And such criticism is no longer purely academic, for to-day there exist large masses of men in every community determined to bring about a "world dictatorship of the proletariat" based on just this principle of mutuality in the relations of men. Is this principle itself rational, and would art survive in a regime which embodied it? These, I repeat, are no longer speculative, but intensely practical problems.

Those who fear for art in a society where the process of democratization should go to its extreme limit of development point to the moving picture, the cheap magazine story and novel, the vaudeville and "musical" comedy, as a hint of what to expect. These, they will say, are the popular forms of art, to the production of which the artist would have to devote his time and skill in return for subsistence. Under the present system the people get what they want, but in a proletarian state nobody would be allowed to get anything else.

Of course, as to what would happen in a workers' republic, were it ever constituted, we can only speculate; but where we cannot know, there hope has an equal chance with fear. We have the single example of the Russian experiment from which to make inferences, the general validity of which is seriously limited by the peculiarities of the Russian nature and situation. But there, at any rate, we do know that efforts have been made to advance general education, to bring the classic literature within reach of the masses, and to encourage opera and drama. In Russia, at all events, the leaders of the revolutionary movement have sought rather to destroy what they believe to be a monopoly of culture than culture itself; and in England also they have a similar aim.

There can be little doubt, I think, that our capitalist economy does promote a monopoly of culture. Through their control of the market, the wealthy are able to bid up the prices of works of art until they are beyond the reach of the less prosperous. As a result, the best paintings and sculptures, with the exception of those that find their way into museums, are accumulated in inaccessible private collections, and opera and music are made needlessly expensive. One very evil consequence is the substitution of a purely pecuniary standard of valuation for aesthetic standards. I know a painter who made the experiment of reducing the price of his pictures to twenty-five dollars, in the hope that many people who really loved art but were unable to pay large prices would buy them, and that thus, by selling many of his pictures at a low price, he would be able to make as much money as if he sold only a few at the prevailing high rates. The experiment failed completely, for people thought that paintings at such a low price must be inferior, and even those who could afford to buy them, would not. The painter now tried the reverse experiment and raised the prices of all his works, with much better success, for people reasoned–the higher the price, the better the picture. But worst of all, through the purely commercial motives governing those who undertake to supply the people with works of art, the public taste is corrupted; little or no attempt is made to educate the masses, but merely to give them anything that will entertain them after a day of fatiguing labor,–anything that will sell. The demoralizing effect of commercialism upon artists themselves is too well known to require more than a reminder; hasty work for the sake of money supplants careful work for the sake of beauty; whole arts, like that of oriental rug weaving, are thereby threatened with extinction; and, instead of producing spontaneous art that would express themselves, people allow themselves to be merely entertained by things supplied to them, nasty and cheap–folk art disappears.

If, on the other hand, the commercial motive were eliminated, who can say what might not result, in each community, from the experimentation of men who could not make money but only honor and a living from the profession of providing people with interesting ways of spending their leisure. The increased efficiency of machine tool work will inevitably make possible a great reduction in hours of labor, when the workers themselves control industry for their own benefit rather than for that of a class bent on still further increasing its own wealth and power. It is entirely possible that the leisure of men will then absorb as much of their devoted energies as work does now, and that they will be educated for the one as well as for the other. It is not impossible to hope that, the machine tool supplanting the slave, the commonwealth of workers will develop as free and liberal a life as existed among the citizens of ancient Greece. Then perhaps each group will have its painters, actors, and musicians just as surely as it now has its judges, aldermen, and police.

It is impossible to judge what art might do for people in a reorganized society by what it does for them now. Art has its roots in interests that are well nigh universal. Everybody loves to dance, to sing, to tell a story; everybody loves either to paint or be painted, to sculpture or be sculptured. Again, everybody is at least potentially sensitive to rhythm, harmony, and balance, and to the beauties of lines, colors, and tones. It is not native incapacity, but rather a failure in aesthetic education due to the one-sided emphasis on work rather than play, industry rather than leisure, success rather than happiness, that is responsible for much of the seeming lack of artistic appreciation among the masses. Under a different social system the people may come to recognize the artist as a fellow-worker, elaborating his products in exchange for other desirable things, and may accord him welcome rather than envy.

However, it will doubtless always remain true that the subtler and more intellectual types of art can never become popular. Like higher mathematics, they will continue to be completely intelligible only to the few. Yet I can conceive of no social system likely to grow out of modern tendencies that would suppress them. The artist in the new state would have his leisure, as other men would, in which he could devote himself to the refinements of his art. It is doubtful whether he would have less time for that then than he has now. How many artists under our present system waste a large part of their lives doing hack work of various kinds to make a living;

only the fortunate few are masters of themselves. Moreover, under any social system, men would be permitted to spend their surplus income as they chose, and the art lovers of the future are as likely to spend it for art then as now. Not being so rich, they could not reward the artist so munificently as some are rewarded now; but even now most working artists are poor, and the impulse to art is independent of large rewards. Heretical and unpopular artists, who could find no public backing, would come to be supported by their own special clients, as they are to-day. In a complex rational society, the principle of mutuality would be transitive rather than strictly symmetrical–a woman would cook for a machine designer although she got no machine in return, provided the designer made one, say, for the shoemaker, who could thus supply her with shoes. Just so, there is no moral objection to the artist's receiving goods and services from people to whose life he contributes nothing personally, so long as these people are compensated by those whose life he does enrich. In other words, part of the reward which the art lover would receive for the work he performed would be paid, not to himself, but to the artist–art would be voluntarily supported by those who appreciated it. No complex social life could be maintained under the principle of strict mutuality, and certainly no system that undertook to preserve the variety and spontaneity of human interests. Only a complete dead-level regimentation of human life in accordance with the average desires of the masses, which is unlikely, would destroy the more intellectual and subtle types of art, and, by the same token, speculation and disinterested higher learning. The higher culture has survived many revolutions; it will survive the next, when it comes.

Chapter XV

The Function of Art: Art and Religion

The distinctive purpose of art, so we have argued throughout this study, is culture, the enrichment of the spirit. But lovers of art have always claimed for it more active and broader influences. To my thinking, most of such claims, especially in our age, like similar claims for religion, are greatly exaggerated. Passion, convention, economic fact in the largest sense, practical intelligence, these are the dominant forces swaying men, not beauty, not religion. Indeed, one who would compare the influence of art upon life at the present time with its influence upon primitive societies might infer the early extinction of that influence altogether. For among primitive men the influence of art is all-pervading. With them art is inseparable from utility and communal activities, upon which it has an immediate modifying or strengthening effect. The movement of civilization, with the exception of the Greek, mediaval, and renaissance city states, has involved a breaking away from this original unity until, among ourselves, art is developed and enjoyed in isolation from the rest of life. Art is valued for its own sake, for its contribution to culture, not for any further influence upon life, and this freedom has come to be part of its very meaning. Instead of being interested only in pictures and statues representing ourselves, our rulers, our gods, or our neighborhood, we enjoy imitations of people who have had no effect upon our lives whatever and scenes which we have never visited, and we repair to museums to see them; instead of employing music to beautify our daily life, we leave that life for the concert hall, where we shut ourselves away for a few hours of "absolute" musical experience. Prose literature and the drama, when inspired by contemporary social problems, offer exceptions to this isolation, for through their ability to express ideas they can exert a more pervasive influence. Although social problems are solved in obedience to forces and demands beyond the control of artists, literary expression is effective in persuading and drawing into a movement men whose status would tend to make them hostile or indifferent, as in Russia, where numerous men and women of the aristocratic and wealthy classes became revolutionaries by reason of literature. And yet the literary arts also have acquired a large measure of isolation and independence. A play representing Viennese life is appreciated in New York, a novel of contemporary manners in England is enjoyed in America. Literature does not depend for its interest upon its ability to interpret and influence the life that the reader himself lives; he values it more because it extends than because it reflects that life. People decry art for art's sake, but in vain.

The development of the relation of religion to life has been parallel to the development of art. Originally, religion penetrated every activity; now, by contrast, it has been removed from one after another of the major human pursuits. Agriculture, formerly undertaken under the guidance of religion; science, once the prerogative of the priesthood; art, at one time inseparable from worship; politics, once governed by the church and pretending a divine sanction; war, until yesterday waged with the fancied cooperation of the gods—even these are now under complete secular control. To be sure, there is some music, sculpture, painting, and poetry still in the service of religion, but its relative proportion is small; kings and congresses still appeal for divine aid in times of crisis, but that is perfunctory; men still pray for rain during drought, but without faith. No one would pretend that our commerce and manufacturing have any direct relation to religion. People still invoke divine authority for moral prescriptions, but the sanctions actually operating are social instincts and fear of public opinion and the law. Religion retains a direct and potent influence only in the institution of marriage, the experience of death, philosophy, and the social life and charities conducted by the churches. Yet even in these spheres the influence is declining, and, so far as it persists, is becoming indirect. Civil and contractual marriage are slowly supplanting religious marriage; there are thousands living in our large cities who do not feel the need of the church to establish and cement their social life; most philosophers disclaim any religious motive or authority for their investigations or beliefs. Only over death does religion still hold undisputed sway.

However, despite the separation of religion and art from life, they may continue to exert influence upon it. But, barring some new integration of the sundered elements of our culture, which we may deeply desire but cannot predict, this influence must be indirect and subtle, and must occur independent of any institutional control. In the case of both it consists in imparting to life a new meaning and perfection, thus making possible a more complete affirmation of life and a freer and more genial attitude and conduct.

For unless the spirit of art or of religion is infused into life, we never find it quite satisfactory. To be sure, men sometimes think they find perfection in certain things–in practical or moral endeavor, in love or in pleasure; but unless art or religion is mixed into them, they always prove to be, in the end, disappointing. No practical purpose is ever quite successful; there is always some part of the plan left unaccomplished; and the success itself is only momentary, for time eventually engulfs it and forgets it. Practical life does not produce any permanent and complete work; its task is done only to be done over again; every house has to be repaired or torn down, every road rebuilt; every invention is displaced by a new one. This is true even on the higher planes of practical life, in political and social reconstruction. Certain evils may be removed, certain abuses remedied, but new ones always arise to take their places; and even when the entire system is remodeled and men think that the day of freedom and justice has dawned at last, they find, after a generation, a new tyranny and a new injustice. The movement of life makes it impossible for any plan to long endure. Hence the disillusion, the feeling of futility that so often poisons the triumphs of practical men. And without the spirit of art or of religion even love does not satisfy. For imagination creates the perfection of its object and, aside from institutional bonds fast loosening, a faith in the continued growth with one another and with a child, which is essentially religious, creates the permanence and meaning of its bond. Love's raptures, in so far as they are instinctive, are, of course, independent of any view of life; but apart from imagination and faith in one another, love does not keep its quality or renew itself in memory, nor can it survive death which always impends to destroy. Men often seek escape from the feeling of imperfection in frivolity, but ennui is the inevitable consequence, and reflection with its doubts cannot be stilled.

By contrast, in the religious experience and in beauty men feel that they find perfection; hence the attitude of self-surrender and joyousness characterizing both. The abandon of the spectator who decrees that for the moment his life shall be that of the work of art, is matched in the mystical experience by the emotion expressed in Dante's line, "In his will is our peace." And in both the self-surrender is based on a felt harmony between the individual and the object–the beautiful thing appeals to the senses, its form is adapted to the structure of the mind, its content is such as to win interest and sympathy; the divine is believed to realize and quiet all of our desires. But while in beauty we feel ourselves at home with the single object, in religion we feel at rest in the universe.

When religion and art are separated from the other parts of life, as they are fast becoming now, the peculiar quality of the experiences which they offer can be rendered universal only by freely infusing it everywhere, through faith, in the case of the one, through imaginative re-creation, in the case of the other. The religious experience is a seeming revelation of a perfect meaning in life as a whole; this meaning must now be imparted to the details of life. By a free act of faith the scattered and imperfect fragments must be built into a purposive unity. The poisonous feeling of futility, will then be lost; each task, no matter how petty or ineffectual, will become momentous as contributing something toward the realization of a good beyond our little existence; and we, however lowly, will find ourselves sublime as instruments of destiny. There is nothing vain to him who believes. And if the believer cannot build a meaning into history and social life as he knows them empirically, he may extend them by faith in a future life, through which his purposes will be given the promise of eternity and the tie between parents and children, friends and lovers and co-workers, an invincible seriousness and worth. Being at peace with the universe, he may be reconciled to the accidents of his life as expressions of its Will.

The method of reconciliation through religion can well be understood by its effect on the attitude towards evil. To one who has faith in the world as perfect, evil becomes an illusion that would disappear to an adequate vision of the Divine. The supposedly evil thing becomes really a good thing–a necessary means to the fulfillment of the divine plan, either in the earthly progress of humanity or in the future life; or if the more mystical types of religion provide the starting point, where individuality itself is felt to be an illusion, a factor in the self-realization of the Absolute. The evil thing remains, of course, what it was, but the interpretation, and therefore the attitude towards it, is transformed. Pain, sorrow, and misfortune become agents for the quickening of the spirit, death a door opening to unending vistas.

The attitude of faith is not embodied in dogmatic and speculative religious doctrines alone; for it finds expression in other beliefs–in progress, in the possibility of a sunny social order, in the perpetuity of human culture, in the peculiar mission of one's race or country. Such beliefs are expressions primarily of faith, not of knowledge; like religion, they are interpretations of life based on aspiration, not on evidence;

and through them men secure the same sort of re-enforcement of motive, courage, and consolation that they derive from the doctrines called religious. But the sphere of faith is wider even than this; the almost instinctive belief that each man has in his own longevity and success, the trust in the permanence of friendship and love, the confidence in the unique value of one's work or genius–these are also convictions founded more on desire than on knowledge, and may function in the same way as religion in a man's life.

The re-affirmation of life which art may inspire is independent of any belief or faith about the world. It occurs rather through the application to the objects and incidents of life of a spirit and attitude borrowed from artistic creation and appreciation. It is a generalization of the aesthetic point of view to cover life as well as art; an attempt to bring beauty from art into the whole of life. Although to-day works of art themselves are severed from direct contact with the rest of life, something of the intention and method of the artist may linger and be carried over into it. Art, the image of life, may now serve as a model, after which the latter, in its turn, will be patterned.

The spirit of art has two forms, one constructive, the other contemplative, and both may be infused into life. When the former is put there, each act and task is performed as if it were a work of art. This involves "throwing the whole self" into it, not only thought and patience, but enthusiasm and loving finish, even as the artist puts them into his work, so that it becomes a happy self-expression. Nothing shall interfere with or mar it, or spoil its value when recalled. The imperfection and transiency of the result are then forgotten in the inspiration of endeavor; and the work or act, no matter how insignificant, becomes perfect as an experience and as a memory. The generations may judge it as they will, but as an expression of the energies of my own soul, it is divine. Of course, from the industry of our time, where most work is mechanical and meaningless to him who performs it, the spirit of art has largely fled. Yet there still remain tasks which we all have to execute, if not in business, then at home, which, by arousing our interest and invention, may become materials for the spirit of art. We have at least our homes, our pleasures, our relations with one another, our private adventures, where we can still be free and genial and masterly. And for our work, art will continue to be an ideal, sorrowfully appealing.

The scope of the spirit of art may be extended beyond the single task or act to embrace the whole of one's life. Impulse offers a plastic material to which form may be given. The principles of harmony, balance, evolution, proper subordination, and perfection of detail, indispensable to beauty in art, are conditions of happiness in life. The form of a work of art and the form of a happy life are the same, as Plato insisted. In order to yield satisfaction, the different parts of life must exemplify identity of motive, continuity and orderliness in the fulfillment of purpose, lucidity of relation, yet diversity for stimulation and totality. There must be a selective scheme to absorb what is congenial and reject the unfit. This sense for form in life may lead to the same results as morality, but the point of departure and the sanction are different. Morality is largely based on conformity, on submission to the general will, and is rendered effective by fear of public disapproval and supernatural taboos; while the aesthetic direction of life has its roots in the love of form and meaning, and its sanction in personal happiness. Moreover, to the reflective person, looking before and after, life has the same sort of reality as a story, and is bound to be judged in some measure like a story. The past and the future live only in the imagination, and when we survey them there they may please us with their interest, liveliness, and meaning, much as a work of art would, or displease us with their vanity and chaos. In this way personality may acquire an imaginative value fundamentally aesthetic. This is different from moral value, which has reference to the relation of a life to social ideals; it is more comprehensive than the religious judgment, which is interested only in saving the soul; because it includes every element of life,–sense, imagination, and achievement, welcoming all, so long as they contribute something to a significant, moving whole.

The feeling for perfection of form and imaginative meaning in life is no invention of philosophers and aesthetes, but part of the normal reaction to conduct. Everybody feels that certain acts, or even certain wishes, are to be rejected by himself, not because they are intrinsically bad or wrong, but because they are inconsistent with his particular nature, and, on the other hand, that there are certain interests that should be cultivated, not because they are universally right or good, but because they are needed to give his life complete meaning. And again, all except the meanest and most repressed souls desire somewhat to shine, if not in the world at large, at least among their friends, and act with a view to appearance and to some total survey of their lives that would consider not merely its goodness or usefulness, but its imaginative emotional appeal. This appeal is the strongest on the death of a great man; this lives longest in the memory. The love of the romantic and adventurous is partly instinctive, but largely imaginative, for it has in view not merely the rapturous pleasures of the hazardous moment, but the remembered delights of recall and expression to others. The love of glory is also imaginative, a feeling for the dramatic extending even beyond the grave. The ambitious man seeks to make a story out of his life for posterity to read and remember, just as the artist makes one out of fictitious material. More might develop out of this love of form and drama in life. We have it to a certain degree of cultivation in picturesque and refined manners, dress, and ceremonial, but even there it is hampered through conventionality and want of invention; further evolved and extended into the deeper strata of life, it would lead to a more interesting and productive existence. Surely, if God is an artist as well as a judge, he will welcome into heaven not only those who have lived well, but also those who have lived beautifully.

There is no necessity, finally, why the constructive spirit of art should be confined to the personal life and should not, in some measure at least, penetrate the community and even the state. By appealing to imaginative feeling, the activities of various individuals and groups, when coordinated and given a purposeful unity, produce an aesthetic effect. The organization of a business or a university may easily come to have such a value for one who has helped to create it, especially if the place where the communal spirit operates is beautiful,–the office, the campus, the shop. Seldom, to be sure, do we find this value in our busy and haphazard America, but in many quarters the intention to create it is awake. As for the state, it is, of course, too little dominated by disinterested intelligence to be beautiful; yet Plato's ideal of statecraft as a fine art still rules the innermost dream of men.

The contemplative spirit of art is perhaps more important than the constructive in its application to life. Not that any sharp line can be drawn between them, for contemplation must always attend or follow creation, to judge and enjoy; yet towards that part of life which we cannot control, our attitude must be rather that of the spectator than the creator. We cannot interfere with the greater part of life; we can, however, observe it and, in the imagination, transform it, where we can then envisage it as we should a work of art. As we watch it, life itself may become beautiful, and instead of giving ourselves to it half-heartedly and with reserve, we shall accept it with something of the abandon of passionate love,–"In thee my soul hath her content so absolute." To this end it is necessary to detach life from our more selfish interests and ambitions, from the habits of thought, annoying and preoccupying, that relate to self alone. To the worldly and self-centered, life is interesting only so far as it refers to pride or ambition or passion; otherwise it is indifferent, as none of their concern. But to the religious and to the aesthetically minded, there is no part of life that may not be of interest; to the former, because they impute something of transcendent perfection to it all; to the latter, because they have set themselves the inexhaustible task of its free, imaginative appreciation.

To this end, it is also necessary, after learning to view life objectively and impersonally, to attend to it leisurely and responsively, as we should to a work of art, allowing full scope to the disinterested feelings of curiosity, pity, sympathy, and wonder to create emotional participation.

Then the world may become for us the most magnificent spectacle of all. To imaginative feeling, every landscape is a potential painting, every life-story a romance, history a drama, every man or woman a statue or portrait. Beauty is everywhere, where we who are perhaps not artists but only art lovers can find it; we cannot embody it in enduring form or throw over it the glamour of sensuous loveliness, but we can perceive it with that free appreciation that is the essence of art. And for this, of course, the artists have prepared us; it is they who, by first exhibiting life as beautiful in art, have shown us that it may be beautiful as mirrored in the observing mind. One region after another has been conquered by them. The poets and the painters created the beauty of the mountains, of windmills and canals, of frozen wastes and monotonous prairies, of peasants and factories and railway stations and slums. Themselves the first to feel the value of these things, through some personal attachment or communion with them, they have made it universal through expression. Their works have become types through which we apperceive and appreciate the world: we see French landscapes as Lorrain and Corot saw them, peasants after the fashion of Millet, the stage after Degas. In vain men have prophesied limits to the victorious advance of art. Just at the time when, in the middle of the last century, some men feared that science and industry had banished beauty from the world, the impressionists and realists disclosed it in factory and steamboat and mine. In this way modern art, which might seem through its isolation to have taken beauty away from the world to itself, has given it back again.

The spirit of art, no less than of religion, can help us to triumph over the evils of life. There are three ways of treating evil successfully: the practical way, to overcome it and destroy it; the religious way, by faith to deny its existence; the aesthetic way, to rebuild it in the imagination. The first is the way of all strong men; but its scope is limited; for some of the evils of life are insuperable; against these our only recourse is faith or the spirit of art. The method of art consists in taking towards life itself the same attitude that the artist takes towards his materials when he makes a comedy or a tragedy out of them; life itself becomes the object of laughter or of tragic pity and fear and admiration. As we observed in our chapter on "The Problem of Evil in Aesthetics," laughter is an essentially aesthetic attitude, for it implies the ability disinterestedly to face a situation, although one which opposes our standards and expectations, and to take pleasure in it. All sorts of personal feelings may be mixed with laughter, bitterness and scorn and anger; but the fact that we laugh shows that they are not dominant; in laughter we assert our freedom from the yoke of circumstance and make it yield us pleasure even when it thwarts us. Laughter celebrates a twofold victory, first over ourselves, in that we do not allow our disappointments to spoil our serenity, and second over the world, in that, even when it threatens to render us unhappy, we prevent it. Fate may rob us of everything, but not of freedom of spirit and laughter; oftentimes we must either laugh or cry, but tears bring only relief, laughter brings merriment as well.

Even with the devil laughter may effect reconciliation. Practical men will try to destroy him, but so far they have not succeeded; men of faith will prophesy his eventual ruin, but meanwhile we have to live in his company; and how can we live there at peace with ourselves unless with laughter at his antics and our own vain efforts to restrain them? Surely the age-long struggle against him justifies us in making this compromise for our happiness. We who in our lifetime cannot defeat him can at least make him yield us this meed of laughter for our pains. People who think that laughter at evil is a blasphemy against the good set too high a valuation upon their conventions. No one can laugh without possessing a standard, but to laugh is to recognize that life is of more worth than any ideal and happiness better than any morality.

And if by laughter we cannot triumph over evil, we may perhaps achieve this end by appreciating it as an element in tragedy or pathos. For once we take a contemplative attitude towards life, foregoing praise and blame, there is no spectacle equal to it for tragic pity and fear and admiration. There is a heroism in life equal to any in art, in which we may live imaginatively, and in so living forgive the evil that is its necessary condition. Or, when life is pathetic rather than tragic, suffering and fading and weak rather than strong and steady and resisting, we may win insight from the pitiable reality into the possible and ideal; the shadow of evil will suggest to us the light of the good, and for this vision we shall bless life even when it disappoints our hopes. The very precariousness of values, which is an inevitable accompaniment of them, will serve to intensify their worth for us; we shall be made the more passionately to love life, with the joys that it offers us, because we so desperately realize its transiency. Our knowledge of the inescapableness of death and failure will quiet our laments, leaving us at least serene and resigned where our struggles and protests would be unavailing. It is by thus generalizing the point of view of art so that we adopt it towards our own life that we secure the catharsis of tragedy. Instead of letting sorrow overwhelm us, we may win self-possession through the struggle against it; instead of feeling that there is nothing left when the loved one dies, we may keep in memory a cherished image, more poignant and beautiful because the reality is gone, and loving this we shall love life also that has provided it.

Finally, in subtle ways, the influence of art, while remaining indirect, may affect practical action in a more concrete fashion. For silently, unobtrusively, when constantly attended to, a work of art will transform the background of values out of which action springs. The beliefs and sentiments expressed will be accepted not for the moment only, aesthetically and playfully, but for always and practically; they will become a part of our nature. The effect is not merely to enlarge the scope of our sympathies by making us responsive, as all art does, to every human aspiration, but rather to strengthen into resolves those aspirations that meet in us an answering need. This influence is especially potent during the early years of life, before the framework of valuations has become fixed. What young man nursed on Shelley's poetry has not become a lover of freedom and an active force against all oppression? But even in maturer years art may work in this way. One cannot live constantly with the "Hermes" of Praxiteles without something of its serenity entering into one's soul to purge passion of violence, or with Goethe's poetry without its wisdom making one wise to live. The effect is not to cause any particular act, but so to mold the mind that every act performed is different because of this influence.

I would compare this influence to that of friends. Friends may, of course, influence conduct directly and immediately through advice and persuasion, but that is not the most important effect of their lives. More important is the gradual diffusion of their attitudes and the enlightenment following their example. Through living their experiences with them, we come to adopt their valuations as our own; by observing how they solve their problems, we get suggestions as to how to solve ours. Art provides us with a companionship of the imagination, a new friendship. The sympathetic touch with the life there expressed enlarges our understanding of the problems and conditions of all life, and so leads to a freer and wiser direction of our own. On the one hand new and adventurous methods of living are suggested, and on the other hand the eternal limits of action are enforced.

Once more I would compare the influence of art with that of religion. The effect of religion upon conduct is partly due to the institutions with which it is connected and the supernatural sanctions which it attaches to the performance of duty; but partly also, and more enduringly, to the stories of the gods. Now these stories, even when believed, have an existence in the imagination precisely comparable to that of works of art, and their influence upon sentiment is of exactly the same order. They are most effective when beautiful, as the legends of Christ and Buddha are beautiful; and they function by the sympathetic transference of attitude from the story to the believer. Even when no longer accepted as true their influence may persist, for the values they embody lose none of their compulsion. And, although as an interpretation of life based upon faith religion is doubtless eternal, its specific forms are probably all fictitious; hence each particular religion is destined to pass from the sphere of faith to that of art. The Greek religion has long since gone there, and there also a large part of our own will some day go–what is lost for faith is retained for beauty.

Bibliography

General Works

English.

SANTAYANA, G. The Sense of Beauty, 1897; Reason in Art, 1906.

MUENSTERBERG, H. The Principles of Art Education, 1905; The Eternal Values, Part 3, 1909.

LEE and THOMPSON. Beauty and Ugliness, 1911.

CARRITT, E. I. The Theory of Beauty, 1914.

KNIGHT, WM. The Philosophy of the Beautiful, Part 1, 1891; Part 2, 1893.

PUFFER, ETHEL. The Psychology of Beauty, 1905.

BROWN, BALDWIN. The Fine Arts, 1892.

ROWLAND, E. The Significance of Art, 1913.

MARSHALL, R. Pain, Pleasure, and Aesthetics, 1894; Aesthetic, Principles, 1895.

SULLY, J., and ROBERTSON, G. C. Aesthetics.

BOSANQUET, B. History of Aesthetics, 1904; Three Lectures on Aesthetics, 1914.

GORDON, KATE. Aesthetics, 1909.

German.

LIPPS, T. Aesthetik, 1903-1905.

VOLKELT, J. System der Aesthetik, 1905-1914.

DESSOIR, M. Aesthetik und Allgemeine Kunstwissenschaft, 1906.

COHN, J. Allgemeine Aesthetik, 1901.

MEUMANN, E. Aesthetik der Gegenwart,1912;Systemder Aesthetik, 1914.

UTITZ, E. Grundlegung der Allgemeinen Kunstwissenschaft, Bd.1, 1914.

MUELLER-FRIENFELS, R. Psychologic der Kunst, 1912.

WITASEK, S. Grundzuege der Allgemeinen Aesthetik, 1904.

GROOS, K. Der Aesthetische Genuss, 1902.

LANGE, K. Das Wesen der Kunst,1901.FIEDLER,C.Der Ursprung der Kuenstlerischen Thaetigkeit,1901.

KANT, I. Kritik der Urteilskraft, 1790; English translationbyJ. H. Bernard, 1892.

French.

TAINE, H. The Philosophy of Art, English translation, 1867.

SULLY-PRUDHOMME, R. F. A. L'Expression dans les beaux arts, 1883.

GUYAU, J. M. Les problemes de l'estetique contemporaine, 1884; L'Art au point de vue sociologique, 1889.

BRAY, L. Du Beau, 1902.

SEAILLES, G. Essai sur le genie en l'art, 1897.

SOURIAU, P. La suggestion en l'art, 1909.

LALO, CH. Les Sentiments esthetiques, 1910; Introduction l'estetique, 1913.

DUSSAUZE, H. Les Regies estetiques et les lois du sentiment, 1911.

FONTAINE, A. Essai sur le principe et les lois de la critique d'art,1909.

Italian.

CROCE, B. Estetica, 1902; English translation, 1909; French translation, 1904; German translation, 1905; Breviario di estetica, 1913.

PILO, M. Estetica.

PORENA, M. Che cos' e il bello, 1905.

Experimental Aesthetics

FECHNER, G. T. Vorschule der Aesthetik, 1876.

KUELPE, O. Der gegenwaertige Stand der experimentellen Aesthetik, in Bericht ueber den 2ten Kongress fuer experimentelle Psychologie, 1907.

STRATTON, G. M. Psychology and Culture, 1903.

VALENTINE, C. W. Experimental Psychology of Beauty.

MYERS, C. S. Introduction to Experimental Psychology, 1911.

WUNDT, WM. Physiological Psychology.

LALO, CH. L'Estetique experimentale contemporaine, 1908.

Works on the Origins of Art

HIRN, Y. The Origins of Art, 1900.

GROSSE, E. The Beginnings of Art, English translation, 1897.

WALLASCHEK, R. Primitive Music, 1903.

BUECHER, K. Arbeit und Rhythmus, 1899.

GUMMEBE, F. B. The Beginnings of Poetry, 1901.

GROOS, K. The Play of Man, 1901.

FRAZER, J. G. The Golden Bough, 1907-1915.

WUNDT, WM. Volkerpsychologie, 1911; Elements of Folk Psychology, 1916.

SPEARING, H. G. The Childhood of Art, 1913.

Additional References for Special Subjects

Chapter Six.—The Tragic.

ARISTOTLE. Poetics.

CORNEILLE, P. Discours de la tragedie, 1660.

LESSING, G. E. Hamburgische Dramaturgic, 1767.

SCHOPENHAUER. The World as Will and Idea; Englishtranslation,Vol. 1, Bk. 3; Vol. 3, Ch.27.

HEGEL, G. W. F, Vorlesungen ueber die Aesthetik, 3ter Abschnitt,3tes Kapitel.

HEBBEL, F. Ein Wort ueber das Drama, 1843.

LIPPS, T. Der Streit ueber die Tragoedie, 1891.

VOLKELT, J. Aesthetik des Tragischen, 1906; System der Aesthetik,Bd. 2, 1910.

BRADLEY, A. C. Oxford Lectures on Poetry, 1909.

BUTCHER, S. H. Aristotle's Theory of Poetry and Fine Art, 1898.

NIETZSCHE, FR. Die Geburt der Tragoedie, 1870.

Chapter Six.—The Comic.

LIPPS, T. Komik und Humor, 1898.

BERGSON, H. Laughter, English translation,1913.

FREUD, S. Wit, and Its Relation to the Unconscious, English translation, 1916.

MARTIN, L. J. Experimental Prospecting in the Fields of the Comic, *American Journal of Psychology*, Vol. 16, 1905.

SCHOPENHAUER, A. The World as Will and Idea, English translation,Vol. 2, Ch. 8.

VOLKELT, J. System der Aesthetik, Bd. 2, 1900.

SULLY, J. Essay on Laughter, 1902.

SPENCER, H. Physiology of Laughter, in *Essays, Scientific,Political and Speculative.*

SIDIS, B. Psychology of Laughter, 1913.

MEREDITH, GEORGE. An Essay on Comedy, 1897.

Chapter Seven.—The Standard of Taste.

TAINE, H. The Ideal in Art, 1867.

LEMAITRE, J. Les Contemporains.

FRANCE, A. La Vie litteraire.

BRUNETIERE, FERD. Questions de critique, 1889.

BABBITT, IRVING. The New Laocoon, 1910.

GATES, L. E. Impressionism and Appreciation, in *The Atlantic Monthly*, July, 1900.

BALFOUR, A. J. Criticism and Beauty, 1910.

PATER, WALTER. The Renaissance, 1873.

SYMONDS, J. A. Essays, Speculative and Suggestive, 1890.

CAINE, T. HALL. Cobwebs of Criticism, 1883.

HENNEQUIN, E. La Critique scientifique, 1888.

SPINGARN, J. E. Creative Criticism, 1917.

Chapter Eight.—Music.

RIEMANN, H. Elemente der musikalischen Aesthetik, 1900.

HANSLICK, E. Vom Musikalisch-Schoenen, 11th ed., 1910.

GEHRING, A. The Basis of Musical Pleasure, 1910.

COMBARIEU, J. Music: Its Laws and Evolution, 1910.

GURNEY, E. The Power of Sound, 1880.

BUSONI, F. Sketch of a New Athetic of Music, 1911.

LALO, C. Esquisse d'une estetique musicale scientifique, 1908.

AMBROS, W. A. Die Grenzen der Musik und Poesie, 1872.

WAGNER, R. Das Kunstwerk der Zukunft; Oper und Drama.

STUMPF, C. Tonpsychologie, 1883, 1890, and articles in *Zeitschrift fuer Psychologie.*

HELMHOLTZ. Sensations of tone, 1895.

MEYER, MAX. Contributions to a Psychological Theory of Music, *University of Missouri Studies*, 1901,1. No. 1;

The Psychology of Music, in *American Journal of Psychology*, 1903: 14.

BINGHAM, W. VAN DYKE. Studies in Melody, 1910.

LIPPS. Zur Theorie der Melodie, in *Zeitschrift fuer Psychologie*, 1902:27.

REVESZ, GEZA. Tonpsychologie, 1913.

SPENCER, H. The Origin and Function of Music.

BOLTON. Rhythm, in *American Journal of Psychology*, Vol. 6.

MEUMANN, E. Untersuchungen zur Psy. u. Aest.d. Rhythmus,in *Philosophische Studien*, X.

STETSON, R. H. A Motor Theory of Rhythm and Discrete Succession,in *Psychological Review*, Vol. 12.

Chapter Nine.—Poetry.

ARISTOTLE. Poetics.

SIDNEY, SIR PHILIP. Defense of Poesy, 1581.

WORDSWORTH, WM. Preface to the Lyrical Ballads, 1800.

SHELLEY, P. B. A Defense of Poetry, 1821.

BRADLEY, A. C. Oxford Lectures on Poetry,1909.

SCOTT, F. N. The Most Fundamental Differentia of Poetry and Prose, *Modern Language Association Publications*, V. 19, pp 250-269,

MILL, J. S. Thoughts on Poetry and Its Varieties, in *Dissertations and Discussions*, Vol. 1.

SANTAYANA, G. Elements of Poetry, in *Poetry and Religion*, 1900.

LANIER, S. Science of English Verse, 1880.

EASTMAN, MAX. The Enjoyment of Poetry.

SOURIAU, P. La Reverie esthetique, 1906.

LIDDELL, MARK H. An Introduction to the Study of Poetry, 1902.

WERNER, R. M. Lyrik und Lyriker, 1890.

LOWELL, AMY. Tendencies in Modern American Poetry, 1917.

GUMMERE, F. B. A Handbook of Poetics, 1895.

ROETTEKEN. Poetik, 1911.

BURKE, EDMUND. A Philosophical Enquiry into Our Ideas of the Sublime and Beautiful, Part 4, 1756.

MACKAIL, J. W. Lectures on Poetry, 1911.

POE, E. A. The Philosophy of Composition; The Poetic Principle.

OMOND, T. S. A Study of Meter, 1903.

VERRIER, P. Metrique anglaise, 1909.

DILTHEY, W. Das Erlebnis und Die Dichtung, 1907.

STETSON, R. H. Rhythm and Rhyme, in *Harvard Psychological Studies*, Vol. 1.

Chapter Ten.—Prose Literature.

SCHOPENHAUER, A. The Art of Literature.

GOETHE AND SCHILLER. Correspondence, passim.

GREEN, T. H. The Value and Influence of Works of Fiction, 1862.

LEWES, G. H. Principles of Success in Literature, 1892.

ARNOLD, M. Essays in Criticism, 1869.

ZOLA, E. The Experimental Novel and Other Essays, translated by B. M. Sherman, 1893.

BESANT, W., and JAMES, H. The Art of Fiction, 1885.

PATER, W. Appreciations, with an Essay on Style, 1889.

STEVENSON, R. L. On Style in Literature, in *Contemporary Review*, 47:548.

BOURGET, P. Etudes et Portraits, 1911.

FLAUBERT, G. Correspondance, published 1887.

ELSTER, E. Prinzipien der Literaturwissenschaft, 1897, 1911.

FREITAG, G. Technique of the Drama, English translation, 1895.

MATTHEWS, J. B. A Study of the Drama, 1910.

JONES, H. A. The Foundations of a National Drama, 1913.

WOODBRIDGE, E. The Drama: Its Laws and Its Technique, 1898.

DE MAUPASSANT, GUY. Le Roman, in Pierre et Jean.

For additional references on Poetry and Prose, consult *An Introduction to the Methods and Materials of Literary Criticism*, by C. M. Gayley and F. N. Scott, 1899.

Chapter Eleven.—Painting.

MEIER-GRAEFE, J. Modern Art, English translation, 1908.

ROSS, DENMON. A Theory of Pure Design, 1907; On Drawing and Painting, 1912.

BERENSON, B. Central Italian Painters of the Renaissance.

POORE, H. R. Pictorial Composition, 1903. VAN DYKE, J. C. Art for Art's Sake,1895.

UTITZ, E. Grundzuege der Aesthetischen Farbenlehre, 1908.

WAETZOLDT, WM. Die Kunst des Portraets, 1908.

WEIGHT, WM. H. Modern Painting, 1915.

LIPPS, T. Aesthetik, Bd. 1, 5ter Abschnitt, Bd. 2, 7tes Kapitel.

GOETHE. Farbenlehre. SOURIATJ, P. L'Estetique du mouvement, 1889.

STRATTON, G. M. Eye Movement, and the Aesthetics of Visual Form, in Philosophische Studien, XX.

COHN, J. Experimented Untersuchungen ueber die Gefuehlsbetonung der Farben, in Philosophische Studien, 10: 522.

BAKER and CHOWN. Experiments on Color, in the University of Toronto Studies.

LEE and THOMPSON. Beauty and Ugliness, in Contemporary Review, 1897.

CHEVREUL, M. E. The Principles of Harmony and Contrast of Colors, 1855.

Chapter Twelve.—Sculpture.

HILDEBRAND, A. The Problem of Form in Painting and Sculpture, English translation, 1907.

RODIN, A. Art, English translation, 1912.

HERDER, J. G. Plastik, 1778.

LIPPS, T. Aesthetik, Bd. 2, 5tes u. etes Kapitel.

LESSING. Laocoon, 1766.

CORNELIUS, H. Elementargesetze der bildenden Kunst, 1908.

Chapter Thirteen.—Architecture.

LIPPS, T. Raumaesthetik, 1897; Aesthetik, Bd. 1, 1903.

SCOTT, G. The Architecture of Humanism, 1914.

ROBINSON, J. B. Architectural Composition, 1908.

VAN PELT, J. V. Essentials of Composition, 1913.

GUADET, J. Elements et theorie de l'architecture, 1909.

VIOLLET-LE-DUC, E. E. Entretiens sur l'architecture, 1863-72.

RUSKIN, J. Seven Lamps of Architecture, 1857.

FRANKL, P. Die Entwicklungsphasen der neueren

Baukunst, 1914.

WORRINGER, W. Formprobleme der Gothik, 1912.

WOELFFUN, H. Renaissance und Barock, 1888.

Chapter Fourteen.—Art and Morality.

PLATO. Republic, Ion, Phaedrus, Symposium, Gorgias.

TOLSTOY, L. What is Art? English translation, 1899.

SCHILLER, F. Letters on the Aesthetic Education of Man, 1793-1795.

MORRIS, WM. Hopes and Fears for Art, 1882.

WILDE, O., MORRIS, WM., and OWEN, W. C. The Soul of Man, The Socialist Ideal–Art, and The Coming Solidarity.

RUSKIN, J. Lectures on Art, 1900.

SYMONDS, J. A. Essays, Speculative and Suggestive, 1890.

PAULHAN, FR. Le Mensonge de l'Art, 1907.

WHISTLER, J. McN. Ten o'Clock, 1888.

GUYAU, J. M. L'Art au point de vue sociologique, 1889.

CASSAGNE, A. La theorie de l'art pour l'art en France, 1906.

Chapter Fifteen.—Art and Religion.

LANG, A. Myth, Ritual, and Religion, 1913.

DELLA SETA, A. Religion and Art, 1914.

HARRISON, J. Ancient Art and Ritual, 1913.

MURRAY, G. Four Stages of Greek Religion, 1912. REINACH, S. Orpheus, 1909.

SANTAYANA, G. Poetry and Religion, 1900.

FRAZER, J. G. The Golden Bough.

HEGEL, G. W. F. Introduction to the Philosophy of Fine Art, translated by Bosanquet, 1886.

MUENSTERBERG, H. Philosophie der Werte, 1908. WUNDT, WM. Volkerpsychologie, 1911.

SANTAYANA, G. Three Philosophical Poets, 1910.

Index